Anna Hanson Dorsey

The heiress of Carrigmona

Anna Hanson Dorsey

The heiress of Carrigmona

ISBN/EAN: 9783741177941

Manufactured in Europe, USA, Canada, Australia, Japa

Cover: Foto ©Andreas Hilbeck / pixelio.de

Manufactured and distributed by brebook publishing software (www.brebook.com)

Anna Hanson Dorsey

The heiress of Carrigmona

The Works of
MRS. ANNA HANSON DORSEY.

ADA'S TRUST. 1 vol. 12mo. Cloth, $1.50.
Apart from the religious principles inculcated by this story, it has a vivid interest and fascinating reality that will hold the reader to the end.

ADRIFT. 1 vol. 12mo. Cloth, $1.50.
This story depicts the gradual passage of a soul from the darkness of error to the light and consolation of the truth.

BETH'S PROMISE. 1 vol. 12mo. Cloth, $1.50.
A story well calculated to captivate the mind and fill the heart with love for all that is good and true.

THE HEIRESS OF CARRIGMONA. 1 vol. 12mo. Cloth, $1.50.
The object here aimed at is to edify and to build up; to conduct the mind into a channel of pure thought.

PALMS. 1 vol. 12mo. Cloth, $1.50.
A powerful narrative of the life of the ancient Romans at the time when Christianity first pierced the gloom of ignorance.

WARP AND WOOF. 1 vol. 12mo. Cloth, $1.50.
"Life is the warp, our deeds the woof, which we weave into a web of grotesque designs and strange patterns of light and shade; symbols of sins, sorrows, joys, and mayhap repentance."

THE OLD HOUSE AT GLENARAN. 1 vol. 12mo. Cloth, $1.50.
An Irish story of the first-class, teaching morals and religion in a most captivating way.

ZOE'S DAUGHTER. 1 vol. 12mo. Cloth, $1.50.
A Maryland story of the days of Lord Baltimore. Its scenes are laid in the classic ground of St. Inigoes. It introduces many historic characters of that locality in the early days.

THE FATE OF THE DANE, and other Stories. 1 vol. 12mo. Cloth, $1.50.
Four of Mrs. Dorsey's best novelettes.

TWO WAYS. TOM BOY. 1 vol. 12mo. Cloth, $1.50.
Two Ways is a story of convent school life, describing a little world in itself. Tom Boy is replete with fun, pathos, and child experience which is not all fiction.

THE STUDENT OF BLENHEIM FOREST. 1 vol. 12mo. Cloth, $1.50.
The hero is of a distinguished Protestant family in old Virginia, whose clear intellect discerns beauties in Catholic teachings, which he heroically follows up until it ends in his happy conversion.

For sale by all booksellers. Sent, post-paid, upon receipt of price. Catalogues of our books mailed free.

JOHN MURPHY & CO., BALTIMORE.

THE HEIRESS

OF

CARRIGMONA.

ANNA HANSON DORSEY,

AUTHOR OF "COAINA," "FLEMMINGS," "TANGLED PATHS,"
"MAY BROOKE," ETC., ETC., ETC.

THIRD THOUSAND.

BALTIMORE:
PUBLISHED BY JOHN MURPHY & CO.,
PRINTERS TO HIS HOLINESS THE POPE,
AND TO HIS EMINENCE CARDINAL GIBBONS.

DEDICATION.

TO THE
REV. EDWARD E. SORIN,

Father-General of the Congregation of the Holy Cross, who, having done for the cause of Religion and Education in the great North-West an apostolic and illustrious work, is spared to see the harvests sown in his youth grow and strengthen, and increase and ripen, until the "desert has been made to blossom as the rose," and his age crowned with a fruition seldom vouchsafed to the servants of God on earth, this story is dedicated with sentiments of profound respect by

The Author,

ANNA HANSON DORSEY.

The Heiress of Carrigmona.

CHAPTER I.

CHE SIN?*

"MICHAEL TRAVERS! Michael! I say are you deaf, man alive, that you sit there like you were in a trance, niver spakin' a word for the last two hours!" said Dame Travers, as she pushed back the spinning wheel, placed both hands on her knees, and fixed a keen inquiring glance on her husband, who sat in his old, high-backed arm chair, by the fire-side, with one foot upon his knee, his arms folded across his breast, and his head drooping forward, as if he were pondering on some subject that both troubled and perplexed him.

"Oh, vo! has the man lost his voice as well as his hearin'? Michael! Michael Travers! stir yoursel' *achree*, and go afther an armful of turf. Don't you see the fire's almost as dead in the grate as it is in your pipe?" cried Dame Travers, more shrilly, for experience had taught her to

---

* Who comes?

dread the dreamy, sorrowful mood that seemed to have fallen on her husband, as the precursor of some approaching misfortune or affliction.

"Erra hould, now, wife," said the old man, rousing himself. "Did any one come over from Carrigmona to-day?"

"Niver a one; but that's nothin' strange, faix! though your own brother lives along with the ould Methodish there, an's as bad a pagan as himsel', sure," said Mrs. Travers sharply. "But what's that got to do with the long face you've pulled on yoursel', and the dead coal in yer pipe? Mightn't I die in sin, but I'm afeard you've run your ould head agin some trouble that you're hidin' from me, Michael, *asthore?*"

"Look you hether, wife," said the old man in a sad, subdued voice, "don't you remimber these forty years back, wheniver any throuble was comin', I felt it beforehand creepin' like a could wind, through my heart an' marrow?"

"Oh, *wirra!* The heavens look down upon ye! Did you have it on ye to-day?"

"Iss, ever since my eyes were opened this blessed day, I felt it. First, it seems to be me; then it seems to be Misther Lacie at Carrigmona; then it seem to be Shaneen * that the black sorrow's comin' to," replied the old man solemnly.

"Christ be good to us!" said Dame Travers, crossing herself devoutly. "Cheer up, *avick.*

---

* Little John.

Mightn't I die in my sins, but to the best of my belief it's just nothin' at all but the could chills of autumn that's creepin' through your ould bones. Give me your pipe, man alive! and let me fill it for yez, then take a smoke, while I brew some bitter yerbs that's a cure for all the disorders of the liver an' stomach, under the sun."

"The MAN ABOVE only knows what it is; but be it this, that, or the other, it houlds a tight grip o' my heart. May the saints above guard *a bouchal dhas* * from the black luck of this life, and show him the way to glory in the next," said the old man, rising slowly up from his chair, and going to the door. "It's as bright as May, wife, but there's a keen cut of wind comin' down the side of Carrigmanne. I'll go out and fetch in some turf."

"Faix, honey, it's the best thing can be done. As you go by, see that the *dure* of the potato house is fastened; and if you meet Shaneen, send him down to the field beyant, to drive home the cows," said Dame Travers, bustling around, as he buttoned his frieze cotamore over his breast, and went out. "I'll give him somethin' to stir up his ould blood, the crayture, an' kape him in good heart." Having pushed back her flax wheel into its place, and swept the hearth, she went to the door and looked abroad, partly from

---

* My handsome boy.

habit, and partly to see if her husband walked with his usual strong, firm step; and seeing that he did, she shaded her eyes with her hand, from the slanting sunbeams, and looked down in the direction of Glendalough, hoping to see the tall, handsome form of her son coming homewards. Perhaps because it was so familiar to her eye, she did not observe the scene of mingled grandeur and beauty that lay spread out around her. The "Farm" lay on a slope, which swept gracefully but boldly down from the mountain, to the broad sandy shores of the Lough.* The cottage was not very spacious, but there was an air of comfort and thrift about it—for Dame Travers was a North-country woman—that more than compensated for its want of size. The haggart and potato-house were well filled with the fruits of an abundant harvest; the turf-stack promised no lack of fuel; and a modest little dairy, half hidden under the low overhanging boughs of an old beech tree, planted more than a century back, by one of Michael Travers' ancestors, with its white-washed walls, its thatched roof, its broad bench covered with clean pails, put there to sun, and the green vines that trailed over the door and windows, bespoke not only industry, but taste. Higher up the mountain, where wild crags and grotesque cliffs usurped the fern, the pine and the heather that lower down clothed

---

* Lough Luggela.

it with verdure, a tiny streamlet, from some hidden spring, gushed from its rocky bed, and fell sparkling, ringing, and frothing from point to point, flashing in the sunlight like a shower of diamonds, or gurgling in the shadow like molten emeralds—and made its way through the midst of the dairy, where a paved channel received it—and went rejoicing on its course down to the beautiful waters of Luggela, into whose bosom it bounded like a laughing child to the embrace of its mother. John Travers had named the beautiful cascade "*The Milk of the Reek.*"* From the open door of the dairy came the notes of a blithe sweet voice singing in spirited strains the old air of *Theela na Guira*. In the fields that stretched away on the hill-side, a small flock of sheep were grazing, and two or three cows, with well-filled udders, stood with contented air, chewing their cud among the stubble. The crimson glory of sunset was over it all, save where the dark, bleak cliffs of Carrigmanne, and the gray vaulted sides of Luggduff frowned down over the quiet Lough, throwing a black shadow far and near over its rippling waters. Beyond stretched away the rugged hills, some covered with verdure, others lifting their bare gleaming peaks, and grotesque, rugged outlines against the sky, while abrupt gorges, and smiling valleys between, softened

---

* The Milk of the Mountain Rock.

and brightened the otherwise savage scenery. Amidst the wild ruggedness of a mountain pass, on the opposite side of Lough Luggela, on a plateau which was densely covered with pine, ash, and beech trees, and a luxuriant undergrowth of holly and fern, and surrounded above, on each side, and below by bare gray rocks, the sharp gables, chimney-stacks, and peaked turrets of Carrigmona could be faintly discerned.

While Michael Travers was filling a basket with turf, at the stack, a young maiden with the bright flush of youth on her soft cheeks, and the fresh light of life in her dark blue eyes, with health and strength developed in every line of her rounded and symmetrical form, emerged from the dairy, and pausing a moment after she had secured the door, to twist up and fasten to the back of her head the mass of golden hair that had fallen in rippling waves and curls over her shoulders, down below her waist, she shaded her eyes with her hand, and looked eagerly and expectantly down towards the Lough. But a bird skimming the waters was all that greeted her sight; and turning away with a sigh of disappointment, she hurried away with fleet steps towards the turf-stack where the old man still lingered over his task.

"Let me help you, Mr. Travers," said the girl. "It doesn't make an ould back any the stronger, to be stooping in that way."

"The heavens look down upon you, Ally,

asthore! but you give me a start," said Michael Travers, raising himself erect, and wiping his forehead. "Have you seen Shaneen?"

"No," she replied, while the roses grew redder in her cheeks.

"Where can the boy be all this time?" said the old man, peering anxiously down through the gathering shadows, towards the valley of the Seven Churches, from under his white shaggy eyebrows.

"Wisha, then, but it's a hard matter to tell. You know the strange gintry that come to these parts to look at the ruins at Glendalough an' St. Kevin's Bed, an' the grand ould Wicklow hills, think the half's not seen if John Travers don't go hither and there with 'em to show what's worth lookin' at," said the girl, proudly. "But hould! there's some one comin' this way! It can't be John, though, for he's as straight as a young ash, and this one stoops. That I ever should have taken him for Shaneen!" she said, turning away with a light-hearted laugh. By this time the basket was filled, and helping the old man to lift it to his shoulder, they returned to the house together, where he busied himself in replenishing the fire, while she remained without to tie up some vines of honeysuckle, that were flaunting over the door. Dame Travers, who was washing some potatoes, and preparing to fry a flitch of bacon for supper, was so full of her household cares as already to have forgotten her late cause of disquiet, when the sound of a strange footstep on the flagged pathway without caused her to turn towards the door, and as she did so, the tall form of a stranger stood upon the threshold. He was clad in a suit of brown from his head to his feet. His face wore a stern and forbidding aspect. His hair, slightly waving over his temples and shoulders, was iron-gray. A black silk handkerchief was tied loosely around his throat, over which fell a broad, square collar, stained with dust. His coat was rounded off in front after the fashion peculiar to the costume of the Dissenters, and altogether his appearance was far from inspiring confidence.

"Good even, madam," said the stranger, in harsh but not discourteous tones; but so unexpected had been his appearance, and so sudden and abrupt was his salutation, that Dame Travers dropped the flitch of bacon she was about putting into the frying-pan, in the ashes.

"A'ra, gal!" she exclaimed, while she attempted to rescue the flitch from destruction, and drop a prim little courtesy at the same time. But the attempt was futile, for she blistered her fingers among the coals, and stumbled over a pail, which brought her all standing before the intruder.

"Will you be good enough to tell me, madam, the nearest way to Mr. Lacie's place? I believe it is called Carrigmona, and is somewhere hereabouts."

"Your servant, sir," replied the dame, bent on being genteel, and making her very best courtesy; "will you please to walk in; there's my husband who has a brother livin' at Carrigmona, can tell your honor all about it."

"Iss, your honor," said Michael Travers, coming forward, and offering his guest a chair, "your honor's not far from Carrigmona, Misther Lacie's place: but it would take a goat's fut to travel there to-night, more by rayson of the steepness an' wildness of the way, than the distance."

"Can you tell me how my—how Mr. Lacie is? I understood that he was in ill health?"

"Faix! it's more than I can say exactly. They say Misther Lacie's been in a bad way this some time back; but it's been two weeks since any news come to us from Carrigmona, though a brother of my own lives there. The docthers say he'll die suddint."

"Is there no possible way of getting to Carrigmona to-night?" asked the stranger, chafing.

"It 'ill be at the risk of your honor's life to try it. If it was not so near night, an' my son, John Travers, was to the fore, he could guide your honor there. But rest aisy, your honor's welcome in God's name to stay where you be until it's safe for you to go. I wouldn't turn a divil of an *informer* out, to find his way through this wild country by night, if he was a stranger in it, as your honor seems to be," said the old man, looking keenly into the stranger's eyes, which, however, did not flinch for an instant.

"Thank you, sir," replied the stranger, laying aside his broad-brimmed slouch hat, and setting his walking-stick in the corner: "I thankfully accept of your hospitality, at least until the moon rises; then I *must* find my way to Carrigmona."

"While I was tying up the honeysuckle," said Ally Kane, the young maiden whom we have described, "I saw a boat comin' round from Luggduff with two gentlemin, an' I think John was rowin' it."

"Oyeh!" said the old man as if suddenly relieved of a weight of anxiety, "of coorse it was Shaneen, takin' some travellers aboard there to St. Kevin's Bed. He's a great scholar, your honor, an' can tell the traditions an' lagends of every ould stone in Wicklow, barrin' the Round Tower at the Seven Churches, an' there's no man livin' can tell the story of it, or the likes of it in all Ireland; an' when the Englishers come travellin' up to these parts, to see the Wicklow hills, an' the ould Abbey, an' the Lough, and the Valley of the Avoca, an' St. Kevin's Bed, the boy's gone, day in an' day out, guidin' them hither an' yon, an' tellin' 'em the history of everything like a book."

"*A bouchal dhas*," said the mother, proudly; "sure an' I've known the strange gintry to wait a week rayther than go without him. Maybe your honor hasn't seen the country!" she said, addressing herself to the stranger, who now sat with his hands folded together, looking intently into the glowing turf fire, as if he were endeavoring to solve some difficult problem.

"Enough to satisfy me. I am not travelling for pleasure," was the curt reply.

"Maybe your honor's the great counsellor that's expected up from Dublin," said old Travers with a sidelong look, but in a deferential tone of voice.

"No, thanks be to God, I don't belong to the Law."

"See that now! That I should be such an ould *bocaun* * as to mistake a gintleman of your cloth for a counsellor, when I might see with the half of an eye sure, by the cut of your honor's coat what you wor. Mr. Lacie's a Methodish hissel'; leastways he's half an' half."

"He's what?" asked the stranger abruptly, as he raised his head and looked full into the old man's eyes.

"Faix then, your honor, there's no disrespect intinded, but he niver goes to Mass, or sees the the inside of a church but twice a year, an' that's on Ash Wednesday, an' Palm Sunday, when he comes marchin' in like a sodger, to get ashes, an' marches out agin'; an' nobody hears of him agin' until Palm Sunday comes round, when be-

---

* Soft, innocent person.

dad! there he is gettin' his bless'd palm as aiger as the best Catholic amongst us. At other times he goes to the Methodish parson's chapel, a mile or so beyant Glendalough;" said the garrulous old man, "an' kapes neither festival nor fast, God help him."

"Pshaw," said the stranger, "Mr. Lacie is right."

"*Wisha*, dear knows! People now-a-days has quare ideas of gettin' safe into the other world, but I'm afeard they're wrong, for all the larnin' an' hocus-pocus they build up their doctrines with.

"Look you hether, your honor!" continued Michael, who dearly loved a bit of argumentation, and prided himself on his theological lore, "the MAN ABOVE gave us one true Faith by which we are to stand or fall. HE planted that Faith in one true Church, that declares on His own word that there's but one God, one Faith, and one Baptism. He says we must hear the Church or be accursed. He says we must be baptized or be damned. How is it, then, your honor, when a man has lived all his days without baptism, without the holy sacraments, an' without the Church, as much as any red pagan in the wilds of Ameriky? As to the Methodishes, that's no faith at all, at all. *Wisha*, but I misdoubt if Mr. Lacie's ever been baptized."

"Is there any law in Ireland to prevent Mr. Lacie's going to the devil his own way?" asked the stranger coldly.

"Oyeh! oh *wirra!* It's to be hoped the blessin' of the poor that he's befrinded 'ill kape him out of that intirely," exclaimed the old man, taken all aback by the question, as well as by the abrupt manner and harsh voice of his guest.

"Humph! you seem to have a good piece of land here," he observed, without noticing the effect his words had caused.

"Yes," answered the old man, with a sigh, "it's been with the Travers, your honor, four ginerations back; but there's no tellin' how soon we'll be put out of it if Mr. Lacie—God preserve him—dies. Our lase expires next Candlemas day."

"It can be renewed, I suppose?"

"If Mr. Lacie lives, your honor—yes."

"There's John's footsteps, Ally," said Mrs. Travers, hastening to dish the potatoes, while Ally scalded the tea, and sat the *cruiskeen* of rich milk on the table. The door opened, and a handsome, muscular young man, whose fine face was flushed with exercise, walked in. On seeing a stranger, he lifted his cap from the dark crisp curls that clustered over his head, and saluted him with a modest and courteous air, in which there was much of natural grace, blended with the dignity of a manly and independent spirit.

"And this is your son, madam?" said the stranger, turning towards Dame Travers, after he had bowed his head stiffly, in acknowledgment of John Travers' salutation.

"Yes, your honor, this is our Shaneen," said the old dame proudly, while the young man passed round, and stooped over for an instant to kiss her cheek, after which he turned to Ally, who stood blushing, as she pretended to arrange the oat-meal cakes on a plate, and stole his arm about her waist, while he whispered something in her ear that deepened the roses in her cheeks to a carnation tint.

"If your honor's not above sittin' at a poor man's table, you're welcome to the best we've got," said old Travers, setting a chair at the board for his guest.

"I am obliged to you for your hospitality, friend," replied the stranger, while a sudden gleam lit up his stern features, and altered their character so distinctly that he looked like a different man; "I am not above doing so, I assure you, and accept a place at your family board with many thanks."

"Take this sate," said Dame Travers, bustling, "it is a warm corner, your honor; and I'll pour ye's out a cup of tay, that the like of's not to be found in all Ireland. My brother-in-law brought it to me from the Injees, when he an' Mr. Lacie came home from furrin parts. An' there's some oat meal cakes, an' fresh butter of our Ally's make—help yoursel', sir,"

They gathered around the table, and each one, except the stranger, made the sign of the cross, and asked the blessing of God on their homely but plentiful repast. There was something in the act and in the momentary silence that ensued, that commanded his attention if not respect; for he sat quiet and motionless, until the voice of Dame Travers asking him if she should put sugar in his tea, admonished him that it was over, when he fell to, with a good will, and partook of the healthy and delicious fare before him, with a zest that showed how he relished it. After the first keen edge was taken off his appetite, he turned to John Travers and inquired, "if it would be possible for him to get to Carrigmona that night?"

"My boat is below on the shore, your honor, and I could row you over the Lough; but it's a rough, wild walk from the Carrigmona landin' up to Mr. Lacie's. If your honor's not afraid—"

"Afraid? What is there to fear, young man? This is not a savage country, is it?" interrupted the stranger.

"No thanks to savage laws that govern it —beggin' your honor's pardon—that it isn't. But some say it's not safe hereabouts at night, on account of some unlawful characters, that scatter here and there at times, burnin' hayricks and the like. Wouldn't it be better for your honor to wait until mornin'?"

"I'd rather not. I must see Mr. Lacie as soon as practicable. I am not in dread of these chaps that you speak of. Is Mr. Lacie a popular man in the country?"

"He's been a good landlord, your honor, an' that's sayin' a dale," said old Travers.

"So, ho! It's an old family, I believe?"

"Oh, vo! Did your honor never hear tell of the Lacies of Carrigmona? They come in wid the Conquest—divil take it—an' married wid the Aidens—all black Presbytarins together—an' for persecutin' the Catholics of Ireland, got a grant of abbeys and church-lands from the crown; but they got a black curse with 'em, bedad, that didn't let such property stick to their name, for one gineration afther another had to sell, sell; they got poorer an' poorer, as might ha' been expected, until it's well nigh all gone except Carrigmona, an' a few farms. The MAN ABOVE only knows who'll inherit it when Mr. Lacie dies, by rayson of there bein' no male heir left of 'em all."

"Has Mr. Lacie no children?" inquired the stranger, who seemed to lend more than a passing interest to the old man's words.

"Iss, your honor, he has one, a poor untrained lassie, that looks more like a wild motherless colt, than a gintleman's daughter. Faith, thin! she can handle the oars, an' scull a boat aiqual to Shaneen there; an' to see her standin' in her shell of a boat when the water is rough in the Lough, her great black eyes wide open an' shinin' like two stars, an' she singin' some wild outlandish song, that sounds, bedad, like the scrame of a young aigle, is enough to scare the wits out of a body, not knowin' but she'll go over every minute, and be drownded. As to the ould churches in the valley, she knows every stone an' inscription thereabouts, from the Cathedral to *Teampul na Skellig*; from St. Kevin's Kitch to the *Rhepart*—"

"But she's good to the poor, God bless her, an' thinks nothin' of walkin' five miles an' more to carry some nice thing to a poor sick body," said Dame Travers.

"That she is; may the heavens look down upon her!—an' has a winsome way of her own, that brings out their griefs, like a good confessor brings out the troubles from a poor sinner's heart," said the old man warmly, for he loved the motherless and neglected maiden of Carrigmona.

"What's that Shaneen asthore, you wor tellin' me about Carrigmona, that you got out of some ould book or manyscript? Maybe his honor'd like to hear it. He's got it at his finger ends, your honor!" said Dame Travers, always glad of an opportunity to bring out the acquirements of her son.

"I shall be glad to hear it," observed the stranger, with an appearance of interest.

"It is not much, your honor. Carrigmona, Mr. Lacie's place, was an Abbey once, founded on land that Brandube, king of Leinster, gave to one Aiden for the Hospitallers Knights. In 1166 Dermot McMurchad, King of Leinster, burnt the little town that was a depindancy on the Abbey of Carrigmona, an' drove out the monks, an' rifled the abbey of its gold an' jewels. Afterwards, struck with remorse, he founded a Benedictine monastery there on the ruins of the ould abbey, that was confiscated to an ancestor of the Lacies by Queen Elizabeth. Then the Lacies an' the Aidens married together, an' Englishers married with their descindants, who in turn mated with the Gentychs, one of the Dutch families planted here by Oliver Cromwell, who has his deserts by this time, anyways."

"So you think," observed the stranger, gravely, "that the Supreme Being withdraws His blessing from those who receive, unjustly, lands and buildings consecrated to His service and glory."

"*Bachal Essu!* there's no mortial doubt of it, your honor. I could tell your honor of more nor fifty proud ould families that's got the same curse on 'em as the Lacies. Look you hether, your honor! surely there's no sin aiqual to *sacrilege*. Christ defend us! Amin!" said the old man Travers, crossing himself devoutly.

"*Che sin?*" ejaculated Dame Travers, lifting her finger and leaning forward, as footsteps rang on the flags without, and glad of an opportunity to change the subject, which she shrewdly judged from the stranger's lowering brows, was becoming distasteful to him. With her keen woman's wit on the alert, and another life com-

.ing into the estate, she did not know how the
conversation might act against their efforts to
procure a new lease; for she had her own suspicions about their guest, which had nothing
clearly defined in them, but were strong enough
to make her wish him to be rather conciliated
than offended. Everything—prosperity, happiness, and comfort—depended on the success of
their efforts to get their lease renewed; hence
they had it more at heart than anything on
earth. For the sake of their son and fair Ally
Kane, his betrothed, they would have made any
sacrifice to gain the desired end. The door
opened, and a tall, stooping figure, wrapped in
a dark frieze cotamore, about whose face a mass
of shaggy gray hair was hanging, came in. An
old otter-skin cap was pulled down over his forehead, quite concealing the upper part of his face.

"*Cead mille failthe*, though you're not the
greatest beauty betune this an' Dublin," said
Michael Travers, rising up, and extending his
hand.

"Uncle Owny!" exclaimed John Travers,
springing from his sweetheart's side to greet the
new-comer.

"Erra, hould now," said the man, pushing
back his cap, "I've not a minit to spare. I've
jist spent myself this fortnight goin' to an' fro
betune Carrigmona an' Glendalough on a wild
goose chase; an' I thought I'd come up an' rest
my ould shins, an' moisten my throat with a

drop of *potheen* afore I trudged back to Carrigmona."

"You're welcome in God's name, brother, for it's not often we lay our two eyes upon ye. How's the Master?" said Michael Travers, taking down a keg, and a small pewter flagon.

"Oh, *wirra!* don't be afther askin'! I don't know but the breath 'll be out of him by the time I get back, an' it'll be as much the fau't of his frettin' to see them he's expectin' these three weeks, as the disease itsel'. God grant he'd come, for I'm heart-sick intirely with these tramps to Glendalough an' back."

"What did you say is your master's name?" asked the stranger, eagerly, he having only heard what the new comer last said.

"I'm not ashamed to tell it to your honor," said the man with a scrape, and a keen, searching glance of the eye. "It is Reginald Lacie, of Carrigmona, at your service."

"Good God!" murmured the stranger, rising hastily from the table. "Friend," he said aloud, "I have come over the sea on business with Mr. Lacie, of Carrigmona. I must see him without delay. Did you say he is ill? And do you intend going to Carrigmona to-night?"

"There's no misdoubtin' your honor's right to see him," said Owen Travers, taking off his cap, and speaking in a respectful tone, "for by the token of the ould Lacie eye that's blazin' undher your black brows, you're the one he's expectin'. Take a dhrop of *potheen*, your honor, for you've got a rough journey before you," he continued, proffering him the overflowing flagon of peat-whiskey, that his brother had just placed in his hand.

"Thank you, I never taste anything of the kind," said the stranger, drily, as he buttoned up his coat.

"Faix, your honor, it's aiqual to a horse an' car; the road we'll have to jog presently 'ud take the breath out of a mule, without a sup o' this to spur him up."

"Drink it yourself, friend. I like to have my wits about me at all times, and more particularly when I have a wild, unknown road in a strange country to travel. An egg-shell full of that stuff would make me too giddy to move a step."

"See that, now, your honor! mine would be the same way without it," said Owen Travers, taking a deep draught from the flagon, and smacking his lips with full content. "Faix, now I'm ready to go to the top of Carrigmanne. Come Shaneen, *avick*, be off with you, an' get your boat in trim, ready for his honor. Goodbye, sister-in-law. Give me a kiss, sweetheart; shake a fist, Mike, old fellow. Now, if your honor's ready, we'll be off."

After they went away, Dame Travers began to clear off the supper table, assisted by Alice. As she lifted her cup, and emptied the dregs into a slop-bowl, something heavy and bright jingled out, upon which she speedily plunged in her hand, and fished up a golden guinea, which their strange guest, unperceived by any of them, had slyly dropped into her cup before he left.

CHAPTER II.

THE PERISHED SECRET.

IN a quaint old room, panelled with oak, which age had darkened and polished, with a ceiling so low that a tall man could touch it with his palm, surrounded by antique furniture and hangings, the richness of which time had faded and mildewed, a man whose years had passed their prime lay tossing uneasily in a fitful slumber, on a bed whose drapery of tattered crimson velvet was drawn back, and twisted around the massive carved posts of the bedstead, as if for the purpose of admitting air. The red flickering light from the capacious fireplace, where two huge logs of fir were smouldering, and bursting out at intervals into fierce jets of flame, revealed features of a high and noble type, which, but for the wasted flesh that covered them, the sunken eyes, the sharp, pinched expression, and pallor, might even still have been called handsome. By the fire, on the hearth, crouched a dwarfed and extremely black negro, who was so intent on stirring a decoction, to which he now and then carefully added some new ingredient, that he did not observe the restless motions of the sick man, who threw his arms about and grasped the bed-clothes, as drowning men clutch at straws; then after a few sobbing sighs, during which time his features were wrung with some mortal pain, he once more lapsed into heavy slumber. We have heard from John Travers that the Lacies at one time intermarried with the Gentychs, and it was at this period that some of the rooms at Carrigmona had been repaired and fitted up by foreign workmen. Over the mantel were three large panels, on which was represented the history of Dives and Lazarus, evidently painted by some skilful Flemish artist. In the centre piece, Dives, clothed in purple and fine linen, sat feasting in his banqueting hall, while Lazarus, smitten by poverty and disease, lay at his gate, where the dogs licked his sores. On the right the scene was changed: Lazarus was seen leaning on Abraham's bosom, surrounded by a company of the bright hosts of heaven, and clouds of splendor. On the left, Dives was seen in hell, lifting up his hands amidst the flames, imploring the aid of Lazarus to obtain a drop of water to cool his tongue in the fierce heat of his torment. Although the colors were somewhat faded, and the smoke of nearly two centuries had blurred and almost obliterated the lesser details of the artist's pencil, the chief characters and principal facts of this old and every-day story were distinctly—and when the red glare of the flames lit up the room with a sudden illumination—almost horribly visible. Between the windows hung a mirror, which was once a marvel of splendor, but was now so tarnished, mildewed, and dim, that for realities it gave back but wavering, grotesque phantoms. Over it drooped a yellow and withered branch of blessed palm. Two or three old portraits of nobles and ladies of the old Cromwellian times, dingy, and showing every sign of decadence like the rest, hung here and there, grasping in their long white hands—for the Lacies were always famous for their beautiful hands—bibles, psalm-books, or swords, the patents of the house of Lacie, by which, through desecration and sacrilege, they had enriched and lifted up their fallen fortunes at the expense of their conscience.

Without, the wind which had risen and now blew with violence through the mountain gorges, crushed the old trees against the window panes, and ploughed up the waters of Lough Luggela, until, like a mimic sea, its waves dashed with a hollow murmur against the rocks below. Now and then, heavy drops of rain lashed the window panes, the *avant-courier* of a storm. The negro having finished his task over the fire to his satisfaction, wiped off the beads of sweat from his wrinkled face, and rising with difficulty, for his feet were both turned inwards, he approached the bed as noiselessly as he could move, to see if his master still slept.

"I am dying, Graff," gasped Mr. Lacie. "I shall never see Hugh Lacie again."

"Lor' mighty, mas'r! what's de use of forever croakin'? You ain't g'wine to die yet. No indeed. Here, mas'r, drink some of dis here hot milk punch. It'll strengthen your innards."

"Thank you, my faithful fellow," whispered Mr. Lacie, who had almost exhausted his little remaining strength in the effort to swallow the proffered nourishment. "I must see him. Why does he not come? I wrote for him months ago, and he said he would come. I *must* live to see my brother."

"So you will, mas'r, so you will," replied the negro soothingly.

"Has Owny Travers come yet?"

"He'll be here presently, old mas'r—go to sleep now."

"No time for sleep, Graff. Owny never staid so late before. Perhaps he's come!" said Mr. Lacie, while a sudden gleam of hope irradiated his features. "What's that?"

"It's nothin' but dat puddle down dar, tryin' to swell herself up to a sea," said Graff, nodding his head contemptuously in the direction of the Lough, the tumult of whose waters came up the steep sides of the rocky hill with a dreary sound. "I shouldn't wonder if he'd bust some time."

"What's that? Listen!"

"It's nuffin', mas'r, but de wind splittin' he sides agin dese wild Irish hills. Golly, it minds me of a steel comb goin' through a nigger's wool."

"Go out, Graff, and see if Owny Travers is coming. My God! if I should die before my brother comes! Raise up my head before you go, and throw a pine knot on the fire. The place seems strangely dark."

"Dar now," said Graff, after obeying his commands, "it's all right now. It is growin' dark, ole mas'r—it's nigh on to six o'clock, sir. Dar! now she blows!" continued Graff, as the resinous wood blazed up and threw out a ruddy glare. "Dat's jolly! it mind's me, ole mas'r, of de time de 'Will o' Wisp' used to lay to under de lee of Sicily, wid the red light from de *wolcano* all over her sails." A deep sigh was the negro's only answer, and he was preparing to leave the room when Mr. Lacie, pallid and gasping, called him back, but a spasm of pain prevented his speaking, and a struggle for breath ensued, which seemed to be the mortal agony. But it passed off, leaving him whiter and weaker than before, and he whispered "Eveleen."

"She out on de cliffs somewhar, ole mas'r. *She* don't mind de wind, nor de rain, nother— I 'spect she's lookin' out for Owny."

"Send her to me—my poor little girl—my poor motherless child," said Mr. Lacie, in tones of anguish. "I am better now, Graff—go."

"Aye, aye, old mas'r," replied the negro, softly, as he went out and closed the door softly after him.

While the master of Carrigmona—Reginald

Lacie—lies silent and alone, cumbered at the last narrow pass with his earthly cares, and a dreary retrospect of the past—and about launching without preparation on the dark tide which would bear him straight on to judgment, we will, in a few brief words, tell what we know of his history. We say what we know, because there was a veil of mystery over certain portions of his life which was never lifted. He had been a wild, disobedient, profligate lad, and in a fit of boyish rage forsook his home and native shores forty years before, accompanied by his foster-brother, Owen Travers. They bound themselves to a foreign sea captain, whose barque lay at Cork, ready to sail. Since then no one had heard aught of him until, one day, about ten years before, he suddenly appeared at Carrigmona, accompanied by a little girl some five summers old, Owny Travers, and the dwarfed negro, Graff. His agent, responsible to his brother in America, Hugh Lacie, from whom he was safely separated by a wide ocean—had carried matters with a high hand on the estate. Mr. Lacie speedily redressed his tenants' wrongs, by a dismissal of the petty tyrant who had so long lorded it with an iron rule over them, mismanaged his affairs, and enriched himself at his expense. They were scandalized at what they called his paganism, for he professed no creed; but they were loyal and grateful, and no Catholic landlord in all Ireland had tenants who would have gone farther to serve him than those of Carrigmona. He held himself aloof from the few gentry who had seats in the neighborhood, and plunged at once into a law-suit with Sir William Erle, for the recovery of a certain portion of the Carrigmona estate, which had been sold by his agent during his absence without his authority. It was the popular belief that Mr. Lacie was rich, but *how* he had acquired his supposed wealth, was a problem; for never a word escaped his lips, or those of his two attendants, to give the slightest clue to the mystery, beyond the fact that he had followed the sea; but whether as a merchantman or a privateer, was never known. He used to go to Dublin twice a year on business, and letters with foreign post marks on them used to come to the little post town near by, directed to him. The ill-disposed used to shake their heads, and say: "If Reginald Lacie was rich, and had got his money by honest trade, he'd not be ashamed to own it." "And, as to religion, faith! it is as well known as can be," said a hanger-on of the Erles, "that two of 'em has sowld their sowls to the divil any way; an' Mr. Lacie's self was only kept out of the scrape by the holy ashes an' blissid palm he got every Ash Wednesday and Palm Sunday."

It was a lamentable fact that Owen Travers, to the scandal of all his family, and his old acquaintances, had given up the practice of his religion, and was classed by them with the worst of pagans; while they regarded the negro, Graff, as a sort of household devil, placed there by the Arch-enemy of souls, to guard against their escape from his clutches. And yet Mr. Lacie was a kind and lenient landlord, dealing out equal justice to all, and demanding strict justice in return; and his motherless child had found her way not only into the poor cabins of the surrounding peasantry, but also into their hearts. She was a frequent attendant at Mass, when the stations were held about the neighborhood, and she had told some one that her mother—a South American lady, named Dolores Villeiano—had been a Catholic until the day of her death; but that was all that was ever heard of the lady Dolores, for the child never spoke of her again, and remained obstinately silent when questioned, or would say: "I have no mother but the Blessed Lady." It was thought strange that Mr. Lacie should allow his child to cultivate her Catholic tendencies, and mingle so freely with Catholics, for it had been almost three hundred years since the head of a Lacie had bowed adoringly to the Sacred Host, or a Lacie's lips had murmured an *Ave Maria;* however, as she did not receive the sacraments, they regarded it as the result of an eccentric negligence, rather than a favorable sign of toleration. Of the house of Lacie, only three now lived: Reginald and his child, and Hugh, who had spent his life in the United States of America, and for whose presence his dying brother was now harassing himself with feverish expectation.

Higher yet the wind had risen; louder roared the waters of the Lough, and the wild blast shivered and moaned through the old trees without, bringing down showers of sere and withered leaves, which came tapping and flitting against the window-panes like stricken birds. The ruddy fire threw a red gleam out of the deep chimney, and lit up the pallid features of Reginald Lacie, which, now at rest, showed the comeliness and old noble type of his race. There was the same high, broad forehead, from which the white hair had fallen back; the high, arched nose; the same symmetrical firm-set mouth, which were seen in the faces of the old portraits hanging around; the same long, shapely hands; and although the flesh was shrunk away from his, the same broad, muscular shoulders. Now and then a spasm of anguish wrung his features, and he muttered strange, sorrowful words, as if some dark, terrible secret were tugging at his heartstrings. But the dead leaves and heavy rain drops dashed in a wild flurry against the casement, and the ruddy fire crackled and blazed like a demoniac *feu de joie* up the broad chimney, until it seemed to mock, with its lurid glare, the mortal who lay dying in its light. Suddenly footsteps rang on the flagged walk under the windows. Mr. Lacie must have heard them in his sleep, for starting up he opened his eyes wide, and exclaiming: "It is he!" sunk back panting and gasping, as if every breath would be his last. The door was opened, and Owny Travers, dripping with rain, came in, followed by the tall gaunt stranger whom he had so unexpectedly met at his brother's cottage, who proved to be none other than Mr. Hugh Lacie; and who now, pale with fatigue, wet, and cold, looked even more stern and forbidding than when we first saw him. He looked like one who had outlived all mundane softness. Creeping slowly in, after them, came a maiden over whose life some fifteen summers might have passed. A faded crimson shawl was thrown over her head, and gathered over her bosom where she held it in her small, slender fingers, from whence it fell almost to her feet, half concealing the dark dingy dress she wore. The symmetry of her delicately-formed feet and ankles was concealed by clumsy woolen stockings, and heavy, half-worn shoes. But through this coarse and faded attire shone a face of wild and touching beauty, from which the raven hair, on which the rain-drops glistened, was pushed quite back. Her eyes, now wearing a sad and startled look, were as dark and lustrous as a fawn's; her nose was neither Grecian nor *retrousse*, but a symmetrical line between the two; her mouth was small, firm, and exquisitely formed, and a dimple on her chin imparted to her sunburnt countenance a rare and beautiful aspect of amiability. These were the features of Eveleen

Lacie, the heiress of Carrigmona; but her face was thin and sunburnt, and there was a shyness and awkwardness in her manner that sadly marred the effect of her natural advantages. She stole round to the side of the bed, and leaning over, smoothed Mr. Lacie's damp forehead, and whispered: "See, dear papa, I have brought him—Owny and I brought him, and you will be much better."

"Hugh," faltered Mr. Lacie, feebly stretching out his hand.

"Reginald!"

Thus spake the two men—brothers who had not looked on each other's face since boyhood—as they grasped hands.

"I am sorry to find you so ill," remarked Hugh Lacie, seating himself by the bedside.

"I am dying, and I fear that I shall not be able to say all that I wish. I must speak with you alone," he said, as Graff, who had come in with the rest, hobbled up to the bedside, with a wine-glass full of milk punch, which he swallowed with difficulty. "Go out, all of you. I must see my brother alone."

"Aye, aye, sir," replied the negro, nodding.

"Eveleen—Hugh, this is my child. Go away now, Eveleen. I must be alone with your uncle. I feel stronger. Go to bed, poor child, for you are worn out with nursing, and watching me;" said Mr. Lacie, laying his hand on the girl's head; and drawing her pale face down to his, he

kissed her tenderly, and whispered "Good night."
Good night it was forever.

"Let me stay, dear papa. I am not weary or sleepy," she pleaded, as she nestled close to him.

"Obey your father, young woman. We have business together," said her uncle, in austere tones.

"If *he* says I *must* go, I will go, but not otherwise," said the young girl, lifting up her head, while her bright Lacie eyes flashed irate fires.

"Yes, go, my love," faltered her father.

"I will go. But, sir," she added, turning to her uncle, "you will please call me, if he grows worse."

"Of course I will; but what good such a slip of a thing could do, if you came, is more than I can tell," was the ungracious reply.

Eveleen shrunk away from her father, after pressing another lingering kiss on his cheek, almost awed and terrified by the austere tone and manner of her uncle, and half tempted to defy him. She only desisted from so doing for fear of exciting her father, and making him worse. She gathered the faded crimson shawl about her, and while a flush of smothered indignation mantled her cheeks, she walked with a noiseless but proud step out of the room. Such tones were new to her, who from her infancy had queened it over the quaint household at Carrigmona like a little despot, and who had been flattered, and humored, and allowed her own way so long, by the three grim old men, that her ideas of the world and its people, beyond the Wicklow hills, were as unreal as any other *chateau d'Espagne.* She had never been thwarted, and it was plain to see that the old Lacie spirit had lost none of its fire by contact with the hot southern blood of the Lady Dolores Villeiano, that flowed in her veins. Owny said it, so did Graff, and they exchanged looks, and chuckled to themselves, as the girl went away.

"You, sirrah, can go to the kitchen," said Hugh Lacie to the negro.

"I stays by de ship, mas'r, till she sink. I ain't gwine away 'less Mas'r Lacie tell me so hese'f; bless God, ain't I," said Graff, doggedly.

"Faix, then, your honor, it'll take Misther Lacie's own ordhers to get me away from him, an' he dyin'," said Owny, winding one of his gaunt arms around the massive bed-post.

"Go, my friends," faltered Mr. Lacie, while a flood of tears obscured his sight—the last he would shed on earth forever—"I have much to say to my brother, and have lost too much time already. When—it—comes—to the last—you shall—be summoned."

"'Taiu't de fust time I laid on de mat at your door for want of a better watch-dog, an' I can do it agin, ole mas'r," replied the negro, passing his rough black hand over his eyes; after which he turned reluctantly away, and went out, casting an angry, defiant look at his master's brother as he went.

"Misther Lacie, *asthore*," said Owny Travers, softly, as he leaned over the dying man, "the heavens look down on your honor; it goes hard with me this day to folly your commands, but I niver put mysel' agin your word yet, an' faix! I won't do it now, that we're so nigh parting. But I'll be jist outside there, under the windy, an' if I'm wantin', all you have to do, sir," he said, turning to Hugh Lacie, "is to put the candle on the windy-sill."

"Very good. I hope you've finished your speeches. The man will die before the long-winded fools can be got rid of. I wonder if there are any more of them," muttered Hugh Lacie, glancing around.

"They have been my best friends through long years of wandering and peril. It seems unnatural to them to be driven away, the fast friends through weal and woe," said Mr. Lacie.

"Pardon me, Reginald. I am like an old file; but I am intent only on serving you—my roughness is less unkindness than impatience," said Hugh Lacie, more gently. "What can I do?"

"You see that I am dying. Well," said Mr. Lacie, drawing a sealed package from underneath his pillow, "I must be brief. In this you will find—my—will—and other—important papers—the certificate—of my—marriage—and of the—child's birth—and baptism. She—will—

be very—rich—but must not know—how rich. She'd squander it—give it away—and be brought to penury. Poverty has been the curse of the Lacies—poverty—and—cursed pride—together. Carrigmona is—yours—during your—life. Be kind to the tenants—to the Travers—in particular."

"Is that all, Reginald?" inquired Hugh Lacie, as the failing man paused.

"No! no! would it were!" cried he, in sudden tones of anguish. His vital energies, collecting their feeble remains of strength for the last struggle, imparted a force of unnatural depth to his voice, while he continued with slow distinctness, and in less broken sentences, to lay bare his heart to his brother.

"I am no priest, Reginald," he replied. "I'd rather not hear it, unless it is something about business that I can set right."

"It is a dark, terrible secret—I dare not take it with me—whither—I—am—going. It would damn me. You must hear it," continued the dying man, as if he had not heard the other's words, and seeming to gather strength as he spoke. "There is a man hereabouts named William Erle, who bought a portion of the Carrigmona domain during my absence abroad. I carried the affair before a legal tribunal—I desired strongly to reclaim it—I had good reasons for wishing it to remain in the family; but by some law quibble he triumphed, and I—lost. That man became my enemy—and I—his. He had a wife and child, money and position; he was a member of the British Parliament; his wife was beautiful and good—his boy noble and handsome; but I hated him, because he had by fraud become the possessor of what was mine; and because, thinking me a poor man, he treated me with supercilious insolence, that stings me even now when I think of it; and last, though not least, because he was wanting in those principles of honor that had been handed down like heirlooms in our family. But—my God!—what—strange — agony is this? Drink — give — me drink!" he exclaimed, as a sudden spasm, one of those wrenching and indescribable pangs caused by the disentanglement of the soul from its bonds of clay, tortured him. Gulping down a few mouthfuls of milk punch, he lay panting for several moments on his pillow, with an increased pallor on his pinched features, ere he recovered sufficient breath to go on.

"You did not murder the man, did you?" asked Hugh Lacie, in his cold, harsh tones, while he almost recoiled from his brother's bed-side.

"There's no blood on my hand, Hugh. Don't fear to touch it," said the fast-sinking man in a sharp whisper; "I did not murder this man. But I connived—in what—has been the—death—of his—happiness. I'll tell you. There was an old crone, a strange and friendless old creature, came down from the north years ago, and took up her abode in an uninhabited cabin that stood alone in a wild and secluded part of the estate. I did not drive her off, but repaired the hut, and allowed her to have whatever she could pick up about the place. The peasants said she was one who had lived with the *good people*,* and knew more than was good for her soul, and avoided her. This woman had a grand-daughter, who was famous in every part of Wicklow for her rare beauty, and old Hulda Bracken loved her with a fierce, fiery love—such love as the tigress of the jungle feels for her young. She watched her with as sharp a care as the wolf-dog who has one ewe lamb under his protection; and woe to the evil beast that with foul intent prowled too near that little fold! Yet that man—William Erle—encompassed her ruin, and the fair child died in giving birth to the offspring of her shame. The old woman buried her with her own hands. She would allow no one to touch her. She shed no tear. Her heart was scorched and seared by the blow, and she spake no word until the clods fell on the rough coffin lid of her child; then she bared her white locks to the wind, and lifting up her voice, she said, in shrill accents, 'This is my hour of desolation. Let William Erle, who has wrought it, look to his.' One night—a few months afterwards—a wild, freezing, wintry night, she came to me:

---

* Fairies.

she told me she was going to avenge—going—child—Erles—stolen—no—more—never seen—"
A sudden change, gray and shadowy, swept over Reginald Lacie's face—his speech failed him—his secret was, after all, about to perish. In vain his brother administered such restoratives as were at hand; the "arrow was fastened;" he spoke no more, but his eyes roved restlessly around, as if in search of some one. He was conscious, but his soul was hungry with some great want, which he could not now make known. Graff and Owen Travers were summoned. When the negro met his master's hopeless and helpless glance, he burst into a passion of tears, and turning to Hugh Lacie, broke out fiercely: "I s'pose you been prayin' wid my old Mas'r."

"Praying! me praying!" he stammered. "I'm no parson. Is my brother a—what do you call it—a pious person?"

"He's a better Christian dan many dat calls demselves 'ligious. He's fed de hungry, an' he's put clothes on de naked, and he's took de prisoner out o' captivity, and he's been good to de poor—so he has; and now you gwine to let him go down to Davy's locker like a old wrack widout hoistin' a signal. Ole mas'r, sir, I dunno how to pray—I'd be as like to cuss if I tried to; but if you'll make a sign, ole mas'r, your ole comrade Owny Travers will try. I heerd him prayin' once in a storm off de Cape of Good Hope. You jest nod your head, ole mas'r."

The dying man, grasping at this last hope, as he drifted out on the death tide, gave the required sign, and turned his sad, entreating eyes towards Owny, who, poor fellow, had long ago forgotten how to string a *Pater Noster* together. But that eye had never entreated or commanded him in vain, and dropping on his knees, while tears streamed over his face, he said: "The Lord have mercy on your soul, Misther Lacie, darlin', and give you a safe voyage to Paradise. May the MAN ABOVE seud his angils to open wide the gates of glory for you, an' the saints make your bed aisy in heaven. You've been a kind friend to me, an' to many others, widdy's, an' orphan's, an' the like; an' I hope in Christ yer honor's good works will meet ye, where you're goin' to." Owen's strange prayer was interrupted by a deep groan, followed by a gurgling sound; and those around saw by the dull, glazed eye—the ashen hue — the motionless breast and fallen jaw, that Reginald Lacie was dead. Even now, in that short experience of eternity, it was made plain to him what was meant by those words, which had been written by the burning pen of one of old: "And if I should distribute all my goods to feed the poor, and if I should give my body to be burned, and have not charity, it availeth me nothing."

And where was Eveleen, who was most of all interested in this event? Owen Travers sought her, and found her kneeling on the floor, her head resting on a chair, asleep. In one hand she grasped a rude Rosary, which some of her humble friends in the valley had fashioned and given to her. The other hung listlessly beside her. The cold, bright November moonlight—for the storm had swept past—fell through the uncurtained window, and lay like a tissue of silver over her, making her face look like rare statuary, and glorifying the tears that lingered gleaming on her pale cheeks. Owny's broad chest heaved—he could not awaken her, to tell her of her desolation; and, almost choked with sobs, and fearing to disturb her, he lifted her tenderly in his arms, and having laid her gently down on her couch, he threw a heavy woolen coverlid over her, and crept away.

CHAPTER III.

EVELEEN LACIE.

THE body of Reginald Lacie, of Carrigmona, was consigned, with all the customary proprieties and solemnities, to its last resting place in the ruinous old vault where reposed all that remained of the mortal part of his Protestant ancestors. The dust of *their* progenitors mingled with the holy soil at the Seven Churches, which was enriched by the bodies of saints, who had, in an age gone by, been deposited there. The stone hatchment over the low door, grim and gray, survived better than the bricks and mortar the ravages of damp and time; for while they showed many an irregular breach along the walls, this insignia of the house of Lacie remained intact, a mockery of human pride, and a scoff at posthumous exclusiveness. This mortuary garner-house was situated in a glen, which was darkened by trees of cedar and pine that projected themselves from the steep, lofty rocks which arose on each side, and met overhead; and its gloom was augmented on the day of the funeral by dark gusty clouds, and the sound of the Lough, which came with a dull, continuous rush, through a narrow ravine that led to the spot. The gentry of the neighborhood came—more, however, to uphold the dignity of their class, than to show respect to the memory of a man they scarcely knew; and Sir William Erle, whom he had most hated in life, was one of the pall-bearers. Hugh Lacie could not gainsay it—he was a stranger there, and had already given offence by sternly forbidding the customary wake, and ordering hot coffee instead of whiskey for those who watched by the corpse— but from under his heavy brows he threw more than one keen look towards the man on whose account his brother had, perhaps, criminally sinned, and whose last moments were embittered by some cruel memory in which he bore part; and even there he could but marvel at his rare dignity of demeanor, his lofty and well-proportioned frame, his pale, handsome features, and quiet air of command; but he did *not* wonder at the look of care, and the impress of some terrible anguish, that was visible in every lineament of his countenance; for he knew too well that there was a cause for it—a mystery, which only his dead enemy, whom he was assisting to bear to his last resting place, could have unraveled. A sermon was pronounced over the Master of Carrigmona, by Parson Westerfield, which the excellent man had written thirty years previous, on the occasion of the death of an individual who had died, it was asserted, in the odor of piety, and which the courtly clergyman never failed to produce when he was called on to perform the obsequies of the rich or well-born of his parish, whether they were saint or sinner. But it was all the same. Such sermons, you know, are not for the dead, but for the living; it being tacitly understood that grief has its vanities, and woe is greedy after mortuary flattery.

Perhaps in all the solemn pageant, the simple, heart-wrung grief of the maiden Eveleen—to whom death, and the eternal separation from the only thing she had clung to in life, was terrible—was the most genuine; and the tears of the negro Graff, and Owny Travers, the most sincere. As to Hugh Lacie, he had been so long a stranger to his brother, that it would be going beyond the mark to say that *grief* had any part in the emotions that disturbed his mind; it was rather a dull, stunned feeling of surprise and dread. The unspoken secret that had died on his brother's lips, involving the happiness of William Erle—the responsibility of the entire charge of a wild, uncultivated young girl—were subjects of grave and perplexing import to this man, whose life had been hitherto undisturbed, and barren of everything like excitement, beyond the clangor and cares of his manufactory. When the rusty hinges of the vault grated, as the ponderous, iron-studded door swung to, leaving Reginald Lacie with but the common hope of all—*resurgam*—amidst the darkness and mustiness of the charnel house, Eveleen, who had, until that moment, restrained her emotion, uttered one loud, wailing cry, and fell lifeless at her uncle's feet. Several gentlemen, among whom was William Erle, moved with compassion for the desolate orphanage of the child, came forward, and offered their assistance; but Mr. Lacie, gathering the slight form up in his arms, thanked them in a manner that precluded any farther courtesy on their part, and strode away with her to the house, where he laid her as gently as he knew how on the couch, in the room where her father had died.

"This is the beginning of my sorrows," he muttered, as he tore down a twig of the blest palm over the old mirror, and thrusting it into the fire for an instant, extinguished the flame in his hand, and held it smoking under her nose. He had an indistinct recollection of having heard, at some period of his life, that burnt feathers were the most efficacious remedy in cases of this kind; but there being none at hand, he fancied that burnt palm would do as well.

"I know nothing of women," he went on muttering: "least of all these kitten women! I'd rather some one had left me an elephant to train; I could beat an elephant, or shoot him if he were refractory; but this thing—" said the old man, lifting up her long, slender hand in his—"Real Lacie fingers! And she'll be beautiful too—all the women of her race were—then there'll be the devil to pay, to make her marry a sensible man, instead of throwing herself away on a puppy. I wish she had died with her mother, and gone to heaven."

Just then Eveleen opened her great brown eyes —the pungent odor of the smoking palm had restored her to consciousness—and gazing at her uncle for an instant, looked towards the mirror, and discovered the spoliation he had been guilty of. She hastily put one hand over her nose, and with the other snatched from him the half-consumed palm which he was holding close to her face, and burst into a passion of tears. Mr. Lacie looked aghast!

"How dare you take them down? *He* put them there with his own hands! You must be a wicked old man to do such a thing, and I believe you are trying to kill me—I do so! No one ever put smoked palm up my nose before, and I wish you'd go away!" she shrieked.

"Eveleen!" said Mr. Lacie, thrusting his hands deep into his pockets, and bending his sternest look on her.

"Yes: you look as if you'd beat me—but that wouldn't do, because I'm a lady, with proud old blood in my veins. Graff says so," she exclaimed with flashing eyes. Mr. Lacie was thunderstruck, and was at a loss what to say or do. He was very much tempted to take her by the shoulders and give her a rousing shake, but she looked so fragile even in her rage, that it seemed as if the weight of his hand must have crushed her; and he was a perfect sciolist in the soft art of winning confidence and inspiring affection. So he could only hold himself very erect and gaze sternly on the excited girl.

"I am not afraid of you. I never was afraid of anything in my life. I hate you; you are so ugly and cross," bolted from her lips.

"Shame on you!"

"Shame! what have I done to be ashamed of?" she asked quickly; while the red blood dyed her hitherto pale cheeks with crimson, impelled thither by her womanly instincts.

"You have just returned from the burial of your father. Such conduct is indecent."

"It is you, then, who ought to be ashamed. You sent me away from his bed-side when he was dying, and pretended that you'd send for me at the last—and you didn't! Fie on you, sir, to tell a lie to a motherless child who had nobody to love her but that father. Then for you to pull down what his own dear hands put up last Palm Sunday, and try to smother me with the smoke! Oh, woe's me! there's no one to care for me or love me now, and I mean to go and throw myself into the Lough," she cried in a wild abandon of grief, as she sprang up, and flew towards the door. Mr. Lacie strode after her, and seized her by the skirt of her dress, just as she—like a wild antelope—was bounding out into the hall; then he grappled with her, and folding his iron arm around her, held her as in a vice notwithstanding her fierce resistance and sundry scratches that she inflicted on his visage with her long Lacie fingers. Firmly, and not relaxing a muscle, he held her, until from sheer exhaustion, her struggles ceased, and her head drooped silently on his shoulder. Then he set her down once more on the couch, and drawing up a chair directly in front of her, took his seat in it.

"Girl," said he, in tones of suppressed feeling, "I am your father's brother—perhaps you did not know it. He has left you under my guardianship; and as he has done so, although the legacy is anything but welcome or desirable, I intend to carry out his wishes. I perceive that you are like a young savage, and if your father were alive, I should tell him that you have been most shamefully neglected. But understand one thing: I am a stern man, used to having my way, and to be obeyed"—

"Did you ever love anybody?" asked Eveleen languidly, but with a quaint, elfish curiosity in the look with which she regarded him.

"Humph!—to be obeyed and treated with respect," said Mr. Lacie, more than ever nonplussed by his niece.

"I won't obey anybody who does not love me," spoke out Eveleen, "and you don't look as if you *could* love anybody or anything."

"Ahem!" said Hugh Lacie, elevating his beetling eyebrows, and letting the light that was hidden far down in his old heart shine out of his eyes, "ahem!"

"I didn't know that you could look that way," said Eveleen, fixing her lustrous eyes full on his; "you don't look like Blue Beard now. Why don't you always look so? and why don't you tell me if you ever loved anybody?"

"You must not be so pert, young woman. It is not handsome," said her uncle, his eyes still visible, "it depends on how people behave whether I love them or not."

"Am I to go away with you?" she asked presently.

"I—well—you'll know in time," he said, really at his wit's end, because, in truth, he had arranged no plans for her future, at least no definite ones.

"I won't go away from Carrigmona. I won't! I will stay where my father is buried. I won't go away!" she exclaimed with a fresh burst of grief, "least of all will I go with you, who don't know how to love me. I am used to being loved, and used to having my own way."

"Miss Lacie, I insist on your going to your own room and lying down. You are beside yourself," said the old man, with a mingling of wrath and pity, "I will send you a cup of tea."

"I'll be glad to go there, sir," she said rising; but she tottered, and would have fallen if he had not caught her, and held her against his breast.

Again he lifted her in his arms, and carried her to her room, where he laid her down on her bed, and was in a quandary what else to do, when Owen Travers made his appearance at the door with Alice Kane. As soon as Eveleen caught sight of Alice, she threw herself on her bosom, and wept bitterly.

"Have some tea prepared for her," said Mr. Lacie to Owen Travers, as he left the room.

"Is the young mistress sick, sir?" inquired Owny, softly.

"Sick or crazy, I don't know which," testily replied Mr. Lacie, walking on.

"Be aisy with her, sir, if you plase. She's had her own way greatly, your honor, an' don't know how to bear the black sorrow that's come on her—the heavens look down upon her"—said Owny Travers, in deprecating tones. The master—the Lord have mercy on his soul—never spoke a hard word to her in her life."

"It's plain to see that between you all, you've made a fool of her: but get her some hot tea—she needs something to stimulate her—she's very weak," replied Mr. Lacie, turning into the sitting-room. Eveleen spent the next day in her own room, with Alice Kane to whom she poured out her grievances, and from whom she received the womanly, tender, and soothing sympathy that her poor young stricken heart needed; but Ally was obliged to go away in the afternoon, and Eveleen, to whom solitude now seemed frightful, wrapped her shawl about her, and went down to her father's room. Her uncle was there, dozing in her father's great chair, beside a table covered with papers. Twilight had crept into the room, but a bright red glow from the fire-place illumined the antique room, and covered the walls with grotesque shadows. Eveleen went softly to the bed, and kissed the pillow on which her father had breathed his last; then, as noiselessly as she could, threw herself on the couch beside the fire, where she leaned listlessly against the pillows, watching with steady gaze the harsh countenance of her kinsman. Sad, and sorrowful memories filled the child's heart, to whom the future seemed like the misshapen, dreary shadows on the wall, and tears rained silently over her cheeks. Just then Graff came in with the supper tray and lights, which roused Mr. Lacie, who started up and looked with a bewildered glance around him.

"I've been asleep, haven't I?" he asked Eveleen.

"Did you not dream something ugly, sir? You looked as if you did."

"Humph! Do you feel better?"

"I am very well, thank you, sir," replied Eveleen, quietly.

"Hey-day—take care," exclaimed Mr. Lacie, as Graff began to push his papers unceremoniously aside. "Leave off. I'll move them myself," continued the business man, taking up each paper, and laying it according to order in a portfolio, which he carefully tied, and laid on the mantel-piece. Graff, with many unfriendly but furtive glances towards the new master, arranged the cold chicken, muffins, toast and tea on the table, and invited Mr. Lacie and his young mistress to take their seats.

"I don't wish any supper, Graff. Do you pour out the tea for Mr. Lacie," said Eveleen in an under tone. Graff remonstrated. "It's no use, Graff, I can't eat. My heart is too full."

"But you see, young Missis, dat ain't gwine to do. Gor Almighty's gone and took ole mas'r to hisse'f, an' it can't be helped;" answered the negro, wiping his eyes with his coat sleeve. "It's umproper, an' unpolite, Missis, for you not to set up an' pour out Mas'r Lacie's tea, cos he's your comp'ny now, an' ole mas'r 'd be shamed in his coffin if he thought comp'ny wor not treated right in his house; besides, little Missis, consider dis is your own blood kin—ole mas'r's brudder. Come, like a lady! Dar now! Dat's right;" said Graff, as Eveleen, convinced by his logic, arose and seated herself at the head of the table, and proceeded with much gravity and decorum to pour out Mr. Lacie's tea. The meal passed in silence, Mr. Lacie being too full of vexatious thoughts to talk—and Eveleen's tears falling without sigh or sob, told that her memory was busy with the dead. Even after the things were removed, neither of them spoke.

Mr. Lacie remained at the table examining his brother's papers, and forgot in the congenial drudgery of business, her existence; while she, lying back on the cushions of her couch, fixed her wild penetrating eye unwinkingly on his countenance, as if she were studying out the problem of his inner life. It was growing late, and he had not yet finished; but continued to unfold, read, fold again, and mark letters and papers, with unflinching patience and diligence. At last he began to read an old letter, one over which his eye seemed to linger. Its contents seemed to touch and soften some vulnerable place in his heart, for his eyebrows lifted themselves up, and his eyes, serene and clear, perused its contents. Suddenly he felt a light touch on his shoulder, and, turning quickly, he saw Eveleen by his side.

"Good night," she said softly, "if you will always look so, I shan't mind going away with you."

"Good night, niece—we shall go in a few days now," he answered.

"Do you never kiss people when they bid you good night? Papa always did!"

"Kiss?" exclaimed the astonished man, who was guiltless of all such tendernesses—not because he was bad or cruel in his nature, but because he was quite unused to them. "Good night, child;" so saying, he touched her cheek with his lips, altogether unconscious whether or no he had performed the act properly.

"You don't know how to kiss, Uncle Hugh, but only keep your eyebrows up, and I'll learn you," she said, as she turned and went away. Owen Travers came in shortly afterwards, to ask if "his honor" wanted anything.

"I was just wishing to see you, Travers," said Mr. Lacie, taking up a folded and sealed paper. "Your brother applied to me for a renewal of his lease."

"Faix, an' he did, an' I hope your honor's given his petition a favorable hearing," replied Owny, with his best bow.

"I could find no reason to do otherwise. It is true there have been several other applicants for the 'farm,' who have offered a few pounds more rent; but it would require some more important consideration than that to cause me to uproot your brother's family from the spot where they have lived so long. Here is the lease—good for an hundred years longer," replied Mr. Lacie, handing it to him. "Take it over early in the morning."

"Bedad, sir, but the fine ould Lacie blood's warm in your honor's heart, an' I hope the heavens will smile upon you forevermore," said Owny Travers, grasping the hoped-for lease, while his lip quivered, and a tear blinked in his small gray eyes. "It would have kilt the ould man outright, an' sent the whole concern to wrack an' ruin, if your honor had turned the craythurs out."

"But tell him," went on Mr. Lacie, as coldly and calmly as if he had just performed the most ungracious act in the world, "that while it is well enough for him to stay here, and lay his bones where he was born, because he is too old for change—this country is no place for that brave, handsome lad, his son. He can never rise from his condition here; a peasant he is, and a peasant he'll die. But there is a land where energy, intelligence, and ambition like his always meet with a just reward. I mean America. I like the lad's looks; and if three days hence he has a mind to go, I'll pay his expenses over."

"It's just what I've been thinkin' of myself, your honor, an' I said as much to John this blessed mornin', but I am pretty sure the ould people will set their two heads agin his goin'. I am goin' anyways."

"You?"

"Look you hither, sir, I've been rovin' so many years that I shouldn't live a fortnight here all alone by myself at Carrigmona, and the master's—no disrespect to your honor—gone. I suppose Miss Eveleen will be goin' with your honor, an' she's been used to seein' me ever since her eyes opened on the light. I think, sir, she'd feel lonesome without me."

"There's room enough there for you too, Travers," said Mr. Lacie, with a grim smile, glad in his secret soul to have a coadjutor in the difficult task of taking charge of Eveleen. "You can retire now. I must finish my task tonight."

"Here's somethin' I forgot, your honor," said Owny, fumbling in his pocket, and drawing out a visiting card—"Sir William Erle called to-day, when you were down at the Seven Churches."

"Sir William Erle. Humph! He did not visit Carrigmona during my brother's lifetime," said Mr. Lacie.

"Faix, sir, it would have been as much as his life was worth to show his face here then. There was something worse than the law-suit betune the two, that was saicret to themselves," said Owny.

"I am not at home to Mr. Erle, if he should call again. He and his children can enjoy what the law has given them from the Lacie domain, but that entails no obligation on me to associate with him," said Mr. Lacie sternly, as the memory of the last hour of his brother's life—its agony, and unrevealed mystery—flashed on his mind.

"Children! your honor. He's as childless this minnit as I am!" exclaimed Owny. "His only child was stole away from him fifteen years ago. The people hereabouts say that the '*good people*' spirited him off; but mightn't I die in my sins, if I don't think some poor miserable body that he laid his cruel hand too heavy on, done it out of revenge! But I beg your honor's pardon for interruptin' you. I pray God you may get a good night, Sir, an' many after it, for the good you've done this day. May your own heart never be troubled, for the sake of them whose hearts this will make as aisy as an old shoe," said Owen Travers, holding up the lease, as he paused an instant on the door-sill.

Reginald Lacie expressly stipulated in his will that his daughter was to reside with his brother, and be reared with strict economy, and be kept in ignorance of her wealth until she was of age, when he hoped—so ran the will—that she would have principles so fixed, and understand the value of money so well, as to know how to take care of it. Mr. Lacie groaned in spirit, when he thought of the stormy future in store for him, with a creature so untamed as Eveleen to deal with. There was an innate chivalry underlying the crust of his nature, which made him shrink from such a contest with a female, although she was a mere child, and his nearest of kin, which his early experience of her violent moods almost caused to degenerate into cowardice. But there was no help for it, and he submitted with an ill grace, as to an evil for which there was no remedy. Chaotic thought banished sleep from his eyes for some hours, and he lay tossing on his pillow, more perplexed and disturbed than if he had suddenly been called to rule an empire, when lo! like an angel of peace, the consoling thought presented itself: "I can send her to a boarding school." The difficult problem was solved—a calm fell over his troubled senses, and a tranquil slumber stole over him.

The turf fire burned bright on the hearth of Michael Travers' cottage, and the light fell on happy faces gathered around the family board. John Travers was at home; he had been lingering around all day, and he now sat leaning back, his arm about Ally's waist, playing with his knife, as if he was only intent on counting the vibrations it made when he struck the point of it on the deal table. Unusually tender and quiet he had been throughout the day, and there was a look of deep thought on his handsome face, which was not sadness, but which was not yet joy. But "Shaneen," thought they, "is such a scholar, an' reads so many ould books, it's no wonder he looks glum with thinkin' of 'em." Now, however, his mother thought there was a troubled look in his eye, and a seriousness deeper than study on his countenance.

"*A bouchal dhas*," she said, cheerily, "have you buried your best friend, that you look so down in the mouth?"

"John, *asthore*, the mother is speaking to you," said Ally, lifting her face to his, and brushing back a curl that had fallen over his forehead.

"*Mahair avourneen*," * he said, with a slight start, "you'll niver hinder me, I know."

---

* Mother darling.

"'That I mightn't die in sin! but the boy's dreaming. An' what is it, sure, that I'm to be after hindering ye!" asked Dame Travers, in surprise. "You've never brought me a sorrowful hour yet, Shaneen."

"Well, now, mother *machree*, look you hether. It might as well out now, in God's name, as at any other time. You all know, as well as I do, how people of our kind is kept down an' trodden on in Ireland. There's no luck or chance for us ever gettin' beyond a certain mark, an' that low enough on the scale. We've got more masters than is good for us; our purses are drained to the last ha'penny for their benefit, an' our veins are drained of our best manly blood to uphold their tyranny. Our souls can't grow to their full stature here—our breath is not our own to spake out the honest thought of our hearts, for fear our masters shouldn't like to hear the words that they know they desarve. I'm goin' away out of it. Mother, father, Ally my girl, I'm goin' with Uncle Owny to America."

"*Oh, ma gra hu!* to leave us in our old age?" cried Dame Travers, half wild with astonishment and grief.

"Oh, *wirra!* hould now with such nonsense. I often heard you talk so before. Young people never know when they're well off. I'd like to know, do you expect to be a lord? I tell you what, Shaneen, what's been good enough for me, and them that lived afore me, is good enough for my son," said the old man, in whose tones bitterness and grief were blended.

"John, *asthore*," whispered Ally, leaning her fair head on his shoulder, "don't go away!"

"It's for your sake, darlin', that I want to go," replied the young man, stooping to imprint a kiss on her forehead. "Father, mother, I'd give my life any minute to keep the wolf from your dure, whether he came in the shape of poverty, sickness, or sorrow; but I can't—an' don't ask it of me—stay here wastin' my life an' manhood amongst the Wicklow hills, though the MAN ABOVE knows I love every stone upon them, an' shall pine many a day for a breath of the sweet-heather on their sides. Faith, I'm as much a man as the dandy strangers that come hether to see the sights, and who look on me, bedad, when I'm tellin' them the legends of the Seven Churches, an' the Lough, an' St. Kevin's Bed, with as much curiosity as if I was a larned pig. I take their shillins with a bow an' scrape, and say 'your humble sarvint,' and so it goes. *That's* the way I'm wastin' my life. Come, now, don't grieve or be angry, but give me the blessin', that I may go to a land where I can win a fair recompense for my labor, an' rise as high as my disserts will let me."

"There's many a one set out with the same intentions, that got nothing but sore disappointment in the end," said old Travers, lifting his head and gazing with a fond, proud look at his handsome son. "Stay where you are, boy, stay by the soil where you wor born, an' by the ould father an' mother that would feel lonesome afther ye. An' look here, Shaneen," said the old man, laying his hand on Ally's head, "did you forget that she an' you wor to stan' up before the priest afther Easter?"

"Father, Ally knows that I love her like my heart's blood, an' she'll be willin' to trust me away until I win what I want, for her sake as well as my own. I want a spot of land that I can call my own, subject to no man's power or whim; where I can dig, an' plant, an' reap, an' have the good of what it produces; where I shall have no taxes, an' duties, an' tithes, an' fees to pay, robbin' me, an' strippin' me, until there's not a shreed of my honest labor left to feed an' clothe me; where I can have civil rights with the best, an' work my way up like a man."

"Christ save the boy!" cried Dame Travers, wringing her hands. "It was pride, alanna voght, that druv the angils out of glory; an' I'm afeard, *acushla*, that it'll be the beginnin' of your downfall."

"Look you hether, John, I'll make you a fair offer," said the old man, in earnest tones, "stay where you are, an' I'll make over everything I own in the world to you;—house, farm, stock, an' all; an' you can marry Ally whinever she's ready."

"Do you think, sir, I'm such an *omadhaun* as

to take advantage of ye in your ould days? I wouldn't rob you in that way, father, for my right hand. Haven't you tilled the land ever since you wor a boy, an' lived under the *latch* of your own roof? It would be a brave sight to see you depindent like, for shelter an' food, if it was your own son that provided it! I'd die first!" exclaimed the young man, with a burst of impetuous feeling. "An' then, *acushla machree*, it wouldn't alter the laws—the oppression, an' the taxation on the poor would go on being just as heavy. I was born for better things than would fall to my lot if I staid. I feel it in my heart, strugglin' an' risin', an' tormentin' me till it seems like it would break. I can never be more than I am if I stay—unless I turned agin my country an' religion. Let me go, father. I shall never be content here."

"I must have a night to think it over, John. It's not so aisy for us, your old mother there an' I, to give *you* up, as it seems for you to give us up," replied old Travers, in reproachful tones.

"It was them books. I tould his reverince, years ago, that no good would come of it!" murmured Dame Travers.

The young man got up, and with his hands thrust into his breeches pockets, walked up and down the room. His face was flushed and hot, and it was evident that he was endeavoring to master a strong emotion. His father's words had stung him deeply. He felt that he deserved not the reproach. They could not understand his manly aspirations or his ambitious hopes; nor could he find language to explain to them, in terms simple but strong enough to suit his purpose, all that he desired and hoped. They had grown old under the system which he felt in every fibre of his body oppressive; they had managed, by dint of tireless industry and excellent thrift, to sustain themselves in comfort, and a certain degree of respectability; they had long ago passed the meridian of life, and were not far off from the "other shore;" here, they had tasted life's simple joys and its bitter sorrows together; under this roof their children had been born; here they had died, one after another, leaving them desolate, until the last one—John —came to cheer their silent and lonely house. Is it strange that the place was precious to their affections, or that they were loth to part with him? So far, he had been the blessing and pride of their lives. He was a dutiful and affectionate son, moral in his habits, attentive to his religious duties, and, in their estimation, learned and wise; while for his good looks, there was not in all Wicklow so handsome a fellow! Nor was he less a favorite abroad. His songs, his skill in wrestling and cricket, his ready jests, and his pleasant, genial temper, made him a general favorite with all, from the priest down to the bare-footed gossoon that drove the pigs and sheep to pasture.

"*Mahair avourneen,*" said John Travers, suddenly standing before her, and bending over to kiss her forehead, "do *you* think it is aisy for me to give you all up, an' go?"

"No, *a bouchal dhas!* no!" she vehemently exclaimed. "It is as hard for you as for us. But for all that, I'll not lay a straw in your way. You've been a dutiful, good son, an' I'll not cross ye. The young are not like the ould, an' the world changes. Go, in God's name—only, Shaneen, avick, you'll come back now an' then?"

"That I will, *mahair avourneen!*" replied he proudly; "an' when I come, you'll not see me what I am now."

"May you never be worse," muttered old Travers, "than your father was before you. The young men now-a-days can't go on quietly in the way of life God has marked out for their feet; they must be flyin' off to strange lands, an' runnin' their heads agin all manner of danger. Oh vo! but it's a livin' wonder they don't set the say on fire! Come, wife, come—it's getting late," he continued, going towards the door, his assumed indignation scarcely concealing the grief and anguish that filled his heart.

The two young people were left alone. Ally's trusting heart, ambitious for her lover, assented to his eloquent arguments, without fully understanding them. She knew that it was something noble and right he was aiming at, and although she could not repress the fond wish that he had been content to remain in Ireland, or stifle a sigh of bitter regret that their marriage, which was to have taken place after Easter, must now be postponed to an indefinite period, she was too true a woman to stand in the way of his plans, or allow herself to become a clog to his advancement.

Michael Travers rode ten miles the next day to consult Father O'Reilly, who had educated the boy, and loved him as he would a younger brother, hoping that he would oppose him; but to his astonishment the good priest approved of his young friend's plan, and besought the old man to place no obstacle in his way. Then he sought Mr. Lacie's presence, at Carrigmona, where, after thanking him in warm and heartfelt terms—in his rude, eloquent way—for the renewal of his lease, he spread his troubles before him.

"Let the lad go. Why should he stay here? He will do well in America, and best of all be *free*. Let him go, Mr. Travers. It shall cost you nothing."

Leaving Mr. Lacie's presence, grieved and crestfallen, he went in search of his brother, all unaware of his intention to leave the country; assured that here, at least, he should find some one to strengthen his position against what he considered his son's wild and foolish scheme. But it was far otherwise. He discovered that

Owny had not only suggested the matter to him, but offered him every inducement to go, and upon his luckless head did the old man empty the vial of his wrath.

* * * * * * * *

In another week John Travers was on his way to America, well equipped for his voyage, and with ample means to pay his way. Far better had he died in the hill-side cottage than have gone. It seemed that the gray winter which was settling down on the hills, and sending its wild shivering breath down into the valleys and glens, had entered in, and frozen into silence the gay, blithe sounds that used to fill it with glee and cheer. Ally's songs were heard at longer intervals, until they gradually ceased. Dame Travers chatted and gossipped but little at her spinning-wheel, and the old man sat pondering and musing for hours in silence beside his hearth. At last letters came form the absent one, bringing sunshine and cheer with them.

CHAPTER IV.

MR. LACIE'S PERPLEXITY.

On the eve of leaving Ireland, Mr. Lacie—for his dead brother's sake—offered the negro, Graff, a support and home as long as he lived, if he chose to accompany him to the United States; but he refused to leave the spot where his master's remains reposed. "He was my best friend in dis life," he muttered, with a look of sullen grief, "an' I'm gwine to stay 'longside his bones. I hates de Irish; but dat's nuffin; I'd stay if I hated dem ten times wus. Let me stay here, mas'r. I'll help to take care of de place, an' won't cost nobody nuffin." Mr. Lacie did not object, and the negro remained at Carrigmona.

Two years had glided by since the events which we have related occured. According to his inspiration that night at Carrigmona, Mr. Lacie placed his niece at a convent school in another city, as soon after he arrived at home as she had recovered from the fatigues of their voyage across a somewhat tempestuous ocean; and amidst the absorbing cares of his business, the clatter and whirl of the machinery of his great manufactory, quite forgot her existence, except when the annual bill for her board, tuition, sundries, ditto, ditto, et cetera, was presented—then he felt as comfortable as if some one had flogged him with nettles, for these bills were so many signs to him of the approach of the time when she must leave school; and what to do with her then, was the question that tormented him. If she had been a boy, he would have put her at once into his great noisy manufactory, and made her what he was himself, an accomplished machinist; but a girl! it quite made him sick. Nevertheless, time rolled on more inexorably than the monstrous iron wheels of his manufactory; and one morning he received a letter, which made him spring round from a model that he had been at work on for more than a year, which he had reason to hope would eventually supersede all other motive power then in use, in its application to machinery, and glare at the youth who handed it to him as if he would annihilate him. His quick eye had detected at a glance the convent seal. He tore it open, and read as follows:

"Sir:—I am extremely sorry to inform you that your niece's health has become so delicate that her physician thinks it advisable for her to withdraw for a short time from school, and travel, feeling assured that change of air and scene will quite restore her. If you desire Miss Lacie to graduate—which she will do with great honor to herself and the institution, next year—

we shall be truly happy to receive her again, as she has not only given us entire satisfaction in her studies, but her moral deportment and amiability of character have endeared her very much to us. Hoping that Miss Lacie may be speedily restored to her usual health, I am, sir, very respectfully yours."

"I wish you had kept her, then. I wish she had taken the veil! What the devil am I to do with a studious, moral, docile, amiable young lady, with the meagrims? I can't travel with her. If she must go, there's no way for it, unless she goes by Adams' Express. I can't watch her and counsel her—I don't know how. I know nothing about women. Hugh Lacie, you are the most unlucky, miserable old wretch alive. Has the bell rung, sir, to stop work?" he said, turning sharply to the young man who had brought him the letter, and who was still waiting.

"No sir—but my grandmother"—stammered the youth.

"Wants money as usual, I suppose? Well, she's old and poor, and must have it," said Mr. Lacie in more subdued tones, as he opened his desk, and counted out some money. "This is Thursday, my lad—here, give her the whole week's wages, and tell her it is the last time I will advance a cent. I won't do it—it's against my rules." The youth received the money in his blackened palm, and if Mr. Lacie had looked up, he would have seen under the mask of coal dust and smut, that covered his handsome features, a crimsoning and flushing which might have arisen from shame or anger. It was hard to tell, for he made no sign and uttered no word, but only bent his head with a proud air, and went out. Mr. Lacie sat down and leaned his elbow on his desk, and buried his face in his hands, to consider what he should do. He was in bachelor's lodgings, in a house where there were no women. He could not place her in a hotel. A boarding house was almost as objectionable. Lodgings—hotel—boarding-house: hotel—boarding-house—lodgings, turned over and over in his mind, like a whirligig, until he was fairly dazed, and almost beside himself. Like an old gray rat in a trap, he ran round and round, gazing with bitter regret on the hole by which he had entered, but by which, alas! he could not escape. He snatched up his hat, and pulling it down over his eyes, went out for no special object but to air his vexation. "I shall write them word to keep her; but no! I'll not murder the poor lass;—but what on earth am I to do? My model was to have been finished this week—those men from England are waiting expressly to see it in operation; and now, faugh! Hilloa!"

"Faix, your honor, I beg a thousand pardons. I was lookin' one way, and your honor the other, and slap we come agin each other like two ingines," said the hearty voice of our old friend

Owen Travers, who was now a thriving fruit merchant in a small way. "May I make so free as to ask when your honor had a letther from Miss Lacie, the darlin."

"No you mayn't. Miss Lacie the darling is just the pest of my life. What am I to do with her when she comes?" he exclaimed gruffly.

"Do, sir? Faix, sir, I don't think that's the way your brother that's dead and gone, Misther Reginald—the Lord have mercy on his soul—would speak about *your* desolate orphan."

"*My* desolate orphan? Begone! Come back here, you crazy, hot-headed Irishman!"

"Wasn't your honor born in Ireland?" asked Owny with a leer.

"Was it my fault if I was? It's because I was that I am forever getting my head into some scrape or other. Yes, I was born in Ireland, sir, and I'm not ashamed of it, though I think she deserves to be blotted out from the face of the ocean, of which she claims to be the gem."

"No she doesn't, sir! She deserves to be crowned—to be free—to be great an' glorious; and I'm ashamed, your honor, to hear a gintleman with the ould dhrop in his veins say such a thing," said Owny, fiercely, as he squared himself before Mr. Lacie. "I'd like to hear another man say as much, bedad!"

"Why don't she be free and great, then? Irishmen can go abroad and fight like the devil in the service of foreign countries; they can govern, rule, and manage everywhere better than they can for their own land; they can win batons, crosses, ribbons and garters, but they win nothing for their own country, except the empty honor of claiming them as her children!"

"It's because they haven't *fair play!*" roared Owny. "Give us fair play, an' we'll sweep the English to destruction, like the waves of the Red Say did the armies of Pharaoh. Give 'em fair play!"

"I can't give 'em fair play," growled Mr. Lacie; "I would if I could. I can't have fair play myself."

"Good morning, Mr. Lacie," said a pleasant female voice at his elbow. "I have not seen you for an age." Mr. Lacie looked up, bowed, and was about rushing off; but the lady, who was in mourning, laid her delicately-gloved hand on his arm, saying: "I think I am going your way, and if you have no objection, I'll walk with you." Mr. Lacie groaned and submitted. He did not even know the woman's name. What right had she to waylay him in that style? He judged, from her weeds, that she was a widow, and perhaps she meant to inveigle him into a marriage with her. A cold shudder passed over him at the thought, for he was well aware that whatever a widow predestines in that line, is inevitable. He must escape, if possible. He thought it would be a good plan to pretend business with Owny Travers; but that worthy, with a leer that provoked Mr. Lacie almost to madness, touched his hat, and walked off with a broad grin on his face.

"Madam," he said, nervously; "I am in great haste. Will you excuse me if I leave you at this corner?"

"I will not detain you ten minutes, Mr. Lacie. I was just on my way to your place of business, when I so opportunely met you. I have a design"—

"I knew it," inwardly groaned the old bachelor.

"Which I will explain," blandly continued the widow, "when we get into a more quiet street; and I hope that you will give me a favorable answer, as much depends"—

Just then a sudden crashing of carts, drays, omnibuses and carriages obviated the necessity of a reply, or he would have burst out with something terrible, for he was wrought up to a high pitch. As it was, he only ground his teeth and registered a vow that he would give a very decided quietus to her hopes, the instant he could.

"Well, madam," he said, in his sternest tone, and with his most austere manner, as they turned out of the noisy thoroughfare into a more quiet street, "proceed with your business, if you please."

"Mr. Lacie, I was left with the barest pittance by my late husband"—she began.

"Who was your husband, madam?" he asked, shortly.

"Is it possible, sir, that you do not remember me? I am the widow of the late William Hunter."

"William Hunter! So? A reckless speculator in fancy stocks. Humph!" muttered Mr. Lacie. "How can I assist, ma'am?"

"My husband, doubtless, made some mistakes, poor man—all are not possessed of your unerring judgment," said the lady. "Had my poor William been blessed with your business talents, sir, his widow and her two helpless boys would not now be compelled to solicit aid."

"The little jade! What an oily tongue she has, to be sure! But I'm on my guard," thought Mr. Lacie, with a feeling of complacency at his own penetration. "Madam," he said, looking at his watch, "I am much pressed for time. I have an engagement at one o'clock. It wants just ten minutes of the time. I am quite willing to lend you a small sum, if you can get a safe endorser."

"Money! Did I mention money?" said the widow, hastily. "I did not come to borrow money, sir. I came for something very different. I heard you had a niece who was about leaving school."

"That is true," groaned Mr. Lacie, "but how did you learn that, ma'am?"

"Owing to the simple fact that my sister is a

nun, and the directress of the school at the convent where Miss Lacie is being educated. She wrote me word that Miss Lacie was leaving the convent in ill health—"

"It is true, ma'am," replied Mr. Lacie, in no amiable mood, "and the news is anything but pleasant to me. I am in hired lodgings, ma'am, in a business part of the city—a bachelor's establishment, where it would be highly improper to bring a young girl. I was in hopes she'd find a vocation for a religious life at the convent. I'm sure it would have been happier for her—and for me."

."Perhaps what I am about to propose, Mr. Lacie, will not only relieve you of your embarrassment, but accomplish my desires at the same time. To eke out my narrow income, I design receiving two or three young ladies, who are situated as Miss Lacie is, into my family, where they will be cared for, and be treated as my own daughters."

"Ma'am," said Mr. Lacie, with alacrity, "it is an old mercantile habit, but I never make a contract with a stranger—excuse me—without suitable references as to that stranger's capability to comply to the letter with every item of it. If you can produce satisfactory references as to the suitableness of the thing in every particular, I shall be prepared to give you a decided answer immediately. You see, ma'am, I feel a deep concern about this unfortunate child who has been thrown on my hands. I promised her father on his death-bed to be a parent to her, only I am at my wit's end how to set about it."

"It is something quite new to me, Mr. Lacie, to be asked for references; but we are strangers— you are the guardian of a young and motherless girl, for whose welfare you are responsible, and I suppose you are right," replied Mrs. Hunter, flushing up, and half inclined to resent what— had she not been a sensible and worldly-wise woman—she would otherwise have regarded as a very impertinent demand. "I believe," she added, "that I can furnish a referee in every way satisfactory. Do you know Rufus Griswold, of the firm of Griswold & Sons?"

"Perfectly well."

"Mr. Griswold has known me ever since I was born. He was my father's friend, and also the friend of William Hunter."

"All right, madam. If we can come to an agreement, I shall be relieved of a most embarrassing—and I may add exasperating—piece of business. I shall see you to-morrow morning, if it will suit your convenience."

"You will find me at Number 95 Elm street; the first house after you turn the corner of Upperton street. Good-morning, Mr. Lacie."

Mr. Lacie nodded his head, tore a slip of paper out of his memorandum-book, wrote Mrs. Hunter's name and address on it, depositing it safely in his *port-monnaie*, and thrust it into his pocket;

then, oblivious of his engagement at one o'clock, which was one of those movable ones which are so convenient—for when did an hour of the day elapse in which Mr. Lacie might not be said to have an engagement?—he hurried off to Griswold & Son's, to make the necessary inquiries in relation to Mrs. Hunter's fitness to become the guardian and chaperone of his niece. Mr. Griswold was a successful merchant, and the representative of a very numerous class in the United States. His ships floated on many seas, and his name was an honored one on 'Change, at home and abroad. He was a sort of Lorenzo de Medici in the germ, and it was a pity that want of early education, combined with unremitting assiduity to business, had prevented the Medici traits from developing in his character beyond certain ideas of profuse expenditure—taste, which, being uncultivated, was gaudy instead of elegant or gorgeous—and a mien and address which was pompous without being dignified. He received Mr. Lacie's visit with unaffected astonishment, and could only interpret the interest which his strange visitor's questions implied in Mrs. Hunter, into a desire to marry her; upon which he launched forth into an unmeaning and pompous strain of eulogium on the lady, compliments to Mr. Lacie's good taste, and congratulations on his approaching happiness.

"Good God, sir," cried Mr. Lacie, almost beside himself, "I don't intend to marry the woman!"

"Pardon me, sir!" said the pompous merchant, "I thought from your seeming interest in the lady that you did."

"No, sir. I simply desire to know if she is a woman to whose care a young and inexperienced girl is to be trusted;" burst out Mr. Lacie.

"Sir, Mrs. Hunter is *sans peur, sans reproche*—that is, she is without stain or blemish; a most discreet, praiseworthy, estimable lady, to whose care I could, without the slightest fear of the consequences, trust *my* daughter if she were motherless. She is a handsome, fascinating woman; of good family, and in every respect qualified to become either the mother or chaperone of your daughter."

"Pshaw! I have no daughter. It is a niece. She'll see but little of me, I assure you, unless she comes down amongst the boilers, pipes, and wheels of my factory; and if she should come too often, there's a way of blowing it up, you know. I hate widows. Good morning, sir."

"I believe, on my soul, he's capable of doing it. The most uncultivated bear, by long odds, that I ever saw," said Mr. Griswold, tossing his ponderous watch-chain and heavily-jewelled seals around his finger, as he walked to and fro. By noon the next day, Mr. Lacie's mind was at rest about Eveleen. He had seen Mrs. Hunter—made all the necessary arrangements—settled an allowance on his niece (from her own fortune) and given the lady *carte blanche* for piano, bedroom furniture, and a supply of such clothing as she might require. Mrs. Hunter—ignorant of Eveleen's wealth—thought Mr. Lacie the most liberal of uncles, and she did not fail to tell him so in the most blandishing way; but he, having fixed ideas on the subject of widows, turned a deaf ear to all of her prettily turned compliments and confined his conversation to the strictest business limits, and his visit to the very briefest time in which the momentous affair could be arranged.

The next day Mr. Lacie dispatched his old confidential clerk, Moses Kugle, to Georgetown convent, to pay Eveleen's school bills, and fetch her home; not home to a warm, loving, kindred welcome; not home to hearts which were longing and yearning to embrace her; not to a home where warm and cherished affections awaited her, and to which her coming would be a realization of the hopes and anticipations of years; not a home where fond eyes "would mark her coming, and grow brighter when she came"— no, there was no home like this awaiting Eveleen Lacie, whose full, warm heart, in all its instincts, hungered and thirsted for love, as a traveler in an arid desert pants for the shadow of a great rock, or the sight of a rippling fount. She did not love her uncle, but she could not help hoping that he would come for her; for many and deep were the plans that she had made

to win his affections—to teach herself to look up
to and love him with filial tenderness—and to
make him at least feel that she was necessary to
his comfort and happiness. Eveleen's nature
was one that gloried in obstacles. Like a mountain torrent, which only makes that which op-
poses its progress subserve its use to increase its
strength and beauty, taking captive its enemy,
and sweeping along its way rippling and sparkling in musical measures, was her will, in which
was blended a powerful energy of devotion, and
a rare and simple tenderness. She had counted
much, therefore, on winning her uncle's love;
for she knew from the glimpses he had a few
times given her of his true nature, that he had
a true and noble heart of his own, only it was
so impenetrable; like one of those patent
money-safes, the locks of which can neither be
picked or blown off—one must have the right
key to open it, and that key she was determined
to find. How great then was her mortification,
when a stranger as old, silent, and stern-looking
as her uncle, came to fetch her away—when she
learned that she was not to live with Mr. Lacie,
and was informed that she was to be placed
under the care of a Mrs. Hunter, a person of
whom she had never even heard before.

"It will be a wonder, though, if I don't match
him," thought Eveleen, as she sat in the cars,
silent and musing, beside Mr. Kugle. The tender
and womanly hearts with whom she had held

such pure and intimate relations for the last two years, their fond, gentle ways, and pious counsels, made the contrast yet more bitter. "My uncle *shall* love me, though—I won't be so desolate on the face of the earth. God never intended it. Can you tell me, sir?" she said, at last, "how Owny is?"

"Who ma'am?"

"Owny Travers!"

"Oh! eh! the old Irishman. He left us—let me see—eighteen months ago."

"He's not dead?" exclaimed Eveleen, springing around sharply.

"Dead! Eh? No, no, he keeps a fruit-stall somewhere," replied the startled Mr. Kugle. "I have not seen him for many months."

"And John, his nephew; where is John?"

"I know nothing about him. It is a little strange, ma'am, for so fine a young lady, who will be a great heiress one of these days, to speak so familiarly of laboring people. Your uncle might not approve of it, ma'am," said the old clerk in words of admonition, which he intended should be kind, but which struck Eveleen as impertinent.

"They are my countrymen, sir, and my friends!" exclaimed Eveleen, with flashing eyes. "I have known them ever since I was born. They used to carry me about in their arms, when I was a child, over the rugged hill-paths of Wicklow and along the beautiful shores of

Luggela. I love them. I love old Owny Travers next to my own father, and I love him more for being an Irishman, because I am Irish to my heart's core; and if I never see my native land again, I shall be none the less Irish!"

Mr. Kugle opened his eyes wide, pulled his cap down lower over his forehead, and braced his elbows to his side, as men do when a tempestuous blast of wind whirls past, announcing a storm; but he did not venture a reply, or speak again until the cars arrived at the depot, when he informed her that the carriage was waiting for them.

"Is my uncle in it?"

"No."

"He's waiting for me at home. Tell the coachman to drive fast."

Although Eveleen had heard that she was not to live with her uncle, she thought surely that she would spend her first evening at home with him, and perhaps the night under the same roof. His reply, however, struck a cold and desolate chill into her heart, and but for very pride she would have given way to a passion of tears.

"Ahem! you are under a mistake, ma'am," said the cautious old clerk. "Mr. Lacie is in lodgings. Mr. Lacie is obliged to be near his place of business—but—ahem!—" halted Mr. Kugle, quailing before the proud silent figure that stood dilating and flashing before him.

"Where did you say I am to go?" she asked in a low voice.

"'To Mistress Hunter's, ma'am. Your uncle arranged it all, and—ahem!—I thought he had explained it all in his note to you. Mr. Lacie thought it was too gloomy and lonesome where he is, for a young lady."

"We will go, if you please," said Eveleen, feeling that the strange home, among strangers, to which she was going, would be far more gloomy and lonesome to her than the dreariest abode where her eyes could gladden and sun themselves on a kindred face. She felt very forlorn and desolate in being thus thrown off on strangers by the only relative she had on earth, and for whom she had been cherishing the most genial and dutiful sentiments. Hence, although Mrs. Hunter received her with bland courtesy; and although the drawing-room into which she was ushered, was warm, bright, and elegant; and although her own apartment, to which she asked permission to retire, was a perfect model of comfort and great taste, all of which her eye—so fond of the bright and beautiful—could not fail to observe; her manner was cold and reserved, and she declined Mrs. Hunter's assistance in unshawling with a gesture at once so resolute and haughty that the bland widow left the room, thinking in her heart that she was one of the most ungracious, disagreeable, and ill-bred young ladies that she had ever met with, and almost regretting that she had become an inmate of her family; while in fact poor Eveleen was under the tyrannic influence of loneliness, anger, disappointment, and longing for kindred love. When left alone she was almost ready to throw herself on the floor and cry like a child. She declined appearing at the tea-table under the plea of headache and weariness, and locking her door she disrobed, and wrapping her *negligée* about her, drew an arm-chair up to the fire, and crossing her feet on the fender, she leaned her head back, and fell into a half dreamy reverie, in which many a vision of the dead past was conjured up. She heard the ripple of the waves of the beautiful Lough—she saw the sunlit peaks of Carrigmanne—she inhaled the fragrance of fern and heather—she saw the gray ivy-clad walls of her old home—the quaint room where she and her father used to sit in the sad twilight and talk together; then came the memory of the last scenes—the death and burial—the voyage across the ocean; and it brought her—here—back to the reality, to her lonesomeness, to her hungering and thirsting for love like that she had known of yore; and with a sob, which ended in a sigh, she knelt down to her evening devotions, feeling a more tender and childlike dependence on her Heavenly Father's care than she had ever experienced before.

"I shall see my uncle to-morrow!" was her last thought ere she fell asleep; but the morrow came and passed—another day, and another—and Mr. Lacie did not come.

CHAPTER V.

A NEW LEAF IN THE LEDGER.

MR. KUGLE, unused to womankind, and unversed in their variable nature, felt an inexpressible sense of comfort on finding himself relieved of Eveleen's presence, whom he suspected of being an unmanageable shrew. He went direct to Mr. Lacie's lodgings, reported her safe arrival at Mrs. Hunter's, laid the receipted bills before him; went patiently over the items, sundries, dittos, et ceteras and all; made the entries in Mr. Lacie's private account book, and was taking up his hat to go away, when Mr. Lacie looked up from a diagram he was examining, and observed rather than inquired, "My niece looks ill?"

"Not at all. They told me at the convent that she got low sometimes."

"Is that all? I'm glad to hear it. Girls soon get over the megrims. Be at your desk early to-morrow, Moses; those English chaps are in for a contract about that new cylinder improvement. It is to be settled to-morrow."

"I shall be there in time. It would be a nice thing, by dunder! to leave you to be cheated, which you will be, surely, if I am not there," said the old clerk.

"Have I ever been cheated, Moses?" asked Mr. Lacie, meekly.

"Not since *I* have had charge of your business, and that's been ever since the first locomotive was built by Lacie & Co. It wouldn't be possible to do it under my nose. But that's not saying people haven't tried to do it, or that you haven't been near falling hundreds and hundreds of times into the snare—only it was impossible, because I was too sharp. People think because I look heavy, and say nothing, that I don't notice, until they find out that I'm the very deuce on thinking," said Moses Kugle, with a guttural laugh. Mr. Lacie loved to humor the old man, who had in truth been all, and even more to him, than he boasted of; he was quite satisfied that he should think himself the pivot on which his extensive and complicated business turned, because this egotism was the sole sunshine of his solitary life, and made him happy.

"They are sharp fellows, those Yorkshire men. I think they might give even the chaps down East some lessons. Yes, be there early, Moses, because when they get me head over heels amongst the cranks, screws, levers, and my new propelling power that I have so much at heart, it'll be all over with me for making a keen bargain."

"Of course it will. You lose your head, sir," said the old German, phlegmatically; "and what you talk about is all Greek to me, for I don't know a cog-wheel from a fly-wheel, or a lever from a pulley, but I know very well when they are watching like cats for the moment when you are the most enthusiastic, and try to clinch the nail on *their* side. Then I put in my word: then I speak out, sir, and bring you to the right point. Ha! ha! I'll be there, sir! These Yorkshire chaps are sharp ones to deal with. Good night."

And Mr. Lacie forgot all about poor Eveleen, until one morning on entering his counting-room he was struck aghast by the sight of a woman, who was comfortably perched on his high office stool, and writing, as he supposed—for he saw the feather tip of the quill pen, just over her shoulder, moving rapidly, and heard vigorous splashing strokes of the nib on the paper of his ledger. His first impression was that some deranged person had got in and taken possession, and he determined to go up softly, lift her down, and put her by force out of his sanctum. But as he looked down over her shoulder he perceived that she was drawing caricatures, the sight of which mingled a feeling of diversion with his wrath and astonishment. There was Moses Kugle —there was no mistaking the long nose, deep-set eyes, and gray moustache—dancing a *minuet de cour* with a donkey, under whose long ears and shaggy mane he recognized his own high-featured, elongated visage. The mysterious artist was just putting the finishing touches to the old clerk, whose arms were formed by two figure fives, his body by number eight, and his legs and feet by inverted sevens. Some involuntary movement of Mr. Lacie's caused the intruder to start and look round. It was Eveleen—she uttered a little frightened scream, and ended by throwing her arms about her uncle's neck, and kissing him. The old man, confused and bewildered by the shock—for he did not recognize the tall, beautiful young woman before him—was almost out of breath; his first thought being that she was a widow, his next that she might possibly be his niece, of whom he had all along been thinking as a little, sunburnt, awkward girl.

"What brought you here?" he asked her, as he pulled up his shirt collar, which Eveleen had crumpled, and smoothed down his thin gray locks. "Are you—"

"I am Eveleen Lacie, and I came to see you, sir!" she said, while an expression, half smiles and half tears, trembled over her flushed countenance.

"Why did you not send for me, child?" he asked, his eyebrows still lowering.

"You knew I was come, sir," she said, with a proud, shy look.

"Yes, yes, but I forgot—I am so much engrossed, child. You cannot understand how much I have to think of."

"I knew that you had forgotten me, sir; but you see I could not afford to be forgotten by the only relative I have on earth; for you know I am very, very poor in those ties which make other people's lives so happy," she said, with daring, but gentle courage.

"So you are, child, and so am I; but I forgot it," said Mr. Lacie, lifting up his heavy eyebrows like a dark cloud from his countenance, and letting his clear, handsome eyes shine out. "I am glad to see you."

"And I to see you, sir, when you look so. Don't let them down again, sir, don't!" she said, smoothing up the shaggy refractory brows with her soft, tapering fingers.

"There, there. Go home now. I'll come and see you this evening," said Mr. Lacie, nervously, "that is, if I can."

"If you don't, sir, I shall come again to-morrow," she said, with an air of quiet determination.

"What! You must not do that. You must never come here again, and scribble over my ledger," he said, pointing to the caricature of Moses Kugle and himself.

"Where is he?" she asked, while every feature quivered with mirth.

"Do you mean Moses Kugle?"

"I mean that respectable old gentleman," she replied, laying the tip of her forefinger on the sketch.

"He's in the office attending to his duty;" said Mr. Lacie, his brows lowering.

"Will you please tell him I'm sorry for behaving rudely to him, the day he came for me? I was sorry and disappointed, for I expected you, sir, and you did not come;" said Eveleen.

"You behaved rudely to Moses Kugle? You should have known better, for you are come of a race whose women have all been noted for their gentleness," said Mr. Lacie, reprovingly.

"Yes, sir. They had English and German blood to chill the warm Irish current that flowed in their veins. But mine is heated by the blood of the tropics, which does not tend to make my character a very passive one;" said Eveleen, quietly. "I could not help drawing him, but I might have behaved better to him."

"You are almost a woman now, niece. I had no idea that you were so grown. You must learn to govern your impulses. It is wrong for any human being to give the reins to their temper and prejudices—extremely wrong. It discovers an absence of principle without which an equilibrium can't be maintained. Did not you learn something like this at the convent?"

"I learned much that was excellent there, sir. I did not become pious enough for the cloister, but I am trying in some sort to be good."

"Have you turned Catholic?" inquired Mr. Lacie, with energy.

"I have never been anything else. My mother was one, and it was the last promise my father made her, when she was dying, that I should be reared in the Catholic faith. But it was neglected, simply because my father did not know the important responsibility which such a promise involved; and Owny—poor Owny!—had grown into a respectable sort of pagan; and so, except what I gleaned now and then from the poor at Carrigmona, and from a few discourses that I heard, but was too young to understand fully, when Father O'Reilly held a station at the Travers 'Farm,' I knew but little."

"You're the first Lacie that ever was a Papist," said Mr. Lacie, frowning.

"Not the first," she said, audaciously. "I am the first since the time of Elizabeth."

"Well, well, I hope you'll be the last. Go home now, and I'll come and see you soon."

"Uncle Hugh," she said; "do you love Ireland?"

"Child!" he said, while the shaggy brows were suddenly uplifted, and the handsome, calm, truthful eyes shone full on her face, "is it any business of yours whether I do or no?"

"Of course it is. And I do know, as well as if you had told me. Now tell me where Owny Travers is?"

"He's in the city somewhere. The noise and smoke of a manufactory did not suit him, so he turned fruit merchant. The fellow's doing well, but he is as hot-headed as a Tartar."

"Please to let him know that I wish to see

him. Where is John—Shaneen, as poor Dame Travers used to call him?"

"Gone West, I believe. I tried to make a man of him, but he thought he'd rise quicker out West. I have not heard from him since he went away."

"Come and see me, Uncle Hugh, and I will sing you some old Irish songs that will make you think you can hear the fir-trees whispering at Carrigmona, and the bright waters of Luggela lapping the shore. Send Owny to see me," said Eveleen, dashing off a tear from her long black eye-lashes.

"You must not come here again, child. People don't know that you're my niece, and as women never come here, it might give rise to unpleasant rumors. I'll come to see you when I can."

"But I'd like to come again!" said Eveleen, looking around.

"For what?"

"I'd like to hear something about all this grand power that I see around me. I'd like to understand it, for I look on it as something very noble, very creative, very sublime!" said the young girl.

"What do you mean, child?" asked Mr. Lacie, looking well pleased.

"Oh, nothing," she said, with a light laugh. "Only those great ponderous things remind me of the genii in the Arabian Nights. They do

4

not seem altogether fabulous when I look on all this iron power."

"Pshaw! genii, indeed!"

"Great genii, who could build up cities in a single night, and transport palaces with their sleeping inmates to the uttermost parts of the earth. They annihilated space, levelled mountains, encompassed seas, and swayed the destinies of kings. I should like to have lived then," exclaimed Eveleen, as holding her skirts close to her, she followed her uncle out through the ponderous iron machinery that was lying around, piled up, and scattered about in seeming disorder.

"Steam does all that. These engines are its servants. Child, you are right. The age of the genii is revived," said Mr. Lacie, who just at that moment stumbled, and was likely to have fallen over an old decrepid woman who was crouching in his path.

"Here again? Begone this instant!" he exclaimed sternly.

"I came to see Jerry, the poor dear," she mumbled.

"I'll dismiss Jerry, if you don't keep away," said the master.

"Don't now, don't, your honor, be after breaking a poor widdy's heart."

"I'm beset by widows high and low, I think. I wish there was a law to burn them with their dead husbands," muttered Mr. Lacie, slyly thrusting a half-dollar into the crone's hand, as he passed her. "Begone, now. You are a disgrace to the honest lad, and ought to be ashamed of yourself to persist in coming here to mortify him in this way. Be off."

The same carriage was at the door that Eveleen had come in; she kissed her uncle's cheek before he could prevent it, sprang in and ordered the coachman to drive home. When Mr. Lacie returned to his sanctum, Moses Kugle was standing at his desk, looking down with a dumbfounded gaze on the dashing caricature of himself and his patron that Eveleen had left on the page of the ledger.

"He'll be sure I did it," thought Mr. Lacie. "I wish the little hussy had been back in Ireland before she did it! Poor Moses, what will he think but that I'm a treacherous, false-hearted old muff, to be amusing myself at his expense in this way."

"Ho! ho! ho! It's capital!—ho! ho! ho!" suddenly burst out the old clerk.

"Moses, I hope, my old friend"—began Mr. Lacie, in a deprecating sort of way.

"It's capital!—ho! ho! ho! Best likeness I ever saw. *She's* been here."

"My niece Eveleen's been here, and she is the author of that ridiculous piece of folly. Of course I was not here when she scribbled my ledger over in that way. I found her here. But she shall not come again."

"Let her! Let her come whenever she wants

to! Ho! ho! ho! It's you, old Moses Kugle, to a T. Don't tear it out, sir!—I like it. But who's the donkey I'm dancing with?"

Mr. Lacie looked—a sudden idea suggested itself. He had not observed it closely. Could it be possible she had *dared* to caricature him in that way? It was even so. His profile and the donkey's were *fac similes*. There was no help for it. She had come into their very stronghold, and made fools of the two solemn, methodical, silent old men, in the very ledger.

"I shall box her ears when I see her!" exclaimed Mr. Lacie, scowling, and trying to look very indignant.

"Don't you, sir! Ho! ho!"

"You're an old fool, Moses!"

"Yes, sir. Ho! ho! It's capital!"

"Ha! ha! ha!" echoed Mr. Lacie, with a saturnine cachinnation. He had never heard his old clerk laugh before; the whole thing was too ridiculous to be resisted. But that was as much breath as he could afford to spare in so unprofitable an investment; so, straightening down his long waistcoat, and pulling up his stock, he said in his usual tones—"Moses, those Yorkshire fellows are haggling yet about that odd thousand."

"It's their way, sir. They'll haggle about the odd ha'penny to the end. But don't give in. Keep up to the line, sir. To my certain knowledge, they expected to pay two thousand dollars more than you have charged them. They are only trying what they can do with you. Bless you, they'd take it for nothing if they could get it," said the old clerk, whose face had suddenly relapsed into its usual look of a cast-iron image.

"Very well. You see them when they come."

"Of course. Dunder! but it's little they'll make out of me," replied the old man, with a keen sparkle in his heavy gray eye. "You have got a great head, sir, for inventions and machinery, but for business—dunder and blitzen! a child could cheat your eyes out."

"That's a fact, Moses. I like to see my inventions in operation; my heart and soul are bound up in their success; and, so they go, I don't care a fig for the money. It's enough to see them fulfilling their mission."

"No wonder she drew you for the donkey," muttered the old clerk, as he bent over the ledger, chuckling until he was purple in the face. "I like her. There's the ring of true metal in her. I knew it from the way she flashed out on me so fiercely about that old Irish fellow, Owny. Ho! ho! ho!"

The next evening Mr. Lacie went to Mrs. Hunter's. A well-bred negro servant, as old and gray as himself, ushered him into the drawing-room. To his infinite relief, the widow was spending the evening out. Eveleen, looking very beautiful, in a rich black and crimson silk, with point-lace collar and undersleeves, was half reclining on a *tete-à-tete* sofa, trifling with a purse she was netting. At a little distance, near the centre table, sat a young lady who was embroidering something very rich and glittering. She had very regular features—a creamy white complexion; her hair was dressed very close to her handsome head, and she wore little jet and gold crosses in her ears, a jet and gold cross for a brooch, and a jet and gold rosary, from which depended a jet and gold cross. Her dress was black silk, with a quantity of cobweb Brussels lace about the neck and sleeves. Her trappings were pious, and her countenance demure; but the spirit of the world and its twin sisters was not to be kept down, masked, or reined in by the outward insignia of piety, and by a thousand and nameless signs, a close observer of human nature could have judged at once how under the calm exterior of Magdalene Estman many dark and evil traits were concealed. Pride, self-love, envy, and bitterness were *her* portion of the bitter cup that her unnatural mother, Eve, prepared for her before she was born. But Mr. Lacie has gone in, his broad, gouty feet falling very softly on the yielding nap of the rich velvet carpet. Eveleen heard the door close, and raised her eyes; in another moment she had sprung up, and before he could prevent it, thrown her arms around his neck, and kissed her cheek.

"This is my uncle Lacie, Miss Estman;" she said with a polite grace, as she led her uncle to the *tete-à-tete*, and made him sit in the corner nearest the fire.

Mr. Lacie made an old-fashioned, Grandisonian bow. Miss Estman bowed her queenly head, scrutinizing the old man closely, and resumed her embroidery.

"I hope you are well?" said Eveleen.

"I am always well. How are you?"

"Very well, thank you—only a little homesick"—she added with something like a sigh.

"Well—home-sick—are you not at home?" he asked.

"Not quite. I am too loyal for that," she replied with one of her bright smiles.

"Nonsense! nonsense! Too loyal for what, I'd be glad to know?"

"To feel at home anywhere on earth but at Carrigmona!"

"You had better try to, as it is not likely you'll ever live there again," said her uncle.

"I think I shall, sir," she replied, in a quiet and determined voice, as she took up a stitch and a bead together in her purse.

"How do you like being here?" asked Mr. Lacie, by way of changing the subject.

"It is very nice, but I'd prefer living with you, sir."

"Such a thing is not to be thought of," said Mr. Lacie in the most positive manner, to put a quietus to her hopes on that point.

"I am sorry for it," she replied with a demure look, while she unfastened a knot in her silk; "for I think we should get on very nicely together."

"It's more than I do, if you are in the habit of playing such pranks as you did yesterday, defacing my ledger and caricaturing Moses Kugle. Let me tell you, Miss, such things don't do."

"I meant no harm," replied Eveleen, with a merry twinkling in her eye, and a dimpling in the corner of her mouth.

"So he said."

"Who, sir?—the cross old gentleman who brought me here?"

"Yes; and if Moses Kugle had not begged you off, and made such a joke of it, I should have been seriously offended."

"Did he really? Then I forgive him!" said Eveleen, magnanimously.

"For what, pray?"

"For lecturing me. Please tell him so, sir, and that I am sorry for having caricatured him."

Mr. Lacie thought her audacious—he had never seen anything like it—but he was amused, in spite of himself, and said:

"I suppose the Donkey was so true a touch of nature as not to demand an apology."

"Dear old Donkey!" said Eveleen, lifting up his dark, wrinkled hand, and laying her soft crimson cheek on it. "I'm going to sing something for you now—something very sweet about our old home on the green cliffs of Luggela." The next moment she was seated at the piano. After a short prelude, which was like a song-bird's flutter from its leafy nest, up through vines and blossoms, into the air and sunshine overhead, her voice arose in rich strains above the instrument. It was a wild air, filled with soft cadences and thrilling sweetness, which melted every now and then into sadness, which, like a weird spell, went down into the old man's heart, and carried him back to his long-ago boyhood, and his tireless rambles through the picturesque glens, adown the heathery braes, and over the beetling cliffs of Carrigmona. But, alas! as the last notes were dying away, and Mr. Lacie, with a softened expression on his countenance, leaned back in pleasant oblivion of all but the rare dream which the song had conjured up in his work-a-day heart, the door opened, and Mrs. Hunter rustled in, all smiles, and welcome. Mr. Lacie suddenly remembered an "engagement," and resisting all Mrs. Hunter's entreaties to remain longer, went out into the hall, followed by Eveleen.

"I must see that you are well wrapped up this bitter night. Where's your comforter, sir? Haven't you got a comforter? Pull up your coat collar, then. I see you need some one to take care of you," said Eveleen, pulling up his coat collar, and with her long slender fingers pressing it against his withered cheeks.

"What nonsense!" growled Mr. Lacie, who, however, obeyed her. "Here, I'd like to have forgotten this. Take it, and mind you don't waste it."

"Yes, sir," replied Eveleen, taking the package —a small one—which he handed to her, without thinking what it was. "Please to send Owny— dear old Owny!—to see me."

"Yes! yes! take care of that money!" said Mr. Lacie, stepping out, and closing the hall door quickly after him.

"Money!" mused Eveleen, as she returned to the parlor. "I wonder what I am expected to do with it? See here, Mrs. Hunter; my uncle has given me a pile of money—what in the world am I to do with it! Here—ten—ten—ten thirty—forty—fifty—sixty—seventy—eighty— one hundred!—one hundred dollars! What on earth shall I do with it?"

"Miss Lacie needs a handsome set of rubies, a jeweled comb, sables, and many other elegant matters," laughed Mrs. Hunter, who was perfectly *au fait* with all that fashion and folly required.

"I have some poor friends at home," mused Eveleen; "they're behindhand with their affairs—some of it would make them very comfortable."

"Miss Lacie may invest her money where treasures corrupt not. I am collecting for the new altar of St. Sebastian," suggested Miss Estman.

"Don't put my name down. Promise me that, and I will give you this," said Eveleen, holding up one of the new ten-dollar bills by the corner. It made a pleasant rustling, and Miss Estman liked the idea of the donations being anonymous; her own name was not down, and making a little mystery, Father Wheeler and the committee would naturally suppose it was her own generous gift; while the sum she had been expecting to be obliged, for the sake of appearances, to subscribe, could now be added to the purchase-money of an elegant set of sables, upon which she had set her heart.

"Miss Lacie is no Pharisee, that is very clear. Of course I will not put your name on my paper, or even speak of it, if you say so;" she said, in her low, clear tones.

"There it is," said Eveleen, folding the bill into a knot, and throwing it into Miss Estman's lap. "Take it, and welcome, on those terms. Don't you think, Mrs. Hunter, that there are a great many little children and sickly women suffering for food and fuel in this large city?" she asked, with earnest simplicity.

"I fancy so. Indeed, there's no doubt of it. You know, my dear, that beggars and paupers are inevitable evils in great cities!" replied Mrs. Hunter, who exchanged looks with Miss Estman.

"Well! I must see. It is so pleasant a thing to give—so pleasant that I shall have no merit in it, you see," said the noble-hearted girl, shrinking with true humility and rare simplicity of mind from any assumption of higher motives than the generous and natural impulses of her heart.

"You are not as generous in your friendships, I fear, Miss Lacie, as with your purse;" said Miss Estman, in her unvarying tone.

"I do not know. I have had so few friends," replied Eveleen, who, having laid the notes smoothly between the leaves of a new prayer-book, which had come home that evening, having been left at the store where she purchased it to have her name engraved on the clasp, took up her *crochet* work, and began to loop in the stitches.

"You had your uncle all to yourself this evening. Monopolies are considered in bad taste by society," said Magdalene Estman, with an air of raillery, while she was in truth quite offended at having been obliged to sit so silent during Mr. Lacie's visit. "Not that I care about making new acquaintances, for the world and I have but little in common."

"I remember now. That was rude," said Eveleen, coloring. "Pray excuse me!"

"No need of apologizing to me, my dear. I only thought it my duty to call your attention to it for your own sake, because the next time you might do the same thing in company with persons who will not be so charitable."

"Thank you," said Eveleen, scarcely knowing whether the interference proceeded from charity or impertinence. But Eveleen was so true-hearted herself—so unsuspicious of guile in others—that she chid herself for the momentary thought, and laying it all to the door of her own ignorance and inexperience, she entered into a pleasant conversation with the two ladies, following their lead, and by the time she arose to retire, she had come to the conclusion that she was only a poor, little, uncultivated, wild Irish girl, and Miss Estman the handsomest, most pious, most intelligent, most discreet, most polished, and most charitable young lady in existence. So she kissed her on bidding her goodnight.

"A most uncultivated little thing," she remarked, after Eveleen went out.

"It's not to be wondered at, poor child. She spent her life, almost all of it, in Ireland, where I am told the people are half wild," said Mrs. Hunter, yawning.

"She affects great generosity," suggested Miss Estman.

"She doesn't know the value of money. I expect she was very poor until Mr. Lacie adopted her."

"I have invited her once or twice to go to early Mass with me, but she declined. I'm afraid she doesn't practise her religion."

"Oh—I don't know. I believe she goes to St. Alphonsus', to the Children's Mass at eight o'clock, generally. You know they have music on the organ, and the children all sing."

"That's the attraction, I suppose. How do you like this stole, Mrs. Hunter?"

"It is very beautiful—extremely rich," said Mrs. Hunter, lifting up an end of the stole, and examining it through her eye-glasses. "I declare, you spend all your time in doing good works."

"You have too good an opinion of me, Mrs. Hunter," replied the young lady, without denying the soft impeachment, however; and having put up her silks, spangles, and tinsel, and folded up her work in a fine damask towel, she arose, and, after kissing Mrs. Hunter, retired to her bed-room.

There are some natures in this world of ours, in the very kingdom of the Church, who, scrupulously observant of the outward duties of religion, bear no fruits to themselves or others, simply because they *have not charity;* who blame and stigmatize those who do not come up to their standard of practice, who cannot, or will not, distinguish between a blunder and a sin, between the frailties of nature and the designs of malice, between light-hearted thoughtlessness and deliberate evil; and who, in their avowed concern for the honor of religion, inflict deeper wounds on it by judging without mercy, and accusing without charity, than the veriest sinners. Of all the triumphs of the devil, it seems to me there is none in which he takes so keen a delight as that of seeing people—who, from the number of masses they hear, and their frequent communions, ought to be almost saints—giving the whisper to lying reports; listening with eager attention to slanderers' tales; circulating by word and look unmerciful and mischievous libels, and judging with harsh lips and envenomed tongues their fellow Christian, who, to the All-seeing eye, may be a very Lazarus at their gate—one of the elect to whom they, in their self-righteousness, refuse a crumb of charity. This is terribly true. These *incubæ* on religion have a real existence; and we—not because it is an agreeable task—call attention to the fact, because Magdalene Estman is one of this class, and—whether laboring under moral obliquity or spiritual blindness—under the cloak of religion she exercised a most evil influence over the life of our heroine, Eveleen Lacie.

CHAPTER VI.

THE SHIP LETTER.

IT is towards the close of a cold March day; a mist fills the atmosphere with gray and shadowy vapors, which partly obscure the wild landscape from view; and gusts of wind, piercingly cold, whirl down through the mountain defiles, and ruffle the dark waters of Luggela, which burst against the shore with a dreary sound. Under a beetling cliff, with the spray dashing over her feet, stands pretty Alice Kane, the betrothed of John Travers, evidently expecting some one, for whose arrival she is both anxious and impatient. Heedless of the cold wind that tosses her golden curls wildly back from her white face; heedless of the spray and mist that saturate her garments; heedless of the gathering twilight, she still lingers beside the shore watching and waiting.

"Mother of God!" she sobbed, as she clasped her hands with a hopeless look over her bosom, "hast thou no hope left for me in my black grief? Oh, Virgin most pure! *a bouchal dhas* was thy child as well as mysel', an' niver an opportunity did he let slip to honor and sarve you. An' Father O'Reilly said often that he had the heart of a child; so he had, an' wasn't

it thy dear Son hissel' that blessed the little ones? An' turn thy eyes, Blessed Lady, on his poor ould mother, that goes cast-down an' sorrowful day in an' day out—Christ help her!—an' by the unspeakable grief that lay heavy upon thy tender heart, when thou didst go seeking thy Son three bitther days, have compassion on her."
Here Ally paused—she thought she heard an approaching footstep, and pushed back the damp curls from her ear, while she leaned forward and listened intently. But it was only some loose pebbles that had fallen with a *thud* from the rocks above on the wet sands. With a shiver she drew her shawl closer about her, and murmured in touching accents—"A long twelvemonth an' niver a word! Oh, Shaneen *asthore!* unless the sod lies heavy on thy *quite* breast, it is a heedless an' cruel trial you are makin' of our love—niver to send a line or word! But I won't believe it of you, John darlin', for you niver was one to put yoursel' before thim that loved you. Surely some one comes! Hist! It is—it is he. Larry, darlin', have ye brought me a letther?" she exclaimed, as a bare-footed *gossoon*, wrapped in a tattered cloak, which was patched with worn-out shreds of every imaginable color, came around the cliff. Without answering her eager inquiry he halted, and began to fumble and search among his ragged garments, pulled out odds and ends of fishing tackle, old cloth, an odd stocking, a tattered red handkerchief, an old

game bag, buttons, rusty nails, and bits of leather—until, having regaled his eyes with a sight of all his possessions, he deliberately restored them to his fathomless pockets; and taking off his frontless cap, pulled up the greasy lining, and drew out a letter, which he handed to Ally. Snatching it from him, as if fearful that it would elude her grasp—like the dreams which of late had so often harassed her—she turned it over, held it out to the fading light to read the superscription, and with a sudden cry of joy discovered by the mark that it was a ship letter. Pressing it to her lips, she clasped it close to her wildly-throbbing heart; then bethought her of the reward she had promised to give the uncouth lad who had brought it, who stood leaning against the cliff whistling "*machro*" with as jolly an air as if he had been a lord instead of a beggar. "There is what I promised you, Larry," she said, laying three bright shillings in his hand; "I would give you ten times as much if I had it, for the sunshine you've brought me this dark day; but, alanna, I'm poor like yoursel'—thanks be to God!—an' I can only pray that the angels will make a bright spot for ye in heaven."

"*Oh, ma gra hu!* D'ye think I'm sich a beggar as that comes to, afther all, Miss Ally?" said Larry with a royal air. "One will do intirely. If the like of us, *alanna voght*, don't help each other, God help us forever! There—take back the two shillins', and don't say Larry Fagan's a misert if he does carry the bag."

"Kape it for my sake, Larry. I don't want it, *asthore*, an' many thanks to you for your good intintions," said Ally, as she wrapped her shawl around her, and bounded away, eager to carry to the sorrowful old man and his wife, at the "Farm," the glad news that a letter had come from America. So joyful and elated did she feel, that the ruggedness of the way homeward, around by the steep mountain path, was quite unnoticed. Her heart, so long heavy and drooping, was all astir with life and hope; it bounded and panted with an emotion almost too intense for its capacity, as the blissful certainty of hearing from her absent lover, of learning the cause of his long silence, of reading over the sweet and tender words which he knew so well how to write, of knowing all about his success and his future plans, possessed it. Poor child! not a doubt of its being from any other than John Travers suggested itself to her. Why should she feel disturbed? The letter was from the United States—it was surely John's handwriting—and she only wished for wings to her feet, that she might fly home more speedily, read all that it contained, and witness the joy of Michael Travers and his wife on receiving tidings of their son.

As Michael and his dame sat beside the smouldering turf fire, saying a few words now and then, darkness and silence crept together into the room; their thoughts had gone far away over the sea after their absent boy, who might even now be dead and laid away among the strangers, for aught they knew to the contrary. In fact, they had every reason to believe that he *was* dead, for not a word, message, or line had they received from him for one dreary year. Previous to that time, his letters had been regular and cheerful; suddenly they were discontinued, and day by day their long-deferred hopes went out, like floating lamps on the waves—went out, or sunk extinguished in the tossing doubts, the alternate hopes and chilling disappointments, which made their life such a weary and cheerless time.

"It is God's will that we should be so tried, wife," the old man said daily; "we set our hearts too much on the lad. We prided oursel's on him, as if he was ours, body an' soul."

As they sat silent and sorrowful in the evening darkness, busy with thoughts that brought no earthly solace to their aged hearts, suddenly a wild, clear lay arose on the night. Blithe and sweet it came trilling on their ears, like the first song of the nightingale. They lifted their heads and listened. It was the very song Ally used to sing when John Travers, their son, would be sculling his boat across the Lough, on his way home in the evening; and which he, in the distance, would take up and sing with her, his clear, manly voice growing louder and louder on the ear, until the keel of his boat cut the white sands of the shore below.

"The heavens look down upon uz!" exclaim Dame Travers, "d'ye hear that?"

"Faix an' I do, surely;" replied her husband in a trembling voice, while he strained his eyes through the gloom, and crossed himself: "Oh vo! how wild and shrill it is! It's nothin' human —God bless us!"

"The Mother of God defend us! it comes through the very *tatch!*" whispered Dame Travers, while she raked the turf, until a ruddy light gleamed out of the chimney. "It sounds like poor Ally's voice, only she is too broken-hearted to sing, an' is in her room beyant cryin' her two eyes out, the craythur!"

"The heavens look down upon uz! there's no livin' mortial could sing like that, wife. It goes an' comes like it was flittin' here and there on the wind. I heard my father say there used to be a *Banshee* hereabouts; he'd heard it cry more'n once, and the night ould Aiden Lacie died—Oyeh! oh *wirra!*" exclaimed the old man, springing back in his chair, as the door flew open, and Ally Kane, speechless with joy, ran in, and threw herself, sobbing, on Dame Travers' breast.

"Cheer up," she sobbed, "there's news!"

"See that now! It's a letther she's got! Tell me, machree," screamed the old woman wildly. "It's a letter from *a bouchal dhas!*"

"It is—it is! I was afeard to tell it to ye's too suddint. But now it's out, an' I'll light a rush, then we'll all read it together," said Ally, rising up and going across the floor with a light, springing step. "Larry Fagan fetched it to me —he's been promisin' an' promisin' to bring me a letther from Ameriky these six months back, an' last night I dreamed that one come, an' I went down to the landin' right agin the road from Glendalough, where *he* used to moor his boat, an' waited there all the afternoon, an' my drame come true—thanks be to God!—for Larry brought me the letther at last."

"God Almighty be praised! Open the letther an' read it—my ould heart is famishin' to hear news of my child—*alanna voght!*" she repeated tenderly.

"The MAN ABOVE knows it's been a sore trial, but it was His holy will for uz to suffer in that way, an' whatever happens is for our good an' His glory—amin," said the old man, in tones of humble thankfulness. Keep that in thy heart, Michael Travers—plant it there like a rock, on which thou mayest climb for safety when the floods come and roll over thee— "Whatever happens is for our good an' His glory!" Do not forget it, when the last blossom of thy earthly happiness withers, and dies by a cruel and untimely frost; and when the staff, on which thou hast been so proudly leaning for years, counting the joys which blossomed on it, and hoping in thy vanity that thou wouldst gather much fruit from it, even in this life, breaks and leaves thee helpless and desolate at the foot of the Cross—remember it is all for thy own good and the glory of God.

The rush was lighted, and Ally, with trembling fingers, broke the seal of the letter, and opened it; but as her eye glanced over the first few lines, a look of strange bewilderment came over her countenance, the color faded out of her cheeks, and she raised her eyes with a wild, pitiful expression, to the two eager faces that were bent forward, with keen anticipation in every lineament, to hear the news.

"What's the matter, *mavourneen?* Why don't you go on?"

"Ally, spake out in God's name," said Dame Travers, in great perturbation. "Let us hear the worst. Is Shaneen sick, or in thruble?"

"It is from Uncle Owny," she murmured, in a low, choking voice; "an' the very first word he writes is to know if John is here. I can't read it—God be good to me! I thought it was from hissel'." And there was a plaintive cadence in the young girl's voice, and such a look of heart-sickness in her wan face, as her head fell back in the chair, that Dame Travers forgot for an instant the maternal pangs that wrung her own heart, to soothe and cheer her with words of hope. The letter was indeed from Owny, who wrote in a way which was calculated to arouse their worst fears for the fate of their son. He informed them that John had left a good situation in Baltimore, and started West some months before. He thought it was a better place for a young man than a crowded city, and expected to better his fortunes, according to the almost fabulous tales of success that he had heard of other poor lads, who had gone out there and made immense fortunes in a few years. He had written from Wheeling, where he staid ten days with a man from Wicklow, named Ennis, since which he had heard no tidings, good or bad, of him. Ennis said that he had started for Cincinnati in good health and spirits, and promised to write, but had failed to do so. There had been some terrible political riots in Cincinnati, and several Irishmen had been killed, whose names no one could ascertain.

"It might be"—wrote Owny—"God above only knows—that the boy came to his death in the scrimmage, if he didn't take it into his head to go home to County Wicklow in ould Ireland, which I hope he did. I have advertised in some of the newspapers, and in the (Boston) *Pilot*, that goes to every part of the round world, and would ferret a man out if he was buried, for information of John Travers; but nothing's come of it yet, and I'm in high hopes that he's home with his sweetheart, and made up his mind to be an honest Wicklow farmer. I'm making a few pennies daily, that I'm saving for them that's to come after me, and you

know there's none nearer to me than the boy—
Christ bring him back to us in safety! I don't
think it's any use to fret or grieve yourself about
not hearing from him (if he's not with you,
which I hope he is), by rayson of the West,
where he started to go, being a great outspread
country as big as all Europe, and England and
Ireland to boot, only there's not so many people
nor cities, but deserts and wildernesses full of
wild Injins, and no way of sending a letter to
absent friends. So cheer up, my dear brother
and sister-in-law, and hope for the best. Miss
Eveleen—God bless her!—is home from school,
and sent for me, but I was away in Wheeling,
and when I come home, and went to see her, the
ould nagur at the dure tould me she was out
shoppin'; but I'm going again and again, until
I see my little *colleen bawn* that I've had many
and many's the time in my arms when she was
a weenie child. Oh, *wirra!* but my heart grows
sick in my body for a sight of the Wicklow hills,
in particular Carrigmanne mountain, when the
sun shines down on the fern and heather. It's
nothing to be in strange countries, and wandering over the say, when a fellow's a young man;
but it seems to me we get tired like childer when
we grow ould, and want to lay our heads down
on our mother's lap. They say Miss Eveleen's
a tall, beautiful young lady, the handsomest of
all the Lacies since the ould Catholic days; and
what will astonish you, she's one herself—goes

to confession and holy communion like the rest of uz, glory to God! I must now conclude, hoping, dear brother, that you will write immediately, and let me know if the boy's at home. Love to my sister-in-law and purty Ally Kane, that's to be my own niece, and believe me your affectionate brother, OWEN TRAVERS."

Michael Travers read the letter through to the end, and although no tear fell from his dim eyes, his voice quavered and his hands trembled so that he could scarcely hold it. Then he folded it up, smoothed it on his knee, and gave it back to Ally Kane, who knelt beside him in tearless woe, leaning on the arm of his chair, with her long golden hair falling in disordered ringlets over her neck and shoulders, while her face looked like a lily that is beaten by the storm and tempest. Her hands were clasped together, and her head dropped forward on her breast. An unutterable grief had fallen on her. Her bright and blissful hopes had been so suddenly extinguished that her heart felt like a "deserted nest, into which the snows of an untimely winter have fallen." Dame Travers, demonstrative under all emotions, sat rocking herself to and fro, wringing her hands, sobbing out her grief in plaintive words.

"I knew it. I knew if *a bouchal dhas* left me, I should never set my two livin' eyes on him agin. He might as well ha' died, and been buried with the rest when he was a wean. It would ha' seemed hard then, but not as bitther or hard as this. Oyeh! God pity me in my disolation this day—there's nothin' left for me to do now, but to go lie down under the sod, with my poor childer beyant there at the Seven Churches. Och! it seems hard, after the pangs of so much child-bearin', an' so many years of sorrow, to be left afther all, disolate in my old age."

"Wife," said Michael Travers, in a choking voice, while his white lips trembled, "it is God's holy will. We are ould; if Shaneen is gone, it won't be long before, with God's help, we'll meet him agin. But that young craythur that loved him aiqual to yoursel', look how white an' still she is, wife; her heart's broke intirely. Spake to her in God's name—don't let Shaneen's darlin' die on our hearth, without a word of comfort from his mother."

"Ally *machree*," said Dame Travers, whose heart gushed over with sudden tenderness, when she heard the words "*Shaneen's darling*," and she rose from her chair, and put her arms about the white, silent form of the girl, and drew her head to her bosom. "Lay your poor head there, *asthore!* Husband! she doesn't hear me! Look how *quite* she is. Ally don't give up so, *achree;* he didn't say *a bouchal dhas* was dead."

"Dead," murmured Ally, leaning her head on Dame Travers' bosom, and shivering as if an ague fit was on her. "Dead." This was all she said. One would have thought to have seen her lying there, so white and motionless in her rare loveliness, with drooping hands and half-closed eyes, that she had fallen asleep from exhaustion, or that she was unconscious; but beneath that spell, every life thought, every mysterious energy of will, every instinct of sympathetic affinity, were stirring with strong and deep impulses, and by slow degrees forming themselves into distinctness of purpose and firm resolve—for something had whispered her that her betrothed was not dead—but beyond that all was turbulent gloom in her mind, like black racks of clouds in December, when the north wind plunges amidst them. It was as if a dark and nameless woe, in which poverty, sickness, loneliness, and ignominy had part, hovered about him, hiding him, in that strange vision, from her sight. The motherly bosom on which she leaned heaved with sobs, and torrents of tears streamed silently over the furrows of the kind face that bent over her, and fell dripping like rain upon her golden hair. The minutes had gone by unheeded. It was past midnight. The rain and sleet lashed the little window panes, and the winds, howling around the peaks of Carrigmanne, and through the defiles of the beetling hills, ploughed up the waters of the Lough with a pitiless roar. Anon, between the wailings of the blast, arose the deep-mouthed howl of John Travers' dog, which he had left at home with Ally, to be taken care of until he came.

Mr. Travers had left the sad group, for whom he had no word of consolation, and thrown himself on the bed, in the next room, without undressing, where he lay, looking his sorrow in the face, and measuring the depths of its bitterness with as much tearless anguish, and as great a desire for submission to the will of God, as it was possible for frail stricken human nature to feel under so cruel a crucifixion. In the language of David, his old, weary heart cried out: "Oh, my son! would that I had died for thee!" but all in vain! He could see nothing beyond the present—there was nothing, seemingly, for him to look forward to in his life; his strength and courage were gone; and he only knew in WHOM he trusted, and that a day would come when the dealings of God with his creatures—which sometimes appear so hard—would be justified to His own glory, and for their eternal good.

"He was good from his youth up. Never did he do anything to anger or grieve me; but was the pride and consolation of my ould age!" murmured the old man, with a soft gush of tears. "God help the poor ould mother, that thought the like of him was niver born—an' no wonder!"

Suppose, old pilgrim, that it had been otherwise with the boy? Suppose his life had gone out, and left no such memories as these to sweeten the bitter cup of separation? Suppose deeds of sin, disobedience and violence, had risen up to appal thee with hopeless fears of his future?

Let not thy heart be troubled, for whatever has befallen the boy, whether he be living or dead, be sure that it is well with him. If dead, he has gone with the sunshine of an innocent life about him, and with clean hands, into the presence of his God; if living, even though surrounded by difficulties, he will triumph in the strength of his integrity, and by his faith in Him who has never failed in the least of His promises.

These were the thoughts, or we had better say, the angel whispers, that came into the old man's heart, softening and consoling it.

There was a slight movement in the next room, and hoping that Ally and his wife were going to bed, he leaned up on his elbow, and saw Ally standing before him, calm but very pale, and with a look so resolute on her countenance that he knew not what to think.

"Go to your bed!—go to your bed, *caen buy deelish*—there's time enough to grieve, *asthore*, in the days to come. It's the will of God for us to suffer; but not His holy will to go agin His laws, an' kill oursels—go to bed."

"Father!" she replied as if he had not spoken, and calling him for the first time by that tender name, which a feeling of maidenly shame had hitherto prevented her from doing, "I'm going away, an' hope you won't cross me. You know what was betune John an' mysel'; we couldn't ha' loved each other more, if we had stood up before the priest; he couldn't ha' been more mine, nor

I his'n, in the eyes of Almighty God, than we wor the day we parted—an' I'm goin' to find him. He's not dead—somethin' tells me that; but I feel like as if there was a black sorrow on him in that strange country, an' I'm goin' across the say to find him."

"See that now! The child's clane distraught—Christ be good to us! Be patient, Ally, honey"—said the bewildered old man, as soothingly as he could. "Surely, *asthore*, you wouldn't be afther lavin' the ould mother desolate?"

"I must go, father. I shall die afore to-morrow night if I stay here. I must go an' find Shaneen, for he's in some great trouble, an' not a friend a-near'st him."

"But how are you to go, *caen buy deelish!* It's a long way, an' woe's me! ther's nobody to tell ye where to find him."

"I'll go. It's no use tryin' to hinder me. If he was dead, it would make a differ—I could pray for his soul as well here as there; but he's livin', and he's my husband, an' nothin' but death shall separate us. I have stood upon your flure, father, since I could totter alone, an' I don't know as ever I contradicted or disobeyed ye's. You tuk me in a desolate orphan, an' made no differ betune your child an' mysel'; an' when he axed me to be his wife ye's niver gainsayed him; an' I'll kneel down at your feet, and ask God, an' the Blessed Virgin, an' the holy angels, to bless ye's now an' forevermore for the good ye's have both done me: but *he's* nearer to me nor all—I must go to him, for it seems to me I hear his voice down in me heart a whisperin', 'Ally, come! come to me!'"

"Don't contradict her, for the love of heaven," sobbed Dame Travers.

CHAPTER VII.

"DELIVER US FROM EVIL."

EVELEEN LACIE'S nature was full of sunshine, which lit up even the commonplace aspects of life with genial brightness, and caused her to distrust with charitable forbearance the suggestions of her keen intuitive perceptions of character, when she came in contact with strangers who made an unfavorable impression on her. This fine and mysterious monitor, which is to some persons such a safeguard, was often rendered useless to her, by an impetuous generosity and an amiable credulity, which found more pleasure in confiding in the professions of others, than in suspecting them. And under all this, there was a blending of Celtic and Milesian pride that not only made her recoil from whatever was mean or unprincipled in thought or act, but roused her at times to resent any undue and tangible interference with her rights. Perhaps her greatest peculiarity of character was strong self-reliance, which, based upon purity of motive, and abstract rectitude of principle, incited her frequently to actions as prompt as the causes which gave rise to them were sudden, without regard to how they might appear to others, or result to herself. Her natural traits were but types of her spiritual life. Genuine and fervent in her religious feelings, constant in her devotion to sublime truths, her reverence for all holy mysteries was too deep for ostentation, or the empty parade of words; it was like a rich flower slowly unfolding its petals in some hidden glen, and sweetening the air with its fragrance, even while it was concealed from the rude and careless gaze of passers-by. She had her failings, but in her soul were the elements that, had she lived in a past age, would have caused her to be numbered in the ranks of the martyrs—so vital and holy, so divine and worthy of all honor and devotion, did she esteem her Faith. Her heart throbbed responsive to all that was noble and good, and she considered it no shame to love and honor virtue in the garb of poverty, or cling with constant friendship to the friends, humble and lowly though they were, who had guarded her infancy, and been the associates of her childhood. Combined with these traits, she possessed a mind of a high intellectual type, and a disposition as free from guile as it was buoyant and cheerful. Having thus given our readers sufficient insight into Eveleen Lacie's character to enable them to understand her motives and sympathize with her, in the events that were developed in her history, we will go on with our narrative.

Eveleen was as contented at Mrs. Hunter's

as she would have been anywhere else in a strange land, under a stranger's roof. She felt heart-sick at times with a yearning desire to see her old gray home, beside the romantic waters of the Lake Luggela: and to breathe the sweet-scented air of the hills once more; and rest her head against the ivy-clad walls of the vault where her father reposed. The cold, formal words of courtesy that greeted her everywhere—the prim Saxon dialect, the measured expressions, the unsympathetic intercourse, and dearth of spontaneity, so unlike the rich, poetical vernacular of home; so different from the blundering, eloquent, heart-touching, gushing accents of her humble and faithful friends among the Wicklow hills—chilled her and often drove her to seek solace in her music, and the books she liked best. It would have comforted her to see her uncle more frequently, but that was impossible; then she puzzled herself to know why Owny Travers did not come to see her, and finally concluded that he was not acquainted with her being there. She saw a great deal of fashionable society at Mrs. Hunter's—people of wealth and position were willing enough to patronize the reputed heiress of old Hugh Lacie; but the fair Irish girl received their attentions with a quiet *nonchalance* which not only surprised but piqued them, while her rare beauty, unaffected gayety, and her highly cultivated talent for music, made them only the more eager to gain such an acquisition to lend *éclat* to their parties. Mrs. Hunter's pleasant and worldly ways amused Eveleen; but Magdalene Estman was a problem to her which she could not solve. There was a velvety softness in her manner and address, an assumption of piety and humility strangely at variance with her sentiments and actions, which struck Eveleen as extremely inconsistent; but as she had expressed great interest in her, and frequently advised her, not only in relation to her toilette, but in the expenditure of her liberal allowance, which she did not disdain to make use of herself when her own scant funds ran low, and seemed otherwise friendly, Eveleen rebuked herself sharply for presuming to call in question her pretensions or her sincerity; she decided such feelings were uncharitable, and strove to banish them altogether from her mind.

Among the most frequent guests at Mrs. Hunter's was Rolfe Estman, a cousin of Magdalene's, a young man of great natural abilities and fashionable pretensions. When he first began to practice at the bar it was predicted by able judges that "if he remained true to himself, he would rise rapidly to the highest eminence in his profession;" but unfortunately he did not, his interest became absorbed by the dice-box, and it was not an unfrequent thing in his daily life for the delirious inspiration of the wine-cup to usurp the divine *afflatus* of genius. Then dark hints were whispered of one who had trusted him too fondly; of a disgraced home and betrayed innocence; but the facts were never generally known, and the story was hushed up. What made all this more scandalous, was the fact that he was by birth and baptism a Catholic; one of those who are pointed at with scoffing finger and sneering lip by Protestants and unbelievers, as an illustration of the insufficiency of the Faith he professed, to preserve him from evil—drawing no distinction between him, who never practised his religion, or allowed its wholesome restraints to control his unbridled passions, and those who, living up to its spirit and precepts, live righteous and holy lives among men. Such cases give the enemies of the Church their highest triumph, because bearing her ineffaceable mark on their forehead, they mock, betray, and crucify her in their lives. But we have no space to moralize over a case which, unfortunately for the interests of religion, is by no means rare. This man, almost shipwrecked in fame and fortune, saw Eveleen Lacie, and when he learned from his cousin that she would inherit all her uncle's immense wealth, the impression that her youth, beauty and intelligence had already made upon him, ripened into a determination to win her if possible. He began by paying assiduous court to his cousin, and taking her into his confidence. Once more he appeared at church, and by a grave and attentive demeanor led his friends to believe that he had "sown his wild oats," and had set about the great work of life in good earnest. There is only one thing we believe that will banish a man beyond the pale of fashionable life—poverty; therefore Rolfe Estman, with all his vices, had not lost *caste*, having still sufficient to keep up appearances, and being not only a brilliant genius, but a handsome and distinguished looking man, Protestant society winked at his sins, and excused his derelictions, because it professed to believe that his creed afforded him ample immunities to go on sinning, if he could only pay liberally for absolution. It was with no slight feeling of triumph that Magdalene Estman received the congratulations of her friends, on having by her influence and example caused the reformation of this fallen and gifted creature. She knew full well how hollow was this pretended reformation, and by what motives it was instigated; but it was to her interest to keep his secret, and tacitly admit the truth of the report, which applied such flattering unction to her vanity, and caused her to be the theme of so many tongues.

From the hour that Rolfe Estman confided his secret to her, Magdalene made overt and ceaseless attempts to win an interest in Eveleen Lacie's heart for her kinsman. Eveleen's attention directed thus incessantly to him, she frankly admitted his many attractions, and confessed that his quiet, high-bred manners and brilliant conversation possessed a peculiar charm for her.

"He has been irregular, poor Rolfe," said Magdalene, one day, when she was sitting with Eveleen in her "study;" "but he is so penitent. Do not you think there is something very noble in the sight of a soul lifting itself up from the abyss into which it has inadvertently fallen? A penitent man is one of the most touching sights in the world."

"When his penitence is genuine," replied Eveleen, all unconscious of the sting her words inflicted.

"Rolfe's penitence is genuine beyond doubt," said Magdalene, heedless of the twinge her conscience gave her; "he made a splendid speech in court yesterday. I read in one of the morning papers, that 'such a brilliant effort of forensic eloquence had not been listened to in the old court-house for many years.' I am very proud of Rolfe!"

"I should like to hear Mr. Estman speak. I believe I heard you say one day that he's a Catholic by baptism; does he practise his religion?" asked Eveleen, in her straightforward way.

"Ah! poor Rolfe! it is that which first led him astray—he neglected the Sacraments. But he is getting on bravely now. Do you not observe how devout he is at Mass?"

"He behaves like a Catholic gentleman, but I do not observe anything peculiarly devout in his manner," replied Eveleen. "The hatred and contempt of Protestants to our holy faith no longer appears strange or unreasonable, when we see those who belong to her fold neglecting her precepts and trampling on her divine sacraments! I do not allude to Mr. Estman particularly, but speak generally."

"They give great scandal," said Magdalene, and changed the subject.

The next day was Sunday. Magdalene came into Eveleen's room to see if she was ready for church, and found her reading.

"Did you know the first bell had rung?" said Magdalene, as she went up to the toilet-glass, and arranged a crimson velvet rose more becomingly against her ivory cheek, tied her bonnet-strings in a graceful bow, and touched her raven hair with bandoline, to make it lie more smoothly on her white, smooth forehead.

"Oh, thank you for coming. I did not hear the bell. I've been poring over one of Carleton's inimitable Irish stories, and almost fancied myself at home again. I believe I have been crying, and must bathe my eyes," said Eveleen. Somewhat careless in the arts of the toilette, Eveleen scarcely looked into the mirror to see whether her bonnet sat crooked or straight on her head; however, if she had been the vainest of her sex, she could not have adopted a style so perfectly in keeping with her strange beauty, or which would have enhanced it more. Her hat was rich and elegant, and her furs, wrappings and dress corresponded with it. She had an innate love for the beautiful, which, with a refined taste, led her to select rich colors, fine materials, and a becoming style, but once purchased they were forgotten, and worn with the same indifference that the plainest articles and most subdued colors would have been.

"After all, you are ready before me, Eveleen—but we can wait a little while; it is in extremely bad taste to go to Church so early," said Magdalene, pulling her jet cross ear-rings more in sight, after which she proceeded to draw on a dainty pair of lavender-colored kid gloves, which fitted her small, but not handsome hand, to a nicety. "Why do you not wear Jouvin's gloves, Eveleen?"

"I do sometimes, but it is cold to-day, and I have on my furred gauntlets," replied Eveleen, holding out one of her hands, the symmetry of which not even the clumsy gauntlets could conceal.

"I believe you draw off your gloves in Church. The gauntlets are more convenient for that," said Magdalene, with an almost imperceptible sneer.

"Yes—a little while before the consecration. I once read, in an old book, that it was a custom in some Catholic countries to do so, as an outward mark of reverence for Him who is coming, and I like it. I try to attract no attention, for I do not think one's piety is at all assisted by singularity," said Eveleen, *naively*.

"Oh, if I had a hand like St. Cecelia's, I'd unglove too; but come, dear, I hear Rolfe's voice in the hall," said Magdalene, going towards the door.

"Is not this the Sunday they are to take up a collection for the College of St. Charles Borromeo?" asked Eveleen, unlocking her drawer, and taking out her purse.

"Bless me! so it is. How unfortunate; but I'll get some change from Rolfe," said Magdalene.

"Don't. Here's my purse; take what you want, and return it when you please," said Eveleen, extending her purse towards her.

"I declare, you are very kind, Eveleen. I shall draw my dividend next week, and pay up," said Magdalene, taking out a gold dollar.

"She may think I do it through vanity," mused Eveleen, as she went down stairs, "but I don't; and I shall continue to draw off my gloves, for nobody sees my hands, which are just as God made them."

Mr. Estman behaved with his usual wellbred elegance on his way to church, and amused his cousin by a description of a wedding in high life, to which she had declined an invitation, because she could not manage to get a white *glacé* silk and a set of pearls, upon which she had set her heart—leaving it to be inferred, however, that she had scruples about going into and mingling in such gayeties. Magdalene led the way up the broad aisle, rustling her brocade, and tossing her plumes, until she came to Eveleen's pew; then she made a graceful genuflection, and, leaning over, opened the door, and invited Mr. Estman in. He made a gesture for Eveleen to pass in, but she told him to enter, then followed them in, latched the pew door, and, kneeling down, reverently and humbly adored the DIVINE PRESENCE on the altar. In a little while she became absorbed in devout attention to the Holy Sacrifice of the altar, assisting, with fervor and recollection, in the efficacious rites. Once or twice she was interrupted in her devotions by a quick gasping sob somewhere near her, but the aisle was so crowded that she could not tell whence it came; but while the congregation stood up to hear the Gospel of the day read from the pulpit, she heard the same sound—as if some one was sinking beneath an insupportable anguish —louder and quicker; and, on turning her head, saw a long, emaciated hand grasping the pew door, as if to sustain the poor body to which it belonged. She now saw a middle-aged woman, on whose wan countenance rested the pallor of consumption, gasping for breath, and almost fainting, in the small crowded space where she stood. To open the pew door, throw her arm about her, and lead her in, was the work of an instant; nor did she observe the look of disgust that flitted over Magdalene Estman's classical face as she put down her hand, and pressed her perfumed silken robe closer to her, to prevent its coming in contact with the soiled and worn garments of the mendicant; but she untied the strings of the forlorn creature's straw bonnet, and wiped off the beaded drops of perspiration from her pale face with her lace-embroidered handkerchief. Some few thoughtless smiles flitted over the countenance of the young folk standing around—not in ridicule of the act, but at the contrast, almost grotesque in its misery, that was presented by the poverty-stricken woman to the elegantly clad ladies who had taken her in; but there were many others who regarded this act of spontaneous Christian kindness with deep emotion, and whispered a hearty "God bless you," on the fair young creature, who, heedless of human respect, and unconscious of attracting attention, had done it. Such acts are rich in benedictions, and while Eveleen, now sitting quietly beside her poverty-stricken guest, forgot her, in her rapt attention to the eloquent discourse on the gospel of the day, a blessing had fallen on her head from those consecrated lips that were now proclaiming with such unction the words of life; and from the incense-clouded tabernacle, so low that no human ear could discern it, yet so loud that all the hosts of heaven heard, came a voice whispering, "Blessed are the merciful;" and although the young maiden did not hear the words, she *felt* the blessing falling like Hermon's gentle dews around her heart. These are some of the beautiful mysteries of the law of mercy. Eveleen's sympathies were deeply touched by the silent, pleading misery of the woman's face. She pictured to herself a comfortless home and half famished children, and felt that their common Father—God—had sent her there, a messenger from Himself, to demand some of her superfluous means for the suffering ones of His fold. But how could she aid the miserable one? She could not talk to her without attracting observation, and appearing ostentatious, and she had left her purse at home. "I will not put this into the collection to-day," thought Eveleen, taking the two dollar and a half gold piece she had brought for that purpose out of her watch pocket. "It will look strange for me to put in nothing, but God read my intention, and I don't care what people may think about it. I will get Father Folliard to hand in my contribution for St. Charles Borromeo to-morrow—the woman must have this to-day." Another idea occurred to her, while the priest at the Altar was reading the last Gospel. She took out her pencil, and wrote her name and address on one of the blank pages of her prayer book, and added these words, "If you need my assistance at any time, send for me." She wrapped the coin up in the piece of paper, and slipping it into the poor woman's hand without being observed, she resumed her devotions. As she turned to leave the pew after the Holy Sacrifice was completed, she was touched to the heart on observing the change that a few moments had wrought in that wan and hopeless visage beside her. The harsh outline was softened, and the pinched, anxious features, no longer haggard and despairing, wore a grateful and tranquil look of repose, and whispering, "God bless you, lady," she bowed her head, and kissed the hem of the young girl's cloak as she went out.

"My dear Eveleen," said Magdalene Estman, in her musical tones, "did you not know that there are seats provided for the poor, when you incommoded yourself so to-day with that filthy woman?"

"I did not incommode myself in the least. There was plenty of room," replied Eveleen.

"The creature was sick, too. I declare it makes me ill to think of taking some disease."

"She looks consumptive," replied Eveleen. "She would have fainted if I had not taken her in."

"Charity's a very good thing, my dear; but, like everything else, charity has its proprieties. Those sort of people are very pushing. I'm afraid I shall be crowded out before long," said Magdalene, in her polished, sarcastic way.

"You are welcome to a seat in my pew, Magdalene, as long as it is agreeable to you," said Eveleen, with a flash in her dark eyes. "I warn you, however, that whenever the poor, the maimed, the halt, or the blind apply to me, either by their necessities or by words, for a seat, you will have to endure their presence."

"A singular taste! Really Eveleen, child, I should be afraid that people would accuse me of having low tastes."

"It is indifferent to me if they do. If what I did to-day is any evidence of low taste, I plead guilty," she replied with spirit.

"And you cannot conceive how odd it looked, when you let the contribution-box pass by without putting anything in," said Miss Estman.

"I shall send a donation to-morrow," she replied quietly, while a crimson hue flushed her face.

"I thought you had forgotten your purse," suggested her friend.

"I did not bring my purse, and applied the money that I brought to put in to a greater necessity than for the purpose for which I intended it."

"Bravo, Miss Lacie! I commend you for doing what you think right, irrespective of the opinions of others," said Mr. Estman, who had been a listener.

But the bravos of Rolfe Estman were as distasteful to Eveleen as were the strictures of Magdalene; and changing the conversation, she talked with them on indifferent subjects until they arrived at home. As they entered the hall from the vestibule, Eveleen heard the sound of an old familiar voice, exclaiming in raised and excited tones:

"I'll not budge for the likes of you until I see her. Take yoursel' off, you black *bocaun*. I'll not swallow the house."

"Owny—dear, dear old Owny!" cried Eveleen, springing forward and grasping his rough hand in both her own. "Oh, Owny Travers, where have you been all this time from your little *colleen bawn?*"

"Faix, your ladyship, if it wasn't for the sound of your voice, that was always like a spring bird's, I'd mistrust my two eyes entirely," said Owny, wiping his eyes: "for surely you look more like the handsome old picture of Lady Grace Aiden at Carrigmona, than the little brown-faced miss I saw last. It's a wonder that such a tall, iligent young lady should remimber the like of me;" said Owny, dashing off the tears that would come.

"How can you be so foolish, old Owny?" said Eveleen, making him sit down on the hall sofa beside her. "As if I could ever be anything but a little child to you. Oh dear!—it almost makes me crazy to get home, to see your honest, familiar old face once more! Tell me all about it! When did you hear? Where is John? How are the two old people at the 'Farm,' and Ally and Graff?" said Eveleen, all unconscious of the tears that were flashing in her eyes, or of the supreme look of wonder and contempt with which Nero, the negro steward, regarded her; or of the meaning glances exchanged between Magdalene Estman and her cousin, as they lingered a moment at the drawing-room door. It would have been all the same to Eveleen if the whole world had been looking on. There she sat, her bonnet thrown on a chair beside her, her furs and cloak unfastened, listening with a heightened color and deep interest to the news which Owny brought her from home. But the brightness faded from her eyes, and the roses from her cheeks, when she learned the sorrowful tidings of John Travers' disappearance, for she knew well how blightingly the trial must have fallen on the foud, humble hearts at the far-off Hillside Farm.

"My poor old friends! Owny, it will kill them if any harm comes to John. Where can he be? I shall speak to my uncle about him," said Eveleen, while her heart throbbed with tender sympathy.

"See that now! Miss Eveleen, honey, I was a stupid old *bocaun* to b'lieve you'd outgrown the remimbrance of ould times. I was goin' to spake to his honor, Mister Lacie, mysel', but of late he's got such a dale of business on his hands, that I couldn't get a sight of him;" said Owny. "I'm afeard some hurt's come to the lad. He's not one that would forget his people, and never sind 'em the scratch of a pen, if he was alive, God have mercy on him!"

"Poor Ally! Owny, John must be found, living or dead;" said Eveleen, in her beautiful, earnest way.

"*Wirra!* It's not so aisy to do, as to say. I've spint a dale of money travellin' hether an' yon, to no purpose; inquirin' of high an' low, if such a one ever come across them; an' offerin' rewards in the papers, hopin' to find him; but I could never get a trace of him beyant Cincinnati. But it's your dinner hour, *asthore*, an' I'll be movin', an' I thank God this day for the sight I've had of your beautiful face. It's been like sunshine to me. May I come agin, Miss Eveleen, *achree?*"

"Come again! Come whenever you can, Owny. It has done me good to see you," said Eveleen, holding the rough hand of the weather-beaten old man in her own, as she walked with him to the door.

"Who in the world can that old fellow be, Magdalene?" said Rolfe Estman to his cousin, when she come back to the drawing-room, after taking off her bonnet and wrappings.

"One of Miss Lacie's Irish cousins, I presume," she replied, with a soft, scornful laugh.

"I'll swear, I've seen that old fellow peddling fruit about the streets!"

"I'm afraid Miss Lacie has low tastes;" observed the young lady with a cold smile.

"It seems so. I should back out, if it were not for the fortune;" he remarked, as he curled his moustache, with a thoughtful air. "I shall certainly lay an interdict on all such low associations."

"Pshaw! She'll learn better. She's unsophisticated now. She'll learn better in time!" said Magdalene, clasping her bracelet. Rather learn *worse* according to your worldly ethics, Magdalene—learn to ignore all generous impulses, all unselfish affections, and all the spontaneity of a humane and lofty nature to become a cold worldling in thought and word! Whited sepulchres are not less common now than of old; men are to be found yet who inscribe their faith on broad phylacteries, and thank God they are not as other men—who lift up their voices and pray in public places, and give alms to be seen of men—whose hearts are cold and bitter, and who, in the effort to serve two masters, have betrayed the Lord of Life, and given themselves up in secret to the world, the flesh and the devil! And there is no help for it. Tares will grow among the wheat until time shall end. Magdalene Estman was yielding her soul, little by little, to these insidious influences; the world engrossed her, and she would fain have led Eveleen into the same perilous way.

Eveleen wrote a letter full of sympathy, and words of endearment and hopefulness, to Ally Kane, after dinner; and when she had sealed and directed it, she put on her bonnet and wrappings, and slipped off to Vespers alone.

The next evening Mr. Lacie called to see her. The old man had begun to feel a strange interest in his beautiful niece, and found a rare and delicious pleasure in listening to her sweet, bird-like voice; in feeling that she was something nearer to him than to the rest of the world; and with singular perverseness, drawing out her best feelings by teasing, and pretending to oppose her views. He troubled himself less and less about the widow, and on several occasions really contrived to answer her civilly when she attempted to converse with him. Eveleen was surrounded by two or three young men of fashion when the old man entered the room in his quaint, dusky suit, and with his prim, formal air; and unable to resist the temptation of saying some rather piquant things to them, which, however, fell harmless against their dull intellects, she joined in the laugh with them, against themselves, and did not perceive Mr. Lacie's presence for several minutes; but as soon as she caught sight of his gray head and his broad brown shoulders, she excused herself to the circle around her, and ran to greet him with a kiss, then winding her arm in his, she led him away to their accustomed seat in the corner. Mrs. Hunter fluttered up and chatted awhile, and one or two of the aspirants for Eveleen's favor sought an introduction to her grim old uncle—who, however, received them with such formal politeness and stern gravity, that they soon glided away, with a discomfited air, to the great amusement of Eveleen.

"Who are all these jackanapes, Eveleen?" he asked in a low voice, while he pinched the tip of her ear.

"They are gentlemen friends of Mrs. Hunter's and Miss Estman's, sir."

"Are they men?" he asked, scanning the dwarfed figures and pale, effeminate faces of the young fops through his spectacles.

"Really, sir—yes—I suppose so!" said Eveleen, highly amused. "You ought to be ashamed, sir. Did you think they were boys?"

"Lord bless you, child, those are not MEN. *They* have no back-bone—no stamina—I could break their necks with your fan-sticks. They are Mollies."

"What is that, sir?"

"A genus that comes between man and monkey. I don't know if it is described in Buffon," said Mr. Lacie, with a grim smile. "Do you think I'd allow you to marry such a thing?"

"I'm sure I do not know, Uncle Hugh. Suppose I can do no better?"

"Die an old maid! Don't for the life of you put yourself in a way to increase the contemptible species. I think it's a sin before high heaven."

"Be quiet, sir. I have no idea of marrying any one. Aha! is *that* a man?" she asked, with heightened color and brightening eye, as the door opened, and the tall elegant form of Rolfe Estman came in, saluting the company in his usual calm, proud, self-possessed way.

"Ahem!—no—that's nearer devil than man," whispered Mr. Lacie. "Ah, little Irish maiden! foolish little bird, let loose from the grey seclusion of Carrigmona! I'm afraid you'll be snared yet, by some cruel fowler who will feel no ruth for your silly, panting, sunshiny heart."

"I think you are mistaken, sir!" said Eveleen, almost startled by his manner and words, in which there was mingled warning and pathos. "I could not love one unworthy of my preference. I should be very careful in making a choice on which my whole earthly happiness depended. But, sir, I think you are very uncharitable. Mr. Estman is considered a talented and excellent young man."

"Eveleen, I tell you, child, place no faith in him. I know him for what he is worth. Here he comes," replied Mr. Lacie.

"Miss Lacie," he said, bowing gracefully, "I am charmed to see you. I thought you were absent when I first entered the room, until I caught a glimpse of your bright face a moment ago."

"Good evening, Mr. Estman. My uncle, Mr. Lacie," said Eveleen in reply.

Mr. Estman bowed profoundly, and extended his hand. Mr. Lacie merely said, "Good evening, sir," and thrust his into his bosom, either not seing the proffered hand, or for some reason determined not to take it. The other, with consummate tact, covered the slight by addressing some complimentary remark to Eveleen, after which he sauntered away.

"Uncle Hugh, was it not very rude to refuse your hand to a gentleman?"

"Child, I never refuse my hand to a gentleman!"

"You would not shake hands with Mr. Estman!"

"No. Do you ever shake hands with him?"

"Sometimes, sir!"

"Don't do it again."

"You are very ill-natured to-night, sir. I must not listen to you."

"Bend down your ear hither, child, That man would not only stake his soul on the toss of a die, but he is the destroyer of innocence!" whispered Mr. Lacie. Eveleen was too much shocked to reply; she only grasped her uncle's hand tighter, and looked with a half-frightened, pitying glance towards Mr. Estman, who was bending over Magdalene's chair, holding a very agreeable conversation with her, if one might have judged by her smiling countenance, and the deep interest with which she listened to what he was saying.

"Could it be, that one who bore with so noble a grace, the 'image and likeness of God' about him, had desecrated and debased it by crime? Was it possible that so fair an exterior covered a heart polluted by evil? Had those soft musical tones ever been raised in blasphemy? Could it be that those dark, bright eyes, which flashed forth the fires of intellect, or beamed soft messages of love at will, had ever lured an innocent heart to ruin? What had he done with his baptismal robe, which he had received unspotted in his infancy? Alas! what foul hand had effaced its purity? By whose consent had it become covered with the mire of pollution?" As these thoughts rushed with vivid swiftness through Eveleen's mind, there came another—"*He has repented*"—and her eyes rested on him with a soft mingling of wonder and compassion in their glance; while a half-tender regret, and the sudden consciousness of a dawning interest in her heart towards him, made the moment a most painful one.

"Don't waste another thought on him!" said Mr. Lacie, who had been watching her countenance from under his bent brows. Eveleen started and reddened.

"I saw Owny Travers yesterday, sir!" she said, in a subdued voice.

"Where on the earth has the fellow been? I have not seen him this age!"

"Owny is in great trouble about John, his nephew—John Travers, whom you know, sir, you persuaded to come over."

"What has happened to John? God bless me! I hope no harm has come to the lad! Where is he?"

"No one has the least knowledge where he is.

He left here for the far West some months ago, and was traced as far as Cincinnati, where all traces of him are lost. They fear that he is murdered, or in prison, or that some other terrible thing has happened!"

"That was a noble lad! Eh, niece, your news troubles me. I besought the boy not to go away. His ambition has been the ruin of him. I will write to my agent, and a gentleman who is a lawyer, and whom I know very well, to make inquiries. I will write to-morrow."

"Thank you, sir. I knew that you would do something to the purpose. But do not go yet. Stay and tell me how my old friend, Moses Kugle, is?"

"Well! he survived the caricatures, and when I told him that I was coming to see you, the ridiculous old fellow hemmed and haw'd, and asked me to give his love to you."

"Give mine to him!" said Eveleen, laughing merrily.

"Come and see Moses. I believe he admires you as much as he does a Dutch tulip."

"Where shall I find him, uncle Hugh?"

"At the factory, of course. Come to-morrow, and I'll show you a MAN—I tell you, girl, a true-hearted, noble man is a sight worth seeing in these degenerate days."

"At what hour shall I come?" asked Eveleen, much diverted.

"Between two and four o'clock. Come in a

carriage, and I'll send Moses Kugle home with you. Good-night. Be wary of that fellow—that Belial!"

"Shall I invite Mrs. Hunter and Magdalene?"

"No!" replied Mr. Lacie with such loud emphasis that Eveleen laughed outright, and the company turned round and stared. Mr. Lacie made his Grandisonian bow at the door, and went away; and Eveleen, at Mrs. Hunter's request, took her seat at the piano.

CHAPTER VIII.

A MAN.

THE next morning, while Eveleen was busily engaged in her room on a piece of fine needlework, Nero tapped at the door, and informed her that "a beggar-boy was waiting to see her down in the hall; but if young Missis chose, he would send him about his business, and save her the trouble of going down."

"It is no trouble at all, Nero. I will come in a moment," she replied to the pompous old African, who looked upon all beggars from a corporation point of view, *i. e.*, as simple nuisances.

When Eveleen went down, she found a child, poorly clad, and with a sickly look, crouching close to the hall stove.

"Did you wish to see me, little boy?" she asked, kindly.

"Yes'm, if that's your name on the paper," he replied, handing her the slip of paper she had given the poor woman in church on Sunday.

"My name is Lacie. I have been expecting your mother since Sunday."

"Mammy was too sick to come. She was raisin' blood all Sunday night."

"I am sorry to hear that. Do you live far from here?"

"'Bout six or seven blocks, I 'spose."

"Wait here until I come down. I'm going up to get my bonnet and shawl to go back with you."

"Mammy 'll be made up, if she can see you, Missy," said the child, while a tinge of red flushed his pale cheeks.

Mrs. Hunter had heard the whole conversation through the Venetian door of the dining-room, and now hastened upstairs after Eveleen to give her the benefit of her advice on the subject. "I hope, my dear Miss Lacie," she said in the most earnest way, "that you have no idea of going with that boy! Indeed, he might lead you into some dreadful place. You can form no idea of their impostures. It will be just as well for you to *send* what you intend giving; but if you will go, I'll get Nero to accompany you."

"I am not afraid, Mrs. Hunter. I promised this poor woman to aid her, and as she cannot come to me, I must go to her. I was always accustomed to visit the poor and sick at home. Good morning. I shall not be away long," said Eveleen, too glad of the opportunity to do a good act, to weigh it in the scales of worldly prudence.

"She's really gone! I declare, she's the most self-willed young lady I ever met with," said Mrs. Hunter, looking after the retreating figure of Eveleen with blank amazement. "I must go and talk with Magdalen, who would not do so imprudent a thing for the world. She tapped at Miss Estman's door, and asked if she might come in.

"Oh, Mrs. Hunter! come in—I thought it was Eveleen!" said Magdalene, when she opened the door and found her hostess there. "Do be seated."

"Thank you, my dear, I have not time. I merely came up to persuade Miss Lacie not to accompany a beggar child home."

"Did she go?" asked Magdalene, without looking up from her netting.

"Of course she went. Between you and me, Miss Lacie does not receive advice kindly. She is very self-opinionated for so young a person. I'm really afraid that her imprudence will get her into difficulties. Now, you know, my dear, there's no one kinder to the poor than I am; there's not a day that I don't give out quantities of cold victuals to beggars; and there's no end to the half-worn underclothes that go the same way—but really, even at my age I should consider it very imprudent to go into the low haunts of these people. There's no telling what characters one might come in contact with there. I offered to send Nero, but she declined. I'm afraid I shall have to speak to Mr. Lacie. Really, the responsibility is more than I like to bear alone!" said Mrs. Hunter, pausing for sheer want of breath.

"I think such a parade of charity is altogether unnecessary, myself. I should certainly feel timid about venturing among such low people. Nothing could be more ridiculous than the affair of Sunday; and I should not be surprised if Eveleen has gone to see something about the woman. As for my own part, I have so little to give that I cannot afford to waste my little on impostors. But she's Irish, you know, and the Irish never think beforehand, but plunge headforemost into whatever they undertake."

Understand, reader, that although Miss Estman was a Catholic, and in her own opinion a very good one, she was one of those—and we are pained to say they are not few—who was conformed more to the spirit of the world than to to the spirit of the Church; who contrived to keep up a certain appearance of piety, and adapt her religion to the maxims of fashion and the requisitions of society; who was more regardful of the teaching of human respect than those of self-denial; more obedient to the suggestions of pride than to the promptings of humility. It was a spirit like unto this, which caused the disciple to murmur because a penitent woman poured costly ointment on the head of Christ, and dictate to Him how better its price might have been applied; which led another to betray Him with a kiss, and one to deny Him with oaths! "His own murmured against Him. His own betrayed Him into our hands! His own denied Him thrice;" shouted the Jewish rabble—"Crucify Him! Why should we be more merciful to Him than those on whom He has lavished His love and benefits? Crucify Him!" And the world caught up the cry, and to this day makes the example of unfaithful Christians the apology for enmity to Christ, and a fresh incentive to the fury with which they crucify Him.

Eveleen Lacie, with a light step, followed the boy down into the city, until they came to the streets which were narrow, and walled up on each side with great dingy warehouses five and six stories high, and presently she saw the river gleaming at the extremity of a long, narrow vista, and a forest of masts belonging to ships and vessels in the docks. Sailors and rough looking men began to cross her path, whistling sea ditties, or trolling the refrain of some low song. Eveleen's brave heart, almost failed her, but drawing her veil closer over her face, she took the inside of the walk, nearest the warehouses, and committed herself to the care of Him whose omnipresent eye watched over her ways. The boy noticed her look of distress, and took hold of her shawl, saying: "We're a'most there now, lady. It's up there in the court." It was with a feeling of great relief that Eveleen followed the child up a narrow filthy street, that led into a dilapidated and dirty court, in which stood what had once been the town residence of one of the signers of the Declaration of Independence, when the city was all on the edge of the river, but which now presented an aspect of ruin and decay from its eaves to its spacious foundation. Its large windows were either stuffed out with old hats and rags, or covered with sea-stained boarding picked up adrift in the docks, and the sculptured stone frames were mildewed and moss grown, while the steps at the main entrance were broken, and the door hanging loose from its ponderous hinges.

"There's the house, lady. Come up the steps careful—they's mighty rickety," said the child, going before her. Up three ruinous, creaking flights of steps he led her until they came to a door on a narrow landing, which seemed to lead to the back of the house, that he opened, and invited her in. Two dim windows, blurred by dust and smoke, admitted a pale and sickly light into the squalid apartment, where, on straw pallet, covered with a ragged quilt, lay the woman she had come to see, but so pale and wasted that Eveleen started back with terror, thinking she was dead; but the noise of the latch startled her from her uneasy slumbers, and opening her great lustrous eyes, she looked up with a wild and frightened glance at her visitor; but she suddenly remembered her, and a smile of welcome dawned over her pallid countenance.

"You are very kind to come, lady," she said, in feeble and faltering tones. "I would not have brought you to such a place, but I was taken worse."

"I am sorry to find you so ill. How can I help you?" said Eveleen, gently, as she knelt down beside her.

"I shall not be here long," she said, while a spot of crimson mounted to her cheeks. "Save me lady, from dying in the street."

"In the street?" repeated Eveleen. "There's no fear of that."

"Alas! it is plain that misery is new to you, lady;" replied the woman, trying to keep back the hectic cough. "I am threatened to be turned out of this poor room before night—unless—unless I can pay the balance of my rent. I have had no work for a month past. I paid my landlord the money you gave me on Sunday, but he wasn't satisfied—God forgive him—and I thought I'd go out and beg it; but the hand of the Lord fell heavy upon me, and laid me here. My poor neighbors—the lodgers in this house—do what they can for me, but they're not much better off than myself, except Mother Garrity's son, and he bought me medicine, made my tea, and nursed me of nights since I've been so bad. But that such things are God's holy will, they would be very hard to bear, lady."

"Make your mind easy, poor woman," said Eveleen, whose countenance expressed all she felt. "What is the amount you owe for rent?"

"Two dollars!" replied the poor seamstress, with a dreary sigh.

"My God!" thought Eveleen. "All this

anguish for the sake of two dollars! Why I gave five, yesterday, for a fan—a gew-gaw—and this poor woman perishing, suffering, and starving for help. "Here," she said aloud, taking five dollars from her purse—"take it as freely as it is offered, and do what you will with it. Do you not need food?"

"May God Almighty bless and comfort you in your hour of need!" faltered the woman lifting up her emaciated her. "He has promised to bless the merciful—and His word never fails—as surely as He has promised never to forsake them that trust Him. The way was mighty dark before me, but you see he sent one of His messengers to comfort me in my extremity. Oh, lady! it is a glorious thing to be one of God's messengers to the suffering poor."

"Do not talk!" said Eveleen, gently, as she wiped off a tear. "You are too weak. You need food—how can I get it for you?"

"Is Jerry here?" she asked the boy. "He never comes until after twelve."

"Jerry ain't home from work yet, mammy."

"We must wait a bit. Jerry will be here presently," she said feebly.

"I'll go down to Mother Garrity's room and see. The bell rung for twelve a bit ago," said the boy, going out. He came back, accompanied by an old withered crone, whose wrinkled visage and bleared eyes, gave her the appearance of the nursery ideal of a "wicked old fairy." She walked with a stick, and as she hobbled to the bed-side, she caught sight of Eveleen, on whose bright face a ray of light which darted with sharp radiance through a broken pane, was shining, and fixing her eyes on her with a keen, searching look, she halted a moment; then turned to the sick woman, and asked, "did she find hersel' better?"

"I'm not in pain now, thank God, Mother Garrity. Sit down; it's a tiresome walk up here, for an old body like you."

"So it is, Martha, honey. I'm out o' breath with it, so I am. What do you want wi' Jerry? Jerry's only a poor lad, that's got enow to do, to support oursel's sure;" she said in a quernlous voice. "Mebbe I can do what you want, if it don't cost nothin', for you—the devil fetch it—I'm as poor as a church mouse."

"Take this, and get her a bowl of good soup somewhere—stewed oysters and bread, or anything nourishing—" said Eveleen, placing the gold piece she had given the sick seamstress, in the withered and dirty palm of the old woman.

"Oyeh! oh!" she said, gloating over the bright coin as it lay glistening in her hand, then peeping curiously into Eveleen's face, "I'll do it, but I'm very poor, an' I 'spose you'll give me sum'at for my trouble."

"Yes, Mother Garrity—a bright dime. This lady has been very good to me, and I can afford to pay you this time," said the seamstress; then added, as the old woman hobbled out—"The poor has to help the poor—she's very old, and strange, but no ways wicked. The people say she hoards, but I don't know." At that moment the nodding grey head of Mother Garrity again appeared at the door, the bloodshot, whitish grey eyes fixed themselves in a deliberate stare in Eveleen's face; a look of intelligence, or rekindled memory, or recognition, flitted over the grotesque countenance; then she withdrew, closed the door, and they heard her hobbling down the steps.

"Have you no one to assist you, Martha?" asked Eveleen, wiping the clammy moisture from the sick woman's face.

"Not a one, lady. My husband was drowned in the dock two years ago. He was a stevedore, and made a good livin'. Then, after he was taken from me, I got work from the slop-shops; but I was never strong, and even with working all day and half the night, the pay was so poor that I didn't make enough to keep the lad and myself. Then an old neighbor got me some private sewing to do for a fine gentleman. I made him a dozen shirts, and it took four weeks to do it—close sewing—for there was a deal of stitching and fine tucks on the bosoms. I carried the work home, but he put me off, and put me off, and at last refused to pay me at all, because, he said, the work didn't suit him. Lady! I saw that man with you last Sunday—God forgive him!—but maybe I shouldn't have told you that," said the woman, with a look of distress, when she looked up and saw the flush on Eveleen's countenance.

"He is nothing to me, my friend—go on."

"There's nothing to tell, miss, only it got me in debt, and I've been going down hill ever since; but our Lord has been very good to me—
—He raised me up a friend in you—I have much to be thankful for."

"What became of your furniture?" asked Eveleen, with abrupt kindness.

"Sold, miss, little by little. One thing after another went, till I was left bare of comforts. But I was thankful and for shelter and this bundle of straw. My poor little Ned picks up driftwood, and the workmen at the ship-yard gives him chips and old waste pieces of timber; so we're in a way provided for."

Just then a quick, firm step sounded on the stairs, and there came a light tap on the door. Eveleen opened it, and some one handed her in a small bowl, filled with something warm. She was turning away, when a voice said in low gentle tones:

"Here is the change, lady, and a small loaf of bread." She held out her hand and received the money and loaf, but, owing to the darkness of the passage without, she could not distinguish the person's face.

"That's Jerry," said the lad, who had just

come in with an armful of chips. "He went to the tavern and got the things for mammy."

"This is chicken soup," said Eveleen, lifting the cover from the bowl, "and very nice." She got a spoon and gave the sick woman—who was fainting and famishing for proper nourishment—a small quantity at a time, which appeared to revive and strengthen her as she swallowed it. By this time it was after one o'clock, and Eveleen recollected her engagement with her uncle between two and four.

"I must go away now," she said, after having made the sick woman as comfortable as was possible under the circumstances, "but I shall see you again, Martha." Martha raised the young girl's hand to her lips, and when she released it felt that there were tears on it—precious tears—and she wiped them off as reverently as if they had been holy water sprinkled there there with benedictions by the priest.

"Good-bye, lady. This is a mighty poor place to invite the like of you into, but I hope I shall see your sweet face many times before I die. Father Folliard is coming to-morrow morning to give the holy communion. I shall offer it for you."

"That will be a great favor, Martha, and I thank you," replied Eveleen, pressing her hand. "I shall come again shortly, and if anything detains me, I will send."

The lad would have gone down with her, but

she told him to remain with his mother, and started to go down stairs, thinking she would walk as far as the next street and take a carriage. She felt very light-hearted, did Eveleen! She had come where Jesus Christ Himself had been, and where He was coming again, to cheer and console His suffering exile. She felt that it was very sweet to follow Him in such hidden paths, and notwithstanding the faults of her nature, and her human frailties, the thought of the Divine Mystery which united her to the poor mendicant she had just left, as closely as members are united to the same body, gave her sweet and blissful emotions, which caused her heart to swell and glow within her. Quite fearless, and unsuspicious of danger, she tripped lightly down the steps until she came to the middle landing, from whence three or four dark, narrow passages diverged; when from a door which opened into one of these, a dark, ferocious-looking man, wrapped in a sailor's pea-jacket, with shaggy hair matted around his face, and a fierce wild look in his eyes, emerged, who sprang across her path, and planting himself before her, gazed insolently at her. Drawing her veil quickly over her face, she attempted to glide past him, but perceiving her intention, he placed his brawny, tattooed hands on each side of the bannisters, and effectually prevented her escape.

"Allow me to pass," said Eveleen, in as firm a voice as she could assume, while she fixed her large bright eyes on his with a look of command.

"I never let a craft loose that I capture—hoist off your topsail, and heave to," said the fellow roughly, while he lifted his hand for an instant to push back his tarpaulin hat. Eveleen, white with terror, observed the movement, and made a spring, hoping to escape past him; but in an instant his brawny hand fell heavily on her shoulder—he dragged her towards him—she screamed for help, and the man, furious at her outcry, lifted her in his arms as if she had been a child, and was about plunging down a deep and narrow stair-way, when some one—a tall, muscular person—sprang after him, clearing three steps at every bound, and dealt him a blow on the back of his head that brought him to a momentary halt.

"Fokes'l Tom, unhand the lady this instant. Do not be alarmed, Miss—the miserable fellow is crazy at times, from a blow he got on his head once, in a storm. Helm up, and be off with you," shouted the young man, while the distraught sailor, trembling like a frightened schoolboy, put Eveleen down as gently as if she had been a young infant, and looked into her deliverer's face with an humble, quailing expression.

"Don't beat me, Jerry—I'll be good," he whimpered.

"Begone, sir. I am ashamed of you, to have frightened a lady in this way, who had come to see your sick sister," said the young man, standing between Eveleen and the sailor.

"I'll never do so again, Jerry, upon my honor. The blood flew up to my head, and then everything got dark," whimpered the shaggy giant.

"Go away now to your room—I'll see you by and by," said Jerry, in more gentle tones. "Come, now, Miss Lacie, you are safe—the poor fellow will be quiet for some time to come."

"I cannot express the gratitude I feel, sir," said Eveleen, now more composed, as she walked by the side of Jerry, on their way down to the front door.

"I am glad I happened to be at home," he replied. "I will attend you to the next street, and call a carriage, Miss Lacie."

"If you please," said Eveleen, who felt some surprise on hearing him address her by name. Twice he had done so; and after puzzling herself a moment or two, she came to the conclusion that he had learned her name from the son of the sick woman up stairs. With a feeling of relief she stepped out of the close, confined atmosphere of the house into the open air. Her companion did not address another word to her, but walked a little in advance, as if showing her the best path over the broken, muddy pavement; and she had an opportunity to scan his face as he now and then turned to see if she needed his assistance, and admire the fine outline of his form. She saw that he was not regularly handsome, although nature had lavished many and noble lines on his countenance; that his eyes were deep and serious, with a penetrating intelligence in them that redeemed them from heaviness; that his mouth was firm set over a square chin, but fashioned to an almost womanly sweetness. Nut-brown hair, glossy and curling, fell waving negligently over his temples and throat. There was nothing in his attire to distinguish him from other young men of his class, only that he wore his grey blouse with an easy grace that caused many a one to say, as he passed to and fro, between his place of business and his poor home: "There goes a noble-looking fellow." He called a carriage; and as he handed Eveleen in, and lingered a moment at the door, Eveleen saw, as she looked full on his face, that strength, energy of will, nobleness of purpose, and intellectual force were there. They might not have been cultivated, or even fully developed; but there they were writ, on every lineament, in bold and true lines, and told with vigorous expression of a settled intent to look life and its difficulties squarely in the face.

"You have been very kind," said Eveleen.

"When you come again, Miss Lacie, to visit the sick and miserable in that poverty-stricken abode, come only between the hours of twelve and one o'clock, when you will be more safe from interruption—at least such as you met with to-day."

"Thank you, I will follow your caution. If

you ever need a friend, and I can serve you, call on me. I have an uncle who may be of use to you." She did not see the peculiar smile that flitted over the countenance of the young man; or the flush that deepened the olive tint of his cheek; she was too excited, and anxious to get away, and when the carriage drove off, she threw herself back against the cushions, and had a good, womanly fit of crying. "I should have followed Mrs. Hunter's advice about taking some one with me. I am so headstrong. I have been terrified nearly to death, and all my happy feelings in doing that poor woman a kindness are so mixed up with the idea of that great shaggy maniac, that I can't bear to think of it. I wonder who in the world that young man is? Blessed Mother! if he had not been there, I might have been murdered! But I cannot give the poor seamstress up. I shall have to go again, but—now I have it!—I'll get Owny to go with me. I never thought of Owny! That arrangement will do nicely!"

Eveleen did not enter into the particulars of her morning adventures to Mrs. Hunter and Magdalene, when they questioned her; she merely told them that the woman she went to see was ill, miserably poor, and she was truly glad she had gone.

"Rolfe is coming to drive us out this afternoon, Eveleen," said Magdalene.

"I have an engagement with my uncle, and must be excused."

"We will defer it until to-morrow," said her friend.

"I beg that you will not. I shall not go at all, I think."

"Rolfe will be disappointed. He wished to show you some beautiful views. However, he has left some exquisite flowers to plead for him. Come up into my room," said Miss Estman, in her gentle, blandishing way.

"Beautiful!" exclaimed Eveleen, as Magdalene gave her the moss-covered basket, in which camellias, heliotrope, half-blown roses, and pale blue hyacinths were arranged in the most artistic manner. "How fragrant! I am much obliged to Mr. Estman."

"And will not disappoint him about the drive?"

"If accepting these flowers involves an obligation on my part to drive out with Mr. Estman, I must relinquish them, dear Magdalene, to you; but I do so very reluctantly," said Eveleen, as she bent over the flowers with an admiring and loving glance.

"Not for the world! How could you draw such an inference? By all means keep the flowers. Rolfe would feel the very keenest mortification if his simple offering of flowers were rejected," said Magdalene, quickly. "He only wishes to do what is agreeable to you."

"Well, as it is very agreeable to me to retain possession of them, I shall do so. Present my thanks to Mr. Estman, and also my regrets,'' said Eveleen, as she went out at the door with the fragrant and beautiful gift. "It can surely be no harm," she thought, "to accept a few flowers, particularly as I want them to put before the statue of our Blessed Lady. I *hope* that my uncle has not formed a correct opinion of Mr. Estman—he is so austere in his notions. I wonder if the poor seamstress could have meant that *he* was the fine gentleman who defrauded her of her just wages! Oh, it is terrible to have such thoughts of people who seem good and friendly!" Eveleen took off her bonnet and wrappings, and looked at her watch. It was nearly two o'clock. She ran down stairs to beg Mrs. Hunter to give her a luncheon, and ask Nero to call a carriage. She wished to be at the factory by two o'clock precisely, if possible; for Mr. Lacie was a minute man, and she did not know how he would fancy being kept waiting. Mrs. Hunter *manœuvred* skilfully to find out what took her to the factory, but in vain; for Eveleen scarcely knew herself, and thought it would be too ridiculous to tell her that she was going there to see—a man. "I have seen one already to-day," she thought, as she mixed some chicken salad, and buttered her bread; "a man—I'd venture to peril my life on it— who will never disgrace the name. I wonder who he can be? They called him Jerry, and he seems connected in some way with that miserable old Mother Garrity—perhaps he's her grandson—but 'a man's a man for a' that!'"

While these thoughts were running through her mind, Mrs. Hunter kept up a running fire of talk, laudatory of her own almsgiving to the poor. According to her own account, one would have thought she fed all the poor in the city, and was the benefactress of mankind. Her egotism was harmless to every one but herself, and evil to her only because it stripped her charities of their merit, and made her almsdeeds mere natural acts. She did not consider the wide difference between the charity which proceeds from natural generosity, and that whose impulses are divine; between the one which has its origin in self-love, and rejoices in laudation, and that which, having God alone for its object, performs its acts in secret; between an amiable desire to be thought well of, and stripping one's self of superfluities! One gives when it is convenient; the other performs some act of self-denial to enable it to give; one shrinks from relinquishing the smallest gratification for the good of the needy, and is only generous when no obstacle exists to its being otherwise; the other strips itself of unnecessary appendage to clothe the naked; deprives itself of luxuries to feed the hungry; foregoes the halls of feasting to visit the sick, and the captive; and if it can do no more, gives a cup of cold water to the suffering, for the love of Jesus, and beholds in every suffering mortal, Him crowned with thorns. The former are useful to the poor, but win no merit for themselves, because they set the mere gratification of natural instincts above the thought of God. These are nice distinctions; such as the world calls *overdrawn*— but it is well enough to consider them, and test them by an application to our own acts.

When Eveleen entered the iron-studded, low-arched doorway of her uncle's celebrated manufactory, Moses Kugle was on the lookout for her, and as her fresh, happy face beamed on him, with a genial look of recognition, a grim smile which would have made a baby cry, so little was it like a smile, relaxed his visage and wrinkled up his eyes.

"I am very glad to see you, Mr. Kugle," she said, shaking hands. "Where is my uncle?"

"He's in the machine-shop. He's going to try his model. I'll tell him you're here," said the old clerk, leading her into Mr. Lacie's *sanctum*. "There's a blank book and some pens, Missy, if you want to draw! Ho! Ho!"

"Mr. Kugle, you shall not go away until you tell me what I must do to merit your forgiveness for my rude demonstration that day," said Eveleen, with a light laugh, while a blush dyed her cheeks.

"Do some more pictures, *fraulein*," said the old fellow, smiling. "Here's your uncle."

"So you've come!" he said, in his abrupt way.

"Didn't you bid me, sir?"

"Yes, but I was afraid you couldn't tear yourself away from the society of your Mollie Hyacinths, with their perfumed whiskers, and lady-fingered hands, that never earned a grain of salt, to come down here amongst the noise, clatter, soot, fire and steam, where only two ugly old gray-beards could speak to you," said Mr. Lacie, glowering, and looking down.

"Uncle Hugh, lift up your eyes this instant, and tell me if you think I am incapable of appreciating the good, and great, and wise?" said Eveleen, with warmth.

"You are like the other chits of your age, I suppose!" said Mr. Lacie, lifting his fine eyes to her face with a glance that belied his words; "but follow me; I'm going to take you where you can look down and see something worth looking at.

"Is it the man?" asked Eveleen, demurely.

"No, miss—that is, it is my model, which is to be tried to-day. You'll see the man at the same time," replied Mr. Lacie, as he turned the key in a side door and told her to follow him. Up a steep, dark, winding staircase they went, until they came to an apartment in which there was scarcely room to turn for the detached pieces of machinery—the finer and smaller parts—that were piled up to the very ceiling. She followed her uncle through this grim labyrinth, until an abrupt turn brought them to a window which commanded an interior view of the workshop below, all alight with lurid forges, and red-hot furnaces, from whose gaping mouths a glare so hot and fierce issued that Eveleen wondered how men could live in the same atmosphere with it and not wither under the scorching heat. But the brawny-limbed, athletic workmen, clad in red flannel shirts and dark tight-fitting trowsers, which were confined over their hips by broad leather belts, moved about with free and agile motions, laughing, talking, singing and whistling, as much at their ease amidst the roar, and glare, and din, as if they had been out in the open fields listening to the singing of birds. It was a wonderful sight to the young girl, to see them contending with the fire and iron, the plunging, ponderous machinery, and the fierce, hissing steam! bending them to their purpose; mastering and managing the senseless giants by the turning of little screws and cranks no bigger than an infant's thumb; applying their brawn and muscle when needful in strong upliftings, or crashing blows with great iron hammers; pouring out the liquid iron like fiery lava into the ponderous molds with ready skill, agile movement, and cautious vigilance! Eveleen's eyes kindled as she gazed down—she did not understand it, but she saw that the result was the triumph of mind over matter; she saw its operations on crude and senseless masses for the purpose of annihilating time and distance, and her heart exulted that so much had been vouchsafed to man; that his mind, faithful to the inspirations of genius, vindicated its divine origin, and carried out in practical and useful plans the most wonderful purposes. The room in which the young girl sat all alone, watching the *Salvator Rosa* lights and shades below, belonged to a house against which Mr. Lacie had built his manufactory, and afterwards purchased to add to it. Her uncle had left her, and presently she saw him busy with one or two workmen, directing and assisting them in the arrangement of some complicated machinery belonging to a small but beautifully-finished engine. This was the model—the pet idea of Mr. Lacie's theories —the *ultima thule*, he thought, of mechanism and steam! But something was found wanting, and, accompanied by the men, he went into another room to fashion it. He beckoned to some one, and pointed to his model, and the next moment Eveleen saw a door, the upper part of which was glass, open, and the young man who had rescued her that morning from the lunatic made his appearance. His grey blouse was confined about his waist by a leather belt, his shirt collar was thrown open, and his hair, curling with moisture, was thrown back, revealing the classic outline of his forehead. There was a ruddy tinge on his dark, noble face, and as he stood surveying the symmetrical parts of the compact and beautiful model, his eyes kindled with interest and pride, and he touched it almost reverently. While thus engaged, a workman—a dull, sickly-looking man—came by with a heavy sledge-hammer in his hand, which he swung carelessly as he walked; and not observing the model, gave it an accidental blow, which broke it. Eveleen, at first indignant, now felt sympathy for him, when she saw his look of wild dismay on discovering the mischief he had done! Suddenly the young man—Jerry—sprang forward, snatched the hammer out of his hand, and pushed him out of sight. Mr. Lacie was coming.

"He'll lose his place. Musther Lacie will turn him adrift, the *bocaun*." screamed a discordant voice behind her. Eveleen, much alarmed, started around, and saw old Mother Garrity, who, leaning on her stick, had been peering over her shoulder, watching the whole scene.

"Be silent!" she said, almost breathless, "my uncle shall know the truth.'

"Eh! Lacie-like—but I wonder who's of 'em you be, wid your wild eyes an' sharp tongue," muttered the crone. "He shan't lose his place for a' that, for he's the aiqual of any Lacie of 'em all."

By this time Mr. Lacie came up, full of the anticipated success and triumph that were about to crown the thought and toil of laborious years. He had succeeded beyond his most sanguine expectations; he had embodied his great idea; and now it only wanted to be set in motion by steam. In a few moments he would see it moving on its plane, with the velocity of lightning.

"Put on the steam, Jerry, as soon as you please," he said, in cheery tones. "Hilloa! Who the devil did this? I'll discharge you, sir! How dare you be so careless?" he exclaimed, white with rage, as he pointed to the broken machinery.

"It was an accidental blow, sir."

"Accidental devil, sir! Begone out of my sight! You are dismissed from my employment this moment. I can't afford to be ruined by accidents."

Just then Eveleen, her face glowing and beautiful in the white light of the furnaces, came swiftly in towards the group. She had seen the young man's noble effort to screen his fellow workman—she saw her uncle's enraged countenance and threatening gestures—she could no longer sit silent and inactive, if she died for it, and allow the innocent to suffer. She laid her long, tapering hand on the old man's arm before he saw her, and was looking bravely into his enraged countenance! "Uncle Hugh, he did not do it," she said.

"There was no one else to do it. Go away, niece. This is no place for you," he replied, sternly, as he tried to shake her off.

"This is a very good place for me just now,

sir. You would be sorry to wrong an innocent man! I saw the whole affair. A workman coming by with that heavy thing in his hand, accidentally struck against your model; *he*, seeing you approaching, took the hammer out of the man's hand, and thrust him out of sight," said Eveleen, earnestly.

"The lady tells the truth, Mister Lacie," said the real culprit, coming forward. "Jerry Garrity did not break the model; I did it, sir, and am sorry for it."

"What's the meaning of all this, young man?" said Mr. Lacie, turning with a stern look towards Jerry, who stood erect, with his arms folded over his breast; "Speak."

"He has a large family dependent on him, sir. I was afraid he might be turned out of employment in the dead of winter," replied the young artisan, firmly.

"And I suppose you thought you wouldn't. You have got a fortune, and have learnt to be a machinist for amusement, I suppose. You both deserve to have your heads broken. Get out of my sight, Fletcher, and don't let me see your face for a month. As to you, Jerry Garrity, set to work and repair the mischief that you were so ready to take the consequences of," said Mr. Lacie, striding out of the shop, followed by Eveleen. He sat down gloomily in his office chair, and she went up and stole her arm about his neck, and, leaning over, kissed him on his forehead.

"Pshaw, my child! *that* don't mend the matter," he said, pushing her from him.

"No, sir; Jerry will mend the model. Do you know, Uncle Hugh, that I have seen some glorious and noble things to-day, that I wouldn't have missed seeing for all the diamonds in Peru?"

"You saw my model smashed!"

"Yes, sir; and I saw a noble-hearted young man take the blame of it on himself, to save his fellow workman and his family from destitution. I saw the man come forward, and generously acknowledge his fault, and exculpate the other; and then I saw an old man, whose hopes were nipped through his doing, and his interests perhaps injured, forgive them both!" said Eveleen, kissing the old brown cheek.

"I didn't say that I'd forgiven the rascals!"

"But you do, notwithstanding—I know you do. I think I've seen all that I came to see, haven't I?" she asked, with sweet pertinacity.

"No," he exclaimed, "and YES. I intended to show you a model man, working a model engine that he had helped me to devise and make. I wanted you to see manhood, without any worldly advantages to help it, dignified by labor, elevated by genius, and glorious with success; but I have been baulked by a clumsy workman— but, pshaw! get home with you—it is growing late."

"I saw man under nobler guises still;" said

Eveleen. "Uncle—Jerry Garrity saved my life to-day."

"Eh! what's that?" said Mr. Lacie, raising his head erect.

Eveleen told her uncle of her adventure with the crazy sailor; upon which he poured out a volley of wrath on her head for her imprudence, declared she deserved to be locked up for a month on bread and water, and concluded his tirade by saying, "Mind how you run your foolish head into any more such scrapes. You'll not always find a noble lad like Jerry Garrity at hand to rescue you."

"It's a great pity he's not a gentleman!" said Eveleen, smiling mischievously through her tears.

"He *is* a gentleman!" said Mr. Lacie, emphatically.

"How can that be, sir, if he's been an artisan all his life? I see that he is both noble and good; but if he should be thrown in contact with well-bred, refined people, you know, sir, their ways are so different, I think he'd feel awkward, and behave so. And then his name!"

"I'll fetch him with me to Mrs. Hunter's some night, and turn him loose among the Mollies who visit there. Then you can judge between them. As to his name, it's a good Irish name, and he'll make it a proud one too, one of these days!"

Eveleen having succeeded in provoking Mr.

Lacie into better humor with his *protegé*, and well satisfied with his threat to bring him to Mrs. Hunter's—a thing she secretly desired, but dared not name—she bade him farewell, and ordering the coachman to drive rapidly home, she got into the carriage, and was soon whirled to Mrs. Hunter's door.

CHAPTER IX.

BITTER DROPS STRENGTHEN THE HEART.

IN the attempt she was making to inveigle Eveleen Lacie into a marriage with her kinsman, Rolfe Estman, Magdalene either lost sight of the turpitude of her conduct, or else she deliberately sinned; for she was fully aware that his reformation was a hollow sham, and his penitence a solemn mockery. She knew but too well that he had almost made shipwreck of his faith, that he held sacramental confession in abhorrence, regarded the Mass as a mere symbol, and in his heart scoffed at all the institutions of that ancient and holy Religion, from which he was in fact an apostate; she knew that his morals were bad, his principles depraved, and his habits worse than irregular; yet for his aggrandizement, and for the sake of her family pride, she attempted to delude herself into a belief in his sincerity, and would have seen, not only without compunction, but with triumph, the destiny of that pure, high-minded maiden linked with his, and her holiest affections wasted on a corrupt and broken cistern; "for, of course," she reasoned, "Eveleen, who is very good, would reform him, and perhaps be the means of saving him." There was no pity for Eveleen's youth and innocence mixed up with her plans—no ruth for the anguish that would blight her temporal happiness, or of the torturing martyrdom that would ensue to that guileless heart in the event of such a marriage; she thought only of self, and of how Eveleen's thousands would build up the fallen fortunes of her family, and lift up once more its crippled pride. "Rolfe and I," she reasoned with herself, "are the last of our name; we are both poor, and if this match can be brought about, it will place me in a position to make an advantageous marriage; and Rolfe—poor fellow—no longer fretted and annoyed by pecuniary embarrassments, will rise to the highest eminence in his profession."

And in pursuance of this aim, she devoted herself to Eveleen—yielded to her opinions,—did a thousand kind, nameless little things for her comfort and amusement—read to her—copied selections from her favorite authors for her—gave her flowers, and assumed towards her the patient tenderness of an elder sister towards a wayward younger one; receiving Eveleen's gifts as if she were conferring a favor, and making use of her purse on frequent occasions, constituting herself Eveleen's almoner, by which means she obtained all the credit of alms-giving, without expense to herself. But with the harmlessness of the dove, there was much of the wisdom of the serpent in Eveleen

Lacie's character. Warned by her uncle, as well as by that mysterious intuitive analysis of character which she possessed in a high degree, Eveleen was on her guard. She regarded Rolfe Estman with a compassionate wonder, for it was incomprehensible to her how a creature of God, so richly endowed with His most precious gifts of intellect and genius—so nobly made in the divine image—should desecrate the one and degrade the other; she pitied the soul that was so ignobly chained to evil habits that it lost sight of the high end for which it was created, and held itself aloof, cowering and defiant, from the only means established to lift up and heal a fallen nature! Sometimes thrown off her guard, she yielded herself to the dazzling charm of his conversation; sometimes, when he affected a sad and weary air—the result, he told her, of midnight studies—he deceived her so far that, in the guileless generosity of her kind nature, she sought to win him from his gloom; but, beyond this, the cause of Rolfe Estman did not prosper; although his vanity, which flattered him that he was invincible, deluded him into the belief that it was only necessary to declare himself to be accepted. Eveleen, unconscious of these machinations against her, sought happiness after her own fashion. We have seen how noble, and good, and generally right she was, in all her impulses; and how, guided by faith, and sanctified by charity, they opened to her many sources of elevated and unspeakable enjoyment; and how, full of an innocent gayety, she was unconscious of any superior excellence in herself, so that one would never have suspected her capable of deep emotion, heroic daring, or self-sacrifice. But we shall see, for Eveleen was but human, and was to have her trials; trials which, however bright the sunshine of our destiny may gleam about us, are coming through the dusky future to meet us with as inexorable a certainty as death or the judgment. There is no escape from these fiery ordeals—these heart-wasting conflicts; but it rests with ourselves whether angels shall walk with us through the flames, and minister consolation to us amidst the gloom of our Gethsemane; or whether we shall be consumed, or perish without hope. God never abandons those who have always abandoned themselves to His divine providence and worked for His interests and glory on earth. To such He reveals Himself—when storms, darkness, and fiery trials assail them—in strength, in fortitude, and, in the end, in peace and consolation.

It is true that Eveleen had her sad moments even now. She often sat alone at twilight, and sent her heart wandering back to her native hills to listen to the musical waters of Luggela, as they toyed with the grim rocks, or melted on the bright sands; to linger around her father's dreary resting-place, and wander through the deserted halls of Carrigmona; and while she sat rapt in such visions, she would weep softly, because she knew they were but visions. The next morning, an early visit to the blessed sacrament, or the Shrine of Our Lady of Refuge, would prove an effectual solace to her heart sickness, and she would return to the every-day routine of her life with renewed hope and courage. She had been twice to see the sick seamstress, Martha Brown, since her first visit, and the poor invalid had so far recovered her strength as to be able to move about her room, which, thanks to Eveleen, now presented a neat and comfortable appearance. Owny Travers went with her each time, but his attendance seemed scarcely necessary, for while she remained every thing was quiet in the great dilapidated house, except an occasional footfall, and the peaceful sound of domestic labor from some of the distant rooms. Once when she was coming away, she met Jerry Garrity entering the house—a sudden light flashed in his eyes, a joyous glow overspread his countenance; he looked as if he would speak; but drawing aside, he bowed, and held his cap in his hand until she passed by.

"I suppose you see him sometimes at the factory, Miss," said Owny, with a shrewd look. "Faix! an' he's the strangest boy!"

"Yes," said Eveleen, without attending to Owny's remarks, for her thoughts were just then engaged in trying to trace out the probable reasons why this young man seemed so closely associated with a class of persons to whom it was very evident he was superior.

"He's poor, an' has to work like the rest of us! but, bedad! he's as proud as the divil—an' as for books, he'll go without his dinner any day, to sit in a corner an' read," continued Owny.

"Have you had any tidings of John, yet?" asked Eveleen, hastily.

"Niver a word," said Owny, sadly. "Did Mr. Lacie write the letther he promised, Miss Eveleen, honey?"

"He has written, but has heard nothing yet," replied Eveleen. "It is a sad thing to come on the two old folk at the 'Farm,' and fair Ally Kane."

"It's the ould story, Miss Eveleen, *asthore*. There's nothin' but trouble in this world. It comes like the waves of the say; sometimes its *quite* like, then it's stormy, and wracks many a brave bonny craft. Now, there's a fellow I took in the other day out of the street—a far-downer, too, the divil fetch him—beggin' your pardon, lady: what must he do, but come stumblin' and staggerin' agin' my door-sill with a fit on him; faith! lookin' like he'd been buried and dug up agin', covered with rags and dirt. I thought —God bless us—I'd let him stay till mornin', when mebbe he'd be strong enough to use his pegs; an' there he is yet, niver spakin' a word when he's awake; and groanin' like a Methodish, an' mutterin' and' screechin' when he's asleep 'till my heart's nearly broke with the pagan. I thought mebbe a priest could do him some good, but you'd ha' thought I brought him a hangman, faith! by the outcry he made; an' Father Folliard tould him to be aisy, he wouldn't stay thin, but he'd be ready to come whin he wanted him, 'for,' said he, 'when it comes to the last the poor priest's sent for to fetch a plank for the drownin' soul.' An' its a true word, if he niver says another, thank God! But I've a mind to send the ould haythen to the poor-house—a miserable *overlooked*, bedivelled sinner—savin' yer presence."

"Don't do it, Owny. That miserable man may bring a great blessing on you. It seems to me there are no blind chances in this world, and whom God sends we have no right to turn away," said Eveleen, in her decided way.

"Faix, then, I'm not a bit of a saint, as your ladyship knows; an' when two tearin' sinners like uz gets together, it's worse nor puttin' two Kilkenny cats in the same bag."

"It is not agreeable, I confess, to associate with those whose faults so closely resemble our own: but it ought to make us ashamed of ourselves, instead of angry with the mirror in which we see our defects. You'll be good to the poor stranger, won't you?" said Eveleen.

"Well, now, Miss Eveleen, I'm no sick nurse!" said Owny with a twinkle in his gray eye.

"You nursed my father!"

"So I did, an' I'd do it agin; he was the best friend I ever had;" said Owny, while he turned to look another way, to hide the tears that had rushed to his eyes. "Tare an' 'ouns, Miss Eveleen, don't bother along with it: I'd nurse the divil hissel' if you'd spake a good word for him, an' I don't know but what I've got him there now."

"Take this to buy something nice for the poor man, or pay for his medicines," said Eveleen, taking some silver out of her purse.

"*Chorp-an-douil*—God forgive me—but do you take me, Miss, for such a skinflint as to begridge a bit an' a sup to the *omadhaun?* Put up your silver—it 'ud burn my fingers."

"Very well," said Eveleen, with a quiet laugh, "I am satisfied for you to have all the merit of your good work. I see we are nearly home now. Let me know the moment you hear from Ireland, or get tidings of poor John Travers!" By this time the carriage in which she had since the first day made her visit to Martha Brown and returned in, drew up to the door, and Eveleen ran up to her room, where she found Magdalene awaiting her with a rich and rare *bouquet* of flowers and a new book of poems, which had been left with Mr. Estman's compliments for her acceptance. Eveleen looked into the book, and saw that it contained the effusions of a satirical rhymer, who, having made one or two popular hits at passing events, found himself famous. This style of reading did not suit Eveleen's bent, and she laid it down, then quietly arranged the flowers on the oratory.

"I fear that Mr. Estman gives himself too much trouble on my account," she observed, as she threw off her wrappings.

"Would that be possible?" asked Magdalene, significantly. Then it occurred to Eveleen for the first time, that by accepting these numerous offerings of flowers and books she was placing herself under obligations to one who might infer that he had a right to expect a higher degree of favor in her regard than she felt disposed to accord him. "This is the last time," she thought; "Mr. Estman must not stand under a false impression with regard to my sentiments. It would be dishonorable to allow him to do so."

That evening Mrs. Hunter's drawing-room was filled with guests, as usual, many of whom were attracted thither by the beauty and accomplishments of the two young ladies under her care, and the reputed prospects of Eveleen as the heiress-expectant of Hugh Lacie's wealth. Among the guests on this evening was a relative of Mrs. Hunter's, Professor Lynn; a man of profound erudition, splendid genius, and pure character, who was not only distinguished for his learning, but also for his urbanity of manner, and his assiduity in contributing to the delights of social intercourse. The childlike simplicity of his manners, which always accommodated itself with rare and beautiful humility to the intellect and capacity of those about him, drew around him on this occasion an admiring circle, who were listening to and questioning him with delighted interest. At his feet, on a tabouret, sat Eveleen, her hands clasped over her knee, and her radiant face uplifted to his, listening to a curious account the Professor was giving of some ancient inscriptions which had been discovered on some broken and defaced stone tablets, which had been found at Thebes, in a tomb. In the midst of his narrative, Mr. Lacie was announced. Eveleen got up to welcome her uncle and introduce him to the Professor, when, to her surprise, she saw that he was accompanied by his *protegé* Jerry Garrity, as self-possessed as if his life had been spent in the highest walks of life; and looking so handsome in a new black suit, that she would have failed to recognize him elsewhere. Eveleen welcomed him with a blush, and a smile.

"You see I've brought him," Mr. Lacie whispered to her, on the way across the room to speak to Mrs. Hunter.

"Yes, sir. I am glad to see him. I hope he will acquit himself creditably among these stylish people," said Eveleen, in a low voice, while a mischievous smile dimpled the corners of her mouth.

"If he don't, call me an old blockhead in future: d'ye hear?"

"Yes, sir," replied Eveleen, well assured, from the young man's bearing, that there was nothing to fear on his account; but without seeming to do so, she kept him in view, and watched, and listened with jealous interest and unconscious pride—as if he were anything to her—to all he said and did. And admirably did he acquit himself. His manliness and innate dignity stood him in the stead of conventional polish, while his intelligence, his knowledge of books, and a consciousness of high aims and pure rectitude, imparted to his manner a self-possession which no degree of conventional polish could have given him. Mrs. Hunter was charmed. Magdalene Estman conversed with him, and imagined she had found her ideal; and Rolfe, observing Eveleen's animated countenance, and her frequently downcast eyes, while the young artisan was talking to her, imagined that he saw in him a dangerous rival. "Who is he!" was the whispered question.

"Do tell us who he is, Mrs. Hunter."

"His name is Garrity, a friend of the Lacies," she answered.

"It is an Irish name."

"Of course. I expect he is a relation. You know the Lacies are Irish."

"Perhaps he is an Irish lord. Lord Garrity! Depend on it, he is."

"He's been accustomed to the best company, that's clear."

These were the whispers that ran round, as
Jerry Garrity, introduced to one and another,
conversed agreeably and without vapidness
with them all, drawing out with rare art their
best points, and giving them a better opinion of
their own abilities than they had before. How
old mother Garrity would have chuckled, had
she heard the gentry's remarks about her handsome boy! As it was, Mr. Lacie overheard
them, and he muttered, "Short-sighted fools! as
if nature's patent of nobility were confined to
class or creed!" But a troubled look passed
over his face, as he looked towards the spot
where young Garrity stood entranced beside Eveleen, listening with kindling eye and absorbed
interest to her clear, sweet voice, and elevated
womanly sentiments. "*That* is not to be," muttered the old man; and he watched his opportunity to step over, and carry one or the other of
them off to another part of the room; but just
then he saw Eveleen introduce him to Professor
Lynn and withdraw to a little distance, and sit
down to listen to the conversation between them.
Mr. Lacie edged his way closer to them—he
trembled for his *protegé* now—he would certainly
get beyond his depth, and make a fool of himself. He wished that he had not brought him.
But the argument began to wax earnest between
the professor and the artisan. He heard themes
discussed that were new to him—he saw how
mind could evoke the powers of mind—he lis-

tened with breathless interest to reasons so full of subtle sophistry and learned logic that he thought they were unanswerable, and was prepared to see Jerry take refuge in flight; but the young man came to the rescue with arguments in support of his theory, so full of force and eloquence—his eyes glowing the while like the fires of his own forges, and his words so full of power and truth, so clear, concise, and to the point, that Professor Lynn gracefully admitted that he was convinced and silenced. "I don't know why it shouldn't be, after all," muttered the old man, as the professor stood shaking the young man by the hand, and every sound was drowned in a clamor of congratulation. "If he *hasn't* got Lacie blood in his veins, he's got what's more noble—intellect." Eveleen sat silent amidst the clamor. She was not surprised at Garrity's triumph. It seemed to her as if she had known him long ago, and was prepared to find him just what he was.

"Have I won?" Mr. Lacie asked her, as he was going away.

"Yes, sir. But perhaps another trial may not be quite so successful."

"That means that I'm to fetch him again?"

"Have you heard from those people in Cincinnati yet, sir?"

"No. It is unaccountable."

"I hope there may be news soon, sir. How does the model work?" asked Eveleen, looking demurely down.

"Like the mischief. Garrity put in an idea of his own when he was repairing her, and it made her perfect. I have received orders for ten of them; and if they are generally adopted, instead of the old, slow-going engines—as they will surely be—I shall take him into the business."

"Suppose you had turned him away, sir?"

"Ahem! get out of the draft, Eveleen," said Mr. Lacie, kissing her cheek—he had learned how to kiss her by this time. "Where is the lad?"

"In the hall, sir. Good night, Mr. Garrity—come with my uncle again sometime," said Eveleen. When she returned to the company, Rolfe Estman seized the opportunity, and drawing a chair beside her, sat down, and hoped "she would allow him to sun himself for a moment or two in her smiles, ere he said good-night."

"You should go to Iceland, Mr. Estman, where they have midnight suns," she said abstractedly, for her thought had—unconsciously to herself—gone wandering out into the night, following with strange interest, and softened memories, the obscure and low-born artisan, thinking how brightly shone the divinity within him, and dignified with its inexpressible grace and influence the whole man.

"I may be frozen nearer home than Iceland, Miss Lacie," said Rolfe Estman, significantly: "only such a winter, coming in the midst of spring-time and flowers, would be too unnatural."

"Yes," replied Eveleen, who took out her little Geneva watch, looked at it, and finding that it had stopped, she wound it up, and having satisfied herself by reference to the French clock over the mantle, that she had set it right, restored it to the fob in the jacket of her dress.

"Is it indifference—affectation—or coquetry?" he thought. "You are weary, Eveleen—Miss Lacie—I will not intrude any longer on you. Have you an engagement for to-morrow?"

"I fear that I have been rude, Mr. Estman," said Eveleen, unwilling to pain one who had shown her so many kindnesses; "Magdalene and I have numerous calls to make to-morrow, and we are going to the St. Cecilia festival at the Archbishop's in the evening."

"Are you free on Thursday?"

"I have no plans for Thursday; my movements will be governed entirely by circumstances."

"I hope I may be allowed to see you on Thursday morning. I have something to say to you, which is of vital importance to my happiness;" he said, in a low voice.

"Yes," replied Eveleen, coldly, while a feeling of repugnance that amounted almost to disgust, chilled her heart. Her uncle's words recurred to her mind—*the destroyer of innocence*—and she shrunk from his touch, as he attempted to lift her hand to his lips. Rolfe Estman's keen eye noted the flitting cloud and almost imperceptible shudder, nor did he forget them.

The interests of a client led him the next day to Mr. Lacie's manufactory, and while he was making notes from Moses Kugle's methodical accounts, Jerry Garrity, his hands blackened, his blouse thrown open at the throat, and his rich hair moist and disordered, came in to speak to the old clerk. They recognized each other on the instant, and while Rolfe Estman, the *gentleman*, drew himself up with a haughty, supercilious air, and scornful smile, scanning him from head to foot with a glance of supreme contempt, the artisan saluted him with an air at once so manly, and full of nature's own dignity, that he could do no otherwise than return the salutation, then turn on his heel, and resume his examination of his client's account. But how his corrupt heart exulted! The rival whom he had feared, and who had caused him to spend so sleepless a night, was only, after all, a low mechanic. It was only one of Mr. Lacie's eccentric freaks to bring him to Mrs. Hunter's; and he felt very sure that if Eveleen, with her high breeding and refined taste, knew it, she would be highly indignant at such an affront offered to her gentility. He would expose him, if he dared thrust himself again among his superiors, to win distinguished attention by his false and presumptuous pretentions to scholarship!

That night Jerry Garrity attended a book auction, and was so fortunate as to be able to purchase two or three rare old books, treating on scientific principles in which he was deeply interested. With his treasure under his arm, he was hastening homeward—to the old dilapidated house, and the ungenial fireside that awaited him in it—when he stumbled over a form that was lying partly in the gutter, and partly on the crossing. It ought to have been moonlight, according to the corporation contract for lighting the streets; but it was both cloudy and foggy, and no lamps being lit, the young artisan had nearly fallen over the prostrate form, as he was walking rapidly along the familiar way, through the dark. A carriage, or vehicle of any kind, driving too near the curb, would have gone over the white, senseless visage, as it lay spattered with the mud and ooze of the gutter. Jerry Garrity stooped down, and, laying his hand on his heart, perceived that he was not dead, but only *kilt* with drunkenness. "Oh, abased manhood!" said the noble young fellow, "how is it that men have so little value for the dignity of their being, so little respect for the immortal life within them, as to brutalize themselves by such low sensuality!" By this time he had lifted the inebriate in his stalwart arms, and borne him to a hack about a half square off, whose lamps were shedding a dim glare through the mist; and as the light fell on the swollen, unconscious face, that rested like lead on his shoulder, he started and exclaimed, "My God!" It was the face of Rolfe Estman! "*She* loves him," he thought, with a pang so keen that his heart throbbed wildly—"she loves him, she who is so true and pure, as to be worthy of an Angel's love—he shall be sacred to me. For her sake I will save him from exposure;" and as tenderly as if he had been his own brother, he lifted him into the carriage, and ordered the driver to convey them to the nearest hotel; and when they reached it, he emptied his purse, and looked over the silver that lay in his hand—it took every cent of it to pay the fare—he did not know when he should have more—but for her sake he gave it willingly, to save from exposure, and what he would have considered disgrace, the man whom he imagined she loved. It is thus that a pure love incites the human heart to acts of rare unselfishness; and it is well in these days of artificial feeling and false sentiment, to draw a distinction between what is real and that which is counterfeit! Having seen Rolfe Estman well cared for, Jerry Garrity went to his cheerless home, where a scant supper, and querulous complaints and mutterings, awaited him from the old crone who was understood to be his grandmother. He tried patiently to soothe her, but when he found it to be of no avail, he took his lamp and went up to his cold, comfortless room under the eaves, where, throwing his cloak about his shoulders, he forgot all his cares in the perusal of the books he had purchased. But some thought obtruded itself—probably the reflection of the morrow's arduous duties—which caused him at length to close them and put them by; and after he had done so, carefully piling them on a table where there were many others, he lifted his flickering lamp, and held it before a crucifix which hung against the wall. Long and thoughtfully he gazed on it; high and holy thoughts swelled in his bosom; the years of patient labor and obscurity that HE had known: the contumely, the scoffs, the ingratitude, the ignominious death!—all swept through that struggling, aspiring mind, like dark, lightning-edged clouds, until, serene and glorious, arose the vision of the Resurrection! "I will be patient," he murmured, as he knelt before the crucifix—"I will be patient, my God: only do Thou send Thy angel to roll the stone away from my heart's dim sepulchre, that I may arise true and strong for the mission for which Thou didst create me—that I may understand Thy will and be true to thy behests! Pardon the outcry of my struggling nature, that sometimes sinks fainting under the cross of poverty and obscurity, as mind and soul together seek to ascend." His voice became silent, but his great soul urged its petition for strength and enlightenment, and at last, in the overwhelming thought of God, its feverish longings for knowledge, and the higher mysteries of science, became assuaged; then a childlike trust came over his spirit, lulling it into tranquillity and submission. "He would forget the first fair dream of his life—Eveleen—he would discipline his heart until it grew strong to endure; he would go on hoping and working patiently; he would repine no more at his dreary poverty, and his hard lot with the bitter old woman who had taken care of him from his infancy—his mother's mother—he must battle with life, and he would do it in the name of God." These were some of the resolves that formed themselves in his mind ere the noble young artisan fell asleep on his bed of straw under the eaves.

Rolfe Estman kept his engagement with Eveleen the morning that he had named, and having proposed in due form, he urged his suit with impassioned eloquence. Sanguine of success, and feeling that his prey was almost in his grasp, nothing could surpass his wrathful amazement when, with quiet dignity, and in the most decided manner, Eveleen rejected his suit, leaving it impossible for him to misunderstand her language or her sentiments.

"He would advise Miss Lacie," he said with bitter sarcasm, as white and almost speechless with rage, he arose to leave her, "unless she desired to establish her reputation as a finished coquette, to be careful hereafter how she received attentions which the dullest female intellect could not fail to understand—thereby misleading her admirers to the fate of which she had just given him so bitter an experience."

Without giving Eveleen an opportunity to utter the indignant reply that arose to her lips, he bowed and left the house, with a fixed determination to revenge the repulse his pretensions had received.

Magdalene's manners grew cold and reserved towards her, and she was obliged to submit to not a few indirect observations, cutting and offensive, which she knew were levelled at her, but which her self-respect would not allow her to appropriate to herself by resenting them. She thought it but natural she should feel her cousin's disappointment, and bore her taunts with as much indifference as she could assume, knowing that without designing it she had been indiscreet at least in permitting the constant attentions of Mr. Estman, while at the same time she could not see clearly how she could have interdicted them. Even Mrs. Hunter was a little stiff; and, altogether, things were growing uncomfortable for Eveleen, who, left much alone, sought in constant occupation a relief from the thoughts that disturbed and oppressed her.

It had been storming for two days, so that it was impossible for her to get out. She was anxious to see her uncle, and confide all her difficulties to him; and still more desirous to seek the solace she generally found in the sacraments of confession and communion; and her thoughts wandered frequently to the poor abode of the sick seamstress, whose patience in suffering and humble submission to the Divine will always edified and strengthened her, even while her affectionate gratitude consoled her.

She was sitting alone in her "study." The wintry twilight had faded, and there was a dreary sound of bitter wind, and wild sweeps of rain and sleet against her window panes. The glowing coals in the grate threw out a cheerful and genial radiance, which lost itself in grotesque and solemn shadows in the distant parts of the room, and flickered here and there on the polished angles of the rich rosewood furniture like great winking eyes. Eveleen was in a mood half sad, half thoughtful. She had been holding a stern inquest over her heart, and the result proved to her that she was in danger of falling into a most unmaidenly error. Too much of her thoughts had been given to one who was almost a stranger to her—one whom she could not avoid seeing stood on the other side of an impassable gulf, which birth, fortune and position had placed between them. How much of that congeniality, so essential to happiness, could she expect to find in a union with one born and educated as he had been, even had no obstacles intervened? It was folly to indulge in such impracticable dreams! She felt that she must discipline her heart to overcome this incipient preference for an obscure and unknown stranger; that to foster it would be to trifle unwisely with her own happiness. Then her heart sought relief in yearning thoughts of home, of the dark glens and fern-clad braes of Carrigmona; she felt that if she were only amidst those scenes, so rich in loving associations, and rendered sacred to her by the dust of her father, she could find strength to battle more successfully with the encroachments of a sentiment that threatened her peace. Then she turned from self to ponder over the sorrows of her old friends in Wicklow, and wonder where John Travers could be.

While occupied with these thoughts, there came a tap at the door. It was Nero.

"Somebody to see young missis!" said the negro.

"Did you bring up a card?" asked Eveleen, fearing that it might be Rolfe Estman.

"Lor' missis, dey never seed a card. It's dat ole Irishman and a gal," said Nero, with supreme contempt, for he had never forgiven Owny for having called him "nigger."

"A girl! who can it be? I'll be down in a moment—or stay, Nero—fetch them up here into my study. "Some person needing assistance, I expect," said Eveleen, after the old negro went down. "I'll thank God for sending me this opportunity to relieve some of His suffering creatures." Eveleen lit the gas, and stirred the fire, and the room looked bright and cheerful. It was furnished like any other drawing-room, and opened into a small sleeping apartment. The large book-cases were filled with books by her favorite authors; her piano, piled with music, stood open; near the window was an *easel*, on which was fixed an unfinished sketch, from memory, of a scene near her mountain home in Ireland; and by her chair stood a parlor work-basket, on which some coarse woolen garments were laid. Eveleen heard footsteps without, and opened the door. Owny stepped in with a bow and scrape, then moved aside to make way for the female standing behind him, who was wrapped in a green cloth cloak, and wore her veil down.

"I wouldn't hev come, Miss Eveleen, *asthore*, but for her—she hasn't been long landed, an' was crazy to see you," said Owny.

"I am always glad to see you, Owny Travers; but who is this? I do not remember—yet there's something strangely familiar—is it any one I know?" said Eveleen, going up to the young woman, who lifted her veil and revealed the wasted but still beautiful face of Ally Kane!

"I hope your not offended with me, Miss, for comin'," said the poor girl, looking down with a quivering lip.

"Offended! Oh, Ally! dear Ally!" cried Eveleen, who, having recovered from her surprise,

threw her arms about her neck, and held her in a warm embrace, while she kissed the pale lips, and smoothed back the damp golden curls—
"Ally! my sister, you are welcome to me. Come, sit here by me—and do you, Owny, sit there—and tell me all about yourself—about home, and the dear hearts in Wicklow!"

CHAPTER X.

THE RESCUE.

"You did right, Owny Travers, to fetch her straight to me. I should have taken it quite unkindly, if you had not done so," said Eveleen, untying the strings of Ally Kane's bonnet, and smoothing back the damp clustering hair from her forehead; all the time feeling a sad surprise at its faded beauty, its aspect of patient sorrow and unspoken grief. "But I fear that the rough sea and confinement on ship-board have not agreed with you, dear. Something has certainly stolen the Irish roses from your cheeks!"

Owen Travers gave his head a rough overhauling with his hand, then jerked it sideways once or twice, and tapped his forehead with his finger; signs which Ally did not see, and which Eveleen did not comprehend.

"It's a poor greetin' to bring you, Miss Lacie, dear; but God help me! the color's not only faded from my cheeks, but the strength itsel' is gone from my heart," said the girl, lifting her wasted hand to her face to wipe off the tears that slowly trickled over it.

Eveleen, still standing beside her, drew her head to her bosom, and smoothed her colorless cheeks caressingly; but scarcely understanding her mood, she did not know what to say to cheer or comfort her, and thought it best to wait until she grew more composed, which she did in a short time.

"I landed yesterday, miss," she said presently, "We had a rough v'yage out; they thought sometimes they'd never see dry lan' agin'. The ship lost a mast an' sprung a leak, an' the great waves rolled over the decks as if they were goin' to swallow us up."

"My poor Ally! I expect you wished yourself back many a time, at your quiet home among the Wicklow hills, during those fearful storms," said Eveleen.

"I didn't mind, miss; I had many things more dreary to think about, sure. I knowed—the Lord have mercy on me—that I was in the hands of Him that made the say as well as the dry lan', an' that He could command it to be still when it pleased Him."

"There is no better courage than that which faith gives us," said Eveleen. "But I rejoice, dear Ally, that you escaped all those perils, and are here really and truly, a living, breathing messenger from Carrigmona. Tell me all about it, and about the good old folks at the 'Farm,' about Graff—dear old Graff—and the tenants generally," continued Eveleen, still wondering at the shadowy wanness of her countenance, but speaking cheerfully.

"The people are all hearty, Miss; an' Graff came down from Carrigmona the night before I came away to send his love to you, an' thank you for the presents you sent him. He is well, an' says he's keepin' watch 'till you come," said Ally, avoiding any particular mention of the Traverses, although her heart was full of them.

"Faithful Graff!" said Eveleen, while tears started to her eyes. "One of those days I shall come. But tell me, Ally dear, about Michael Travers, and the good old dame."

"The're as well as could be expected, Miss—the Lord look down on their sorrows!—seein' the black grief that's come upon their ould days," she replied in a low voice, while her lips quivered.

"True—I had forgotten that," said Eveleen with tender concern. "Poor John! have they heard no news of him yet?"

"Not a sign of any, lady," sobbed the girl.

"They will miss you sadly, Ally," said Eveleen, gently, and wondering why she should have left them in their sorrow.

"I have come to look for him, Miss Eveleen, *asthore*. Only for that, and the hope that I should find him, I'd niver have left them," she said, more calmly.

"The heavens look down upon you, *caen buy deelish*—an' how in all the world do you expect to find him?" suddenly burst out Owny, unable to contain himself a moment longer. "That's the question, Miss Eveleen, *deelish*—how she's to begin to do it in this great, wild, ramblin' country's more than I can understand at all."

"Niver do you fear, Misther Travers, for He that put the thought into my head, guides the swallows through the air, where there's no track to show 'em the way, an' He'll help me. I have no fear, an' if I don't find him, I'll only be doin' right by them that's been everything to me," said the girl, with a look of calm content and trust.

"You ain't a swallow!" said Owny, shaking his head.

"I have no fear, Miss Lacie, *asthore*," said the poor girl, never heeding Owny's petulant remark; "no fear, by rayson of a drame I had on the v'yage. It was a dark night, an' the tempest was ploughin' up the say till it seemed to grow higher than the highest cliffs of Carrigmanne, when all at wonst, I saw our Blessed Lady, with a bright light about her, walking on the black waves; an' she called me by name, an' says: 'Ally Kane,' says she, 'don't be afraid; I will protect you. You'll find John, but you'll not hinder him, for he's carryin' my SON'S cross, an' you know,' says she, 'it is very heavy.' Then a fog seemed to rise between us, but I know by that token that I'll find John."

"I hope you will, Ally darling—I hope so from my heart. My uncle is much troubled about John, and he has written to people in Ciucinnati, where he was last heard from, to make very particular inquires about him, and we must hope for the best. Your dream was certainly a consoling one," said Eveleen, brushing the unbidden tears from her cheeks. Owny caught her eye, and again tapped his forefinger in a very significant way, to indicate his belief in her being a degree light-headed on the subject; but he said nothing.

"There's but little doubt of my findin' him," continued Ally, with a calm and undiminished trust. "I have no misgivin's about that, but by token of the heavy cross she tould me he's bearin', I know he's steeped in trouble, an' maybe nigh unto death."

"God's ways are mysterious, dear Ally, and there's nothing left for us but to submit to His holy will. I sometimes think we are like blind men, led by one who sees and knows the way that is best for us to go in, and who, to avoid our destruction, is oftentimes obliged to lead us through thorny places and over rough roads. There are none of us exempt from trials. Each one has his own bitter cross to bear in one shape or another," said Eveleen gently, without, by even a word or sign, seeking to impair the high trust and simple faith she had in the success of her almost hopeless mission.

"That's true for you, Miss Lacie, *asthore*. His holy will be done," said Ally Kane, folding her pale hands together. "All the tenants," she said, after a pause of several minutes, "are hopin' you'll come home an' reign ever em—not that they had a bad time, for the agent's not as bad as some of his kind, but they've never forgot you, lady, an' would rather have their own lawful ruler over 'em."

"Some day or other I shall come," murmured Eveleen, with a prophetic feeling in her heart, that that day was not far distant. "You are staying with Owny, I suppose, Ally?"

"Faix, Miss, it ain't manners to take the word out of her mouth, but I'll tell you the truth. She's at my poor bit of a place; but by rayson of that pagan that's in it, an' havin' only one bed, she slept on the bare boards last night, an' I'm goin' to the station to get some of the pollis to take him away. Bedad, it would rouse the dead to hear him."

"Not to-night, Owny—it is bitter cold, and rain and sleet are both falling—he might die. Don't, my good Owny! You may depend Almighty God will reward you for your hospitality to this unknown stranger."

"Oh, no! if it wasn't so much begridged, it might fetch a blessin'. Divil take him, savin' your presence, I b'lieve he's murdered somebody that's tormenting him," exclaimed Owny, nodding his head. "But there's no gainsayin' you, Miss—there never was, you know, when you was only knee high to a pig."

"That's right. You know poor wanderers like the one you have are God's guests."

"Oh, *wirra—*"

"And Ally must be mine to-night," continued Eveleen; "I would keep her altogether, but I am only boarding, you know, and she might have to mix in some way with the negro servants. But to-morrow I shall see Martha Brown, who, I am sure, will be glad to receive Ally, and share her room with her."

"You mean the seamster, Miss?" asked Owny.

"Yes. Her poor place is fixed up right snugly now, and she will know how to comfort Ally, for she's had her own sorrows;" replied Eveleen.

"That's a bright thought," said Owny, musingly. "She'll be better satisfied with her own kind."

"Yes, many thanks to you, Miss Lacie, darlin'. I couldn't rest in a great fine place like this, where folk are expected to look happy, an' do like the rest," said Ally. "It's only two or three days I shall stay. I must be going to look afther John."

"I'm to settle for boord and lodgin', Miss," said Owny, tapping his forehead with a disconsolate look.

"Better leave that to me, Owny," replied Eveleen, in a low voice.

"Look you hether; Miss Lacie, I'm a poor man, I know, but I've got as much honest pride as the next one. I've turned her out of my own house—sich as it is, with only one room an' a shed where I cook—an' she's a stranger in a strange lan', all for the sake of a villian that I nivir set my two eyes on 'till he came stumblin' agin' my dure, an' hope I may nivir see the like agin'; an' I'm not agoin' to let her cost no man a penny, nor woman either, for that matter. So good night, 'till I see you to-morrow. Ding it," broke out Owny Travers, starting out.

"Come back here, old Owny," said Eveleen, holding out her hand with one of her brightest smiles; "that does me good. I like one of those old-fashioned tiffs — I almost expect to hear Graff growling behind you. Have your own way. But can you take a note from me to my uncle early in the morning?"

"In course I can, Miss. I'll go to-night if you like."

"It will do in the morning. I wish my uncle to come here to-morrow. Perhaps he has heard something from Cincinnati." While she unlocked her *escritoire* to write a note to Mr. Lacie, Owny and Ally Kane conversed apart in whispers, he urging upon the sorrowful girl to give up what he deemed a hopeless design, and she in a calm spirit of reticence asserting in a few, but decided words, her determination to prosecute it at all hazards.

"Is it any wonder, muttered Owny—"the heavens look down upon me!—that I niver made sich a fool o' mysel' as to get married? I nivir seen a woman yet that hadn't the obstinacy of a mule or a pig," he added, running his hand frantically through his grizzled locks; "'an the more you thry to argy them out of their tangents, the more bent they are, bedad, on goin' head foremost into difficulties. There, *caen buy deelish*—it's natural, I s'pose, an' he your first love too—don't now, don't!" plead Owny, wiping off the tears from Ally Kane's thin white cheek with a large crimson silk handkerchief, which he kept for show in his breast-pocket.

"Here is the note, Owny; give it to my uncle yourself," said Eveleen, placing the billet in his hand, "and if you can, bring me word if he can come to-morrow. I'll take good care of Ally," she added, laying her hand kindly on the drooping head of the girl.

"Good night, Miss Eveleen, *machree*—the sight of you this night carries me back to the time when you were a little wean, an' used to rule us all from your father—God ha' mercy on his soul!—down. 'Fraid of nobody nor nothin', from the ould gray aigle on the cliff to the tossin' waters of Lough Luggela, an' never will be to the best of my belief," said Owny, looking with a proud look at his *Ban Tierna*.

"Of no one but myself, old Owny—I'm coward enough to be afraid of myself sometimes," she replied, with a smile, half merry, half sad.

"Och, thin, I'd like to see the thing that can scare you, miss, that's all. You'll see me airly, Ally, *asthore;* it's no use to be grievin' an' droopin'; cheer up *alanna!* there's day break at the end of the blackest night," said Owny, as he backed himself out of the room, and closed the door.

By this time the tea-bell rang, and leading Ally to the sofa, where she insisted on her reclining until she came back, Eveleen went down, her heart so overflowing with genial kindness to all the world that she quite forgot Magdalene Estman's wrathful mood and its cause, until she was reminded of it by seeing her cold averted face, and could not help observing the supercilious manner in which she replied to her observations. To say that Eveleen Lacie was wounded, would not, perhaps, define her feelings justly; for there was a mingling of surprise and indignation with it, which, however, she, from higher motives than mere self-respect, kept in check. She directed her conversation to Mrs. Hunter, who was also, she thought, more restrained than usual in her manner, and she was really glad when the meal was at an end.

"Mrs. Hunter," she said, as she pushed back her chair, "I have a friend in my apartment who will spend the night with me; may I ask the favor of you to send up a cup of tea and a muffin?"

"A friend! La! Miss Lacie, I'm surprised that you did not invite your friend to table with you!" replied Mrs. Hunter, exchanging looks with Magdalene Estman—for they were both fully aware of the condition of this friend, having by dint of cross-questioning Nero when they came, ascertained that.

"My friend—none the less my dear friend, because she is so—is a poor and respectable peasant girl from Ireland; and even had I been disposed to claim a seat at your table for her, such is her humility and delicate sense of propriety, that she would have refused; besides which, I respect her too much to have placed her in a position which would have subjected her to the smallest discomfort," replied Eveleen, with becoming spirit.

"La me, Miss Lacie! of course the girl is perfectly welcome to her supper; but hadn't she better come down? I declare I don't know what Nero'd say, if I sent him up on such an errand?" said Mrs. Hunter, fluttering.

"I will not trouble Nero, Mrs. Hunter. If you will be kind enough to pour out the tea, I will take the things up myself," replied Eveleen, with dignity, while her eyes kindled with suppressed indignation; "and you will please," she added, "charge it to my weekly account." The words were no sooner out than she wished them unspoken, for she felt instantly that they were susceptible of an implied taunt, which referred particularly to Mrs. Hunter's needy position. That lady, however, made no reply, but bridled up and tossed her head, and poured out the tea with an energy that made a little tempest in the cup, and dropped the sugar in with a wrathful precision which reminded one of those little episodes which are not of unfrequent occurrence on the Bosphorus, when faithless *odalisques* tied up in sacks are dumped into the sea. Eveleen placed some muffins, cake and butter on a plate, and, having arranged everything nicely on a small waiter, she went up stairs with it, glad to escape from the atmosphere of ill-feeling that she felt was around her.

"Really, Miss Lacie's conduct is extraordinary!" exclaimed Mrs. Hunter.

"Miss Lacie has extraordinary tastes for a lady of her degree, I must confess," observed Magdalene Estman, trifling with her teaspoon.

Then followed a low-toned conversation between the two ladies, confidential and refreshingly malicious, in which Eveleen's shortcoming were judged without mercy. Mrs. Hunter had never really liked Eveleen, but she had an eye on Mr. Lacie's wealth, and hoped by winning the confidence and affections of his niece, to make a conquest of him. But so far her designs were utterly fruitless, as far as he was concerned; for Mr. Lacie, except when brought in contact with her as her guest, or when he came to settle her bills, which business was always got through with by him in the most formal and laconic manner, avoided her, and was deaf and blind to all her charms and blandishments. Baffled, and secretly exasperated by her disappointment, jealous of Eveleen's influence over the unmanageable old millionaire, and without the slightest personal interest in her, she entered with zest into all Magdalene Estman's spite, and without committing herself, gratified her own resentment by indulging hers. Hence her somewhat changed demeanor, and her careless indifference to her wishes that morning.

But all unconscious of being the object of such feelings, Eveleen sat talking with Ally Kane, until a clock from a neighboring steeple tolled half-past midnight—talking of their far-off home, among the wild Wicklow hills; of their sorrows; of their friends of long ago; of the dead and buried; of the living and sorrowful, until the conversation again came round to the subject of the strange purpose which had brought the girl across the wide ocean to wander in hopeless search in a strange land for her missing lover. An indescribably tender pity sprang up in Eveleen's heart towards her; she listened with keen sympathy to the simple history of her alternate hopes and fears, and with a soft gush of womanly feeling put her arms about her, and told her to regard her henceforth as a sister and a friend. The next morning, before she had left her room, she received a brief note from Mr. Lacie, informing her that he could not possibly see her that day; and after breakfast, which passed in the interchange of cold civilities, and a faint offer from Mrs. Hunter to send Miss Lacie's friend's breakfast up—which offer Eveleen pleasantly declined, saying she would take it up herself, but would be obliged to Mrs. Hunter if she would send Nero to call a carriage, as she intended going out in half an hour, which was promptly done—she went, accompanied by Ally Kane, down to Raynor's court, at the entrance of which they got out of the carriage—the court being too narrow to admit of its turning round—and walked together over the broken and frozen footway to the house where Martha Brown lived. At the door stood Mother Garrity, with a red shawl about her head and shoulders, her white grizzled hair frowzed over her deep gray eyes, which blinked and glared on the passers-by, and her shrunken hands clasped together over the knob of a stout stick on which she leaned. She was crooning some old by-gone tune to herself in Irish, which melody was frequently interrupted by alternate fits of coughing and noisy pinches of snuff, which she scraped together with her long skinny fingers from the depths of a Scotch mull that hung at her girdle. Altogether her aspect was so weird and revolting that Ally shrunk to one side, and Eveleen pulled down her veil as they approached her.

"Hech!" she exclaimed, jerking aside Eveleen's veil, as she was passing; "is it a Lacie you be?"

"My name is Lacie," replied Eveleen, with gentle dignity.

"Mate wid your own kind, thin! The aigle

niver mates wid the rook," she muttered violently. "Mate wid your own kind, lady, if you want the dead to rest in pace!" The old crone's words sounded harsh and dreary to Eveleen, although it occurred to her instantly that she must have heard from Jerry that she was the niece of Mr. Lacie, and that her strange warning proceeded from that feudal regard for family pride which is so characteristic of the Irish peasantry, who always entertain a genuine contempt for people who don't know who their grandfathers were—yet her heart thrilled with a foreboding of ill, which suddenly overclouded her dreamland of hope and happiness.

"Thank you for your counsel, good woman," she said gently, as she flitted past her.

"Aye, an' heed it! The Lacies be a proud ould race, proud to their own undoin', but ne'er a one of 'em ever married beneath 'em yet. It 'ud be better for you, lady, to wrap your shroud about you, than to wear the bridal robes at the altar wid a man that's not of your own degree."

"Cóme Ally," whispered Eveleen, with a sudden shiver, as she drew her companion away, "let us leave her. She is evidently in her second childhood. Poor old woman!"

"Ye may fly from me, but ye canna fly from the bitter repintance that goes wid an unaiqual match. Better die! better die!" she screamed, lifting her wrinkled, trembling arm towards them, as they fled up the dark stairway, never pausing an instant until they came to Martha Brown's door. The poor woman received her young benefactress with genuine tokens of welcome, and when she learned that it was in her power to do her a favor, her satisfaction was extreme. Ally's pale, sorrowful face had interested her the first moment she saw her, and she told Eveleen in her simple, homely fashion, that she was glad to have some one to keep her company, and would not only willingly share her room with her, but treat her like a sister. The room was clean, comfortable and cheerful, wearing quite another aspect from the one it had when Eveleen first visited it; and it was soon arranged that her son should sleep in a large closet hard by, and Ally should occupy his bed. Eveleen sat an hour with them for the purpose of teaching Mrs. Brown a new *crochet* stitch, and giving her directions about assorting the various shades of silk that were to be wrought into future purses with gold and steel beads. She had not only taught the poor woman this branch of light fancy-work, but had furnished her an outfit of materials for the purpose, and persuaded the proprietor of a fashionable jewelry establishment to buy at a reasonable price all that she could furnish of this sort of work—not so fatiguing, and far more profitable than plain needle work. Mrs. Brown was delighted with the new occupation, and having much natural taste for such things, she soon excelled her kind instructress in the rapidity and neatness with which her work was executed.

Twelve o'clock surprised her while thus engaged, and taking leave of Ally Kane, she kissed her cheek, bade her be of good cheer, and having promised to see her the day following, she shook hands with Mrs. Brown and hurried away.

Lingering on the steps Eveleen leaned over the rickety banister to see if Mother Garrity was still at the door; but she was not there—to her great relief—and with light and noiseless footsteps she hastened out of the house. Looking down to pick her way over the mud and ooze —the warm rays of the sun having melted the frozen pools—she did not observe the approach of another person up the narrow, irregular court, until a voice, which she knew but too well, in grave and gentle tones bade her "Good morning." She lifted her eyes, and Jerry Garrity stood before her. A warm flush mounted to her face, and with a gentle inclination of the head she would have passed him, but owing to the narrowness and filthy state of the footway, it was impossible.

"Is my uncle well to-day, Mr. Garrity?" she asked, to cover the awkwardness of the encounter.

"He is well, but very busy, Miss Lacie," he replied. "Be careful—the pavement is dreadfully broken, and the thaw has made the walking in this miserable place almost impossible."

"Thank you," she replied, essaying to pick

her way among the black slimy puddles. "It was quite frozen when I came here this morning."

"Allow me to help you, Miss Lacie," he said, holding out his hand, when he saw how impossible it would be for her to make any further progress, in consequence of a black turbid torrent that now guttered and widened òver their path, owing its impetus to a descent from a street above, which was some six or seven feet above the level of Raynor's court.

Eveleen placed her hand in his—there was no help for it—and he swung her lightly over, regardless of his own feet, which were completely hidden under the black streamlet. He walked by her side, watching where she placed her thinly-clad feet, and without speaking; while she, glad to be so guarded, yet wishing with a pang that he were gone, knew not what to say or how to act. Had it been any other than he, there would have been no difficulty; she would have said frankly "Hold my hand and do not let it go until I get safely over this, then I will not longer trouble you;" but she could not speak so to him, so shy and sensitive, so proud and gentle as he was. If they were widely separated by fortune and position, she would not thrust him further away still by conventional *hauteur*, and assumed coldness of speech; he should not think of her, when he saw her no more forever, as scorning his companionship. The dreary time would come soon enough, when he would have to be to her like unto a dream; she would not anticipate it, and embitter her hereafter, by repulsing him, when it would be, perhaps, the last time they would ever meet. Again he held out his hand to assist her, and confidingly she nestled hers within it, saying in a gentle voice:

"I have a favor to ask you, Mr. Garrity. I have just left a young woman—one of my early friends from Ireland—with Mrs. Brown for a few days. May I ask you to extend your protection to her, if she should need it, while there?"

"You may, Miss Lacie, and depend upon it, that the slightest wish of yours is entitled to my sacred obedience," he replied, still holding her hand, and guiding her along the ruinous pavement. By this time they came near where the carriage awaited her, and as she stepped up to it, and was in the act of getting in, Rolfe Estman came up, and greeting her with his usual high-bred grace, made a motion to assist her in; but with a cold and distant bow, she turned her head away from him, and with her hand leaning on the strong clasp of Jerry's, sprang in and closed the door after her. In another moment she was driven out of sight.

"You should choose a more romantic place than the precincts of Raynor's Court, to hold a tryst with a lady of Miss Lacie's degree," said Rolfe Eastman, surveying Jerry with a sneer, from his head to his feet.

"Miss Lacie, was here on an errand of mercy, and I met her quite by accident—so much in justice to her: and now," said the young man, while his eagle eyes flashed, and his fine sinewy form dilated to grand proportions, "if you ever dare, or if I ever hear of your presuming to cast such an insinuation again on that lady in connection with myself, or any one else, you shall rue the day that you were born."

"Base cur, get you out of my sight, lest I chastise you with this," exclaimed Rolfe Estman, turning white with rage, while he lifted his heavy jewel-headed cane over the noble young fellow's head. In an instant, and with a calm, quick, determined gesture, Jerry Garrity seized the cane, and breaking it into splinters with a single wrench, he threw it into the gutter, leaving his antagonist unarmed.

"I have been accustomed, sir, to working in iron until my muscles have grown into steel; and I could as easily fling you in yonder muddy ooze, as I lifted you a few nights ago, from where you lay in drunken unconsciousness, exposed to the danger of having your life crushed out in the darkness by every wheel that passed by. Good-day, sir," said Jerry Garrity, turning slowly away, with ineffable scorn in every feature.

"I'll see you again, you low bully, and throw that lie in your teeth," exclaimed Rolfe Estman, in suppressed tones of baffled rage.

"And I will have proof forthcoming, which

will cast it back with a vengeance. You'll find me at my old post in Mr. Lacie's manufactory," replied Jerry, walking away neither faster nor slower than his usual gait.

"And so it was he who picked me out of the gutter that night? Rolfe Estman, thou'rt indeed fallen, to be indebted to such a hind as this! But I'll be revenged! How dare the contemptible mechanic lay his sooty fingers on a gentleman?" muttered the unprincipled man, as he slowly walked away from the scene of his discomfiture. "And on you too, proud Eveleen, I'll have a most sweet revenge. I'll go this moment to my pious cousin Magdalene with what I have seen to-day; and I have no faith in woman, but that before to-morrow night you'll be glad to hide your head from the scorn of your sex."

Oh, rare gentleman!—oh, honor to your lordly sex!—oh, apt illustration of modern chivalry!—beware, for it was written long ago by an inspired pen, that "He who layeth a snare for others, falleth into it himself." He who forsakes his religion and its practices as you have done, giving its precepts the lie with every profane breath you draw, hurling defiance at God in every act, and trampling with brutal feet on the Divine Sacraments instituted for your salvation, must in the end be abandoned to the devices of his own wicked heart, and given over to the curse of a reprobate spirit, without a single claim on which to found a hope of the protection of Divine Providence!

Jerry Garrity walked towards his poverty-stricken home full of exceeding joy!

He had seen Eveleen, he had held her hand in his, she had turned to him as if for protection, and afterwards he had defended her from a vile aspersion. If he never saw her again, and if even in his day-dreams she was never anything more to him than now, this memory would still dwell within him and brighten up the waste places that a blighted hope had made in his heart. His religion was not a mere outward profession of faith, or a yoke which made him restive, but it was in truth a living, vital principle, which had imparted strength and blessing to his struggles, and given him the victory in many temptations, and would still be his aid and stronghold in this ordeal; but hereafter when his pure but hopeless love for Eveleen should become the basis of the highest and best earthly aims of his life, not one, he vowed, should be unworthy of association with her memory, nor would he ever engage in any plan, or pursue any success, of which he would blush to tell her the history. Full of such thoughts—the fruits of a pure love—neither the discomforts of the poor home nor the querulous complaints of the old crone—his grandmother—disturbed his sweet but sad tranquillity; and, when having finished his simple meal, he walked back through the noisy, crowded thoroughfare to the scene of his daily toils, they went with him, nor forsook him even when he stood amidst the clangor of machinery, the fierce ringing blows of iron hammers, and the loud roar of blazing furnaces. Like low sweet music they pervaded his inner life, in strains as sweet as those which sometimes arise in dreams over the graves of perished hopes!

Eveleen was no coward by nature, but when the breakfast bell rang next morning at the usual hour, she lingered some moments, from an unwillingness to come in contact with persons who had, in the most unjustifiable manner, changed their behavior towards her, to a degree which was not only embarrassing, but offensive; and being sensitive and impulsive, she felt *afraid* of being betrayed into saying, or doing something resentful, which would involve not only regret on her part, but perhaps the humiliating necessity of an apology; for Eveleen was too true and faithful a Catholic to have held back, in such a case, from a duty which religion demanded of her, however painful it might have been to her human pride.

Standing on the threshold of the door, she blessed herself devoutly, and hoping that the blessed sign of the cross would be as a shield and guard to her, she placed herself under the protection of the Adorable Trinity whose divine name she had invoked, and whispering a prayer that her soul might be preserved in patience, let whatever would happen, she went down.

Mrs. Hunter barely returned her courteous

morning salutation, and Magdalene Estman fixed her great black eyes in a broad insolent stare on her face—deigning her no other recognition—as she seated herself at the table. Eveleen's heart began to surge tumultuously, but she restrained its resentful impulses and held in check the emotions they gave rise to.

"We shall have fine weather now, I think," she observed, looking towards a window, through which a flood of sunlight poured in, "I never saw a more beautiful morning."

"Ahem! Yes—very," said Mrs. Hunter. Then there came a pause. Eveleen, guiltless of offence, felt she would be compromising her dignity as well as assuming that she had given them some reason for their strange conduct, by noticing it; and she concluded not to do so, unless urged to do it by demonstrations still more offensive; then, she thought, in justice to herself, it would become her duty to ask an explanation. And she rightly concluded that if her rejection of Rolfe Estman had incensed Magdalene to this extent, and led her to the very verge of open insult, however much she might regret it, she was in no wise accountable for it.

"I believe that you were at the wedding last night, Mrs. Hunter," said Eveleen. "I hope you had a pleasant time."

"Oh, yes, very! Eva Sanders is one of the finest girls I ever knew. Everybody loved and admired her."

"She was *prudent*, also, Mrs. Hunter, was she not?" asked Magdalene Estman, with a sneer.

"She was a very discreet young lady. Of course she was," replied Mrs. Hunter, with a simper.

"I suppose she never made a cloak of charity, to have clandestine meetings with her lover."

"Dear me, Miss Estman, no—of course not. Bless me, Miss Lacie, what ails you?"

Eveleen had risen from her chair. Her encounter with Rolfe Estman the day before, and her unexpected meeting with Jerry Garrity, suddenly presented themselves before her mind, and furnished her a clue to the insinuations and taunts just levelled at her. She leaned her hand on the back of her chair, for she trembled excessively, and fixing her eyes full on Magdalene Estman's, asked her in a low, calm voice to explain her gross insinuations.

"By what authority does Miss Lacie ask an explanation of my words?" she inquired in her smooth, silvery voice.

"Because I have reason to believe they were intended for me. If they were not, why should you evade an explanation?"

"Dear me, young ladies! I had no idea! Don't quarrel! Bless me, Miss Lacie, you look very white! Pray don't quarrel with Miss Estman," said Mrs. Hunter, fluttering, and turning red.

"Madam, I must indeed forget my self-respect when I condescend to quarrel. Give yourself no uneasiness on that score," returned Eveleen, in the same low tone. "I simply and civilly ask an explanation of what I deem a most offensive insinuation against myself."

"Bless me, Miss Lacie, don't get so high! Sit down. I declare I intended to tell you myself in a private way."

"I prefer standing. What did you intend telling me, madam?"

"Well, you know, Miss Lacie, that I am as it were, responsible for your—oh—the manner in which you conduct yourself while under my care. I thought at first I'd speak to Mr. Lacie, who has a legal right to restrain you," blundered Mrs. Hunter.

"Why did you not do so, madam? you would have found a warm defender for me, who would have shielded his orphan niece from insults."

"Oh my, you are too severe!"

"Once for all, Mrs. Hunter, speak out. I demand it. What is it that you have heard disparaging to me?" asked Eveleen, calmly.

"Well, you see, Miss Lacie, people will talk, you know," replied Mrs. Hunter, who could no longer escape, and who was quite cowed by the manner of Eveleen; "and, to be plain with you, your fondness for low people, my dear, and your frequent visits to an obscure house in Raynor's Court have been commented on, and very much wondered at, indeed; but I hinted that it might be some harmless Irish eccentricity—dear me—"

"The result of early associations," suggested Magdalene Estmane.

"Exactly, early associations. But I told everybody that you were very lavish of money and very charitable, and although you were dreadfully imposed on in many instances, *that* never deterred you from assisting the needy. Indeed, I defended you through thick and thin, until I heard that you went to Raynor's Court to meet that young fellow your uncle brought here one night, which I didn't take kindly, as it turned out that he was only a mechanic. But I didn't believe a word of it, until I heard from an eye-witness that you met him there yesterday."

"I am no longer surprised that a well-bred *gentleman* like Rolfe Estman should have been so unceremoniously rejected," sneered Magdalene.

"Rolfe Estman!" repeated Eveleen, looking proudly up, " has proved by this base attempt to impugn my fair name, his high claim to the name and character of a gentleman! I should not go too far if I were to say that I consider his having ever presumed to aspire to my hand as degrading to me."

"Child," suddenly exclaimed a harsh, familiar voice behind her, "come out from among them!"

Mrs. Hunter shrieked and upset the teapot in her lap; Magdalene Estman started and arose from her chair; and Eveleen threw herself in her uncle's arms, as he stood in the door-way, and nestled her head on his shoulder.

"I came here to see my niece this morning," said Mr. Lacie, looking from one to another of the frightened women with a lowering frown, "and the negro man told me that you were at breakfast; so I walked in—and I'm glad I did— just in time to hear the base calumnies that you have dared to utter, ma'am, to this innocent, high-minded child—which malicious falsehood, I am happy to say, I am able to refute. And I tell you plainly, miss, that I'd rather see her married, this day, to old Owny Travers, poor and ignorant though he be, or to the poorest apprentice that hammers iron in my manufactory, than mated with that smooth-faced scoundrel, Rolfe Estman. As to Jerry Garrity—he holds about the same relation to him as the devil does to an angel! And I want you to inform your honorable kinsman, that by a certain nefarious act of his, I have him completely in my power. A certain spurious paper has come into my hands, which places him at my mercy. I know the history of my child's visits to Raynor's Court. My old clerk has rooms there. His eye has been on her. Pish!—did you think I'd leave a tender inexperienced thing like this unguarded? And now, in conclusion, unless you retract what you have said in reference to my niece, and give up the author of this malicious calumny, I'll institute a suit for *slander* against ye both, before another hour rolls over my head!" said the enraged old man.

"I'm sure I'm very glad to hear Miss Lacie exonerated from blame!" whimpered Mrs. Hunter, frightened almost to death.

"Excuse me, I have no concern as to whom Miss Lacie does or does not marry," said Magdalene Estman, loftily, as she endeavored to pass by Mr. Lacie.

"It seems to me, Miss, that you've got crosses all over you—in your ears, on your breast, and even on your fingers; but may be they are only *Egyptian* crosses, to signify some sort of belief in a hereafter. I'm not pious, but I know well enough that the MAN who died on the Cross didn't consecrate it with His blood to make it the sign of a creed of slander, calumny, and the injuring of another by stealth. But I've got nothing to do with your crosses, only to advise you to take them off, or act more like a Christain. Nay, young lady, you do not pass out of this room until this foul charge against my niece is stifled. Eveleen, fetch me pen, ink and paper."

CHAPTER XI.

A LETTER, AND WHAT CAME OF IT.

"SIR!" exclaimed Magdalene Estman, gasping with rage, "I question whether or no you have a legal right to act as you are doing, insulting and brow-beating two defenceless women!"

"If that is the difficulty, it shall soon be obviated. These unjust and malicious falsehoods must and shall be retracted within an hour. I am going for my lawyer. Do you retire to your room, Eveleen, until I return," said Mr. Lacie, putting on his hat.

"Uncle," said Eveleen, laying her hand on his shoulder, "don't stir. These ladies, I would fain hope, have acted more from thoughtless impulse than malice. Appearances are probably against me, innocent as I am in fact. I am sure they are quite willing to do me justice, and avoid any unnecessary exposure."

"Of course," said Mrs. Hunter, with alacrity; "certainly. I'll sign a paper, or do anything you suggest, Mr. Lacie, to give satisfaction. I was misinformed as to the motives, as well as the facts. I'm sure I'm sorry, but my sense of propriety—"

"Pish, madame! That's enough," exclaimed Mr. Lacie. "What do you say, Miss?"

"I simply repeated to Mrs. Hunter what I had heard, and advised her to speak to Miss Lacie—*that* was my duty," said Magdalene Estman, who, although she was burning inwardly with hatred and revenge, was quite willing to retreat from the dangerous ground on which she stood; for it was very evident to her that Mr. Lacie was not a person to be trifled with.

"And who, I demand to know, instigated by malice, dared tell you that my niece had clandestine meetings with Jerry Garrity in Raynor's Court?" he asked, sternly.

"He must defend himself, and take the consequences of his own act if he has deceived me," she replied; "it was Rolfe Estman."

"As I supposed. I'll deal with him as he deserves. Where is the pen and ink—fetch it quickly, child," said Mr. Lacie, turning to Eveleen.

"Use this desk, sir—you'll find paper and everything you need in it," said Mrs. Hunter, opening her writing-desk, and glad to escape—on any terms—from the disgrace of a public exposure of the case.

Mr. Lacie sat down and wrote a formal—and to them humiliating—retraction of all they had said or insinuated against Eveleen; that he requested them to read and sign, which they did, and soon afterwards left the room, considerably crestfallen, but secretly enraged and mortified beyond expression. Eveleen, who, until now, had been supported by an indignant and roused feeling of excitement, was conscious of a revolution, which left her scarcely able to stand. Mr. Lacie stood scowling on the rug, with his back to the fire, and did not observe how pale she was, until, as she attempted to reach the lounge, she staggered and would have fallen if he had not sprung forward, and having caught her, supported her head on his shoulder.

"It is all over now, sir—I'm better," said Eveleen, in a faint voice, as she lifted her head, and having walked a few paces, fell into a chair. Mr. Lacie saw a decanter of sherry on the sideboard, and striding across to it, and pouring out a glassful, handed it to her, with the laconic command to drink it, which she did, and felt revived.

"You were imprudent, Eveleen child, in going so often into such an obscure place. You were right in theory, but wrong in practice. It is only the sácred garb of a Sister of Charity which can fully protect a woman in such a haunt as that in which your pensioners live. You had no business to recognize Jerry Garrity, or be seen with him there; though Moses Kugle, who knew how it all happened, says you were not to blame. The world hates charity any how, and particularly that which is done in secret, and will, if possible, revenge itself on those who reproach it by practising its maxims;" said Mr. Lacie, gravely.

"I believe, sir, I am right before God in this matter; therefore, although I have been outraged by the false insinuations it has exposed me to, and grieved by the injustice and ingratitude I have so bitterly experienced this day, I will endeavor to bear it in a patient and forgiving spirit, because I would not willingly waste the merit this may otherwise obtain for me. It is the best way I can show my gratitude to Almighty God, for having delivered me from a snare as hidden as it was evil," said Eveleen, firmly, while at the same time she distrusted her own ability to do so.

"If you mean by bearing it patiently, to forgive those two women, and to treat them as if they had been writing an epic in your praise, instead of seeking to tarnish your fair fame, I hope they'll beat you. I don't approve of such things. When people behave ill, they ought to be made to feel it."

"That is the code of the world, sir, which is at variance with that of Christianity. These trials are tests of our fealty to God, and it seems to me that when they come, although all human feeling and inclination may be against us—aye, even our own cowardly hearts—there is but one thing to be done, and that is to ignore all human considerations at whatever cost, to be loyal to our own Divine King;" said the young girl, whose high sense of Christian duty led her to distinguish the right of God to tribute as at least equal to that of Cæsar.

"I know nothing about such subtleties," said the old man, on whose brow a storm still lowered; "I know only this—I have checkmated and silenced those two women. I would take you away immediately, but I am worldly-minded enough to know that it would excite remark, which might or might not be unfavorable to you. And I know this. It was no idle threat, when I said Rolfe Estman was at my mercy. I have at this moment in my possession a draft which he forged some months ago. With this I will effectually silence him, and, it may be, consign him to the penitentiary. A mean, cowardly scoundrel! to seek, out of revenge, to injure a woman. The despicable dog! But I must go—and mind, if these women begin to show their nails under their velvet paws again, let me know it. I won't have you scratched!"

"I don't think I shall be scratched, sir," said Eveleen, with a low laugh—she could not help it—"but I shall be lonesome enough. I know that. For you know, sir, that you are so in love with Moses Kugle and your inventions that you haven't time for such trifling, as to come and see me oftener than once a week."

"You shan't be lonely, child. I will come," said Mr. Lacie, lifting up the storm-cloud from his brow. "But, hilloa! what brought me here? God bless me—yes—here's a letter—a letter from my agent in Cincinnati," suddenly exclaimed Mr. Lacie, fumbling in his pockets. "It was knocked clear out of my head by those feminine cats."

"Sir!"

"Angels, then, my dear, if it will suit you better. Aha!—here—read it," said Mr. Lacie, handing the letter—which he at last found in his hat—to her.

"All efforts," said the letter, every word of which Eveleen read with the keenest and most painful interest, "all efforts to discover any trace of the young man—John Travers—have been in vain. We have spared neither pains nor money (according to your instructions) to find him, but both money and time have been wasted. We put the ablest detectives about here on the trail, but without success. The only chance—and it was only the shadow of one—that presented itself was this. There's a young fellow in prison here, under sentence of death for murder. We heard that he was an Irishman and a Catholic. There was no positive proof, we learned, that he committed the crime, but the *circumstantial evidence* justified the verdict of the jury. Many of the community believed him innocent, but in the end there was no question of his guilt. I went to the prison for the purpose of asking the unfortunate criminal if Hanlon was his real name; for I thought that, for some motive best known to himself, he *might have assumed a fictitious one.* He was sitting at a table reading when I entered. He arose and returned my salutation respectfully, and invited me to take a chair. I saw at once that he belonged to what the Irish call '*the bettermost class*' at home, and I was almost afraid that my conjectures were right as to his identity with the one I was seeking. I stated my business, and asked him 'if Hanlon was his real name?' He said—'unfortunately it was.' I asked him 'if he had ever known one John Travers?' He raised his head suddenly, gave a wild, startled look about him, then leaning his forehead on his head, replied, 'No. The name was strange to him.' I told him that 'Travers' friends were uneasy about him, not having heard anything from him, or of him, for more than a year.' I watched him as I spoke, and saw the veins in his neck and forehead throbbing and swelling as if they would burst; and it was several minutes before he spoke. At last he said, 'You will excuse me, sir, but my health has got very bad since I've been in prison. Something's the matter with my heart. I had a spasm in it just now. I know nothing about John Travers. It's likely he's dead. I am sorry to appear rude, sir, but you will please to leave me, if you have nothing further to say, for I hear my confessor's footstep in the corridor.' I offered him my hand, which he took, saying, 'I would not take an honest man's hand, sir, if mine was stained with murder, as they say.' And, sir, there was a manly truthfulness in every lineament of his thin, pale face that forced me, in spite of my cooler judgment, to believe him. This is all. It may be that he is John Travers, after all. I have my own suspicions about it."

"My God!" exclaimed Eveleen, dropping the letters in her lap.

"Aye! what do you think of that?"

"It can't be, sir—and yet, merciful God! there's a something that makes me fear that it is he. Poor Ally! poor broken-hearted old father and mother! Uncle! if it takes all that I have on earth, he must be saved!" said Eveleen, earnestly and sorrowfully.

"Child, it would not be wasted if it saved John Travers' life—if this be he—but it is too late for even bribery now. If it be really he, sentence has been already passed, and he only awaits its execution. It is too late, I say. And even had we heard the news in time, you know that the laws are so justly administered, there's so much equity and probity about our courts, so much impartiality, and even-handed justice, that beyond paying for the services of talented counsel for the accused, money would have been useless. Juries are incorruptible—of course they are. No doubt, the fact of this poor young fellow's being a poor, unknown Irishman, without friends, facilitated the ends of justice, and gave him the benefit of law to its uttermost limits. Ding it! the law is so fond of vindicating its majesty, and, at the same time, making an example, that in its zeal it is just as likely as not to kill the lambs, because the wolf has muddied the fountain. I take off my hat to the law!" said Mr. Lacie, with a cold, sarcastic look.

"I do not understand you exactly, sir," said Eveleen, looking puzzled, unable to determine whether her uncle had uttered a bitter truth, or meant a cutting irony.

"It is not necessary that you should, child," he replied, taking up his hat. "Circumstantial evidence! It makes me sick! I'm now going to look for Owny Travers."

"If you find him, sir, please tell him to fetch Ally Kane to me to-day. I promised to see her, but I cannot go there again!" said Eveleen, while a shade of annoyance flitted over her face.

"Child!" said Mr. Lacie suddenly, while he gathered both her hands in his, and fixed his softened eyes on her face, "tell me truly—dost thou love the lad?"

A crimson hue dyed her face, but she looked down, never uttering a word.

"Aye! aye! I see how it is," said Mr. Lacie, sadly. "It is no shame to thee, child, for he's a most noble lad; but thou must forget him. It can never be."

"Never," murmured Eveleen, in a low, firm tone, "never!"

Mr. Lacie put his arm about her, and drew

her to him, with a feeling of inexpressible pity, and kissing her head, as it lay throbbing on his bosom, he released her, and went away with rapid steps out of the house. Quick walking soon brought him to the dwelling of Owny Travers, whom he hoped to find, that he might show him the letter from his man of business in Cincinnati: but the door was opened by a rough, stupid-looking lad, who informed him that "Musther Travers was abroad."

"Very well, my lad. When he comes in, tell him to come, without loss of time, to Lacie's factory. Can you remember that?"

"Be you Musther Lacie, sir?" asked the boy, scratching his head, and throwing an anxious, frightened glace over his shoulders into the room beyond.

"God bless my soul! what's that?" exclaimed Mr. Lacie, springing backwards from the door, as a shrill, dismal, prolonged howl sounded from within, while the lad, in his hurry to get out, fell headlong under his feet, where he lay squirming and twisting, and holding fast all the time to Mr. Lacie's leg, at the imminent risk of throwing him into the gutter. "Get up, you young rascal—it's over now—and tell me what it means."

"It's *him*, sir," said the lad, who arose slowly to his feet, and cowered up against the wall of the house.

"A dog, is it?"

"Agra! but I wish it was no worse than a mad dog, sir," replied the lad, whose teeth were still chattering.

"Is any one sick here?"

"Iss—mebbe. Sick or *overlooked*, one or t'other. Only that he's tied I'd be afeerd of my life. It's bad enough to see the eyes of him! Faix, sir, you ought to see 'em; they look like two glarin' coals of turf; an' it's too bad intirely for a poor man like Musther Travers to have the trouble an' expinse of a stranger that he don't even know the name of. There he goes ag'in!" cried the lad, plunging head over heels out into the middle of the narrow, unpaved street, as another yell, more furious and horrible than the last, resounded through the small tenement. Without a thought of what the consequences might be to himself, and impelled by a feeling of humanity, Mr. Lacie stepped in, thinking he might render some sort of assistance to the miserable wretch, whoever he was, and saw a man, squalid-looking, and emaciated to a fearful degree, who was corded down with strong ropes to the bedstead, tossing his grizzled head from side to side on his pillow, and snarling and snapping like an infuriated dog whose chain galls him; while his eyes, large and unnaturally bright, glared, and rolled round their orbits in a terrible manner. He suddenly ceased his contortions when Mr. Lacie approached the bedside, and fixed his wild, stormy eyes with a bewildered but wistful expression on his face.

"Do you want water?" said Mr. Lacie, holding a mug of water towards him; but he remained silent. "Can I be of any service to you, friend?" he then asked.

"Friend! friend!" he muttered in a shivering tone, which he gradually raised to a howl of agony, "are ye a divil or a priest, come to make mock of me? If you're a divil, shake hands wid me, for the sign of hell is on my hands! See it! It drips! It flames! It is red! It looks like blood! It makes all the world an' the sky red! Away, priest! down wid the papists! hurra! for the jolly Orangemen!"

"He's crazy," said Mr. Lacie, turning away with a shudder, and making the best of his way out of the house, glad to be released from a presence which mingled in its influence the spirit of the infernal deep, with the most revolting phase of mere brute life. He gave the boy a piece of silver, and telling him to watch the house, and deliver his message faithfully to Owny Travers, he walked briskly away towards his place of business, wondering what on earth Owny had burdened himself with such an inmate for. But he was once more within sight of the massive and blackened walls of his manufactory, and already heard the panting of its fiery heart, which exhaled itself in fierce white jets of steam, which, meeting only the bright sunshine, and the calm of a tranquil atmosphere, melted away in soft undulations and vapory traceries in the fathomless depths above. Their mission of power was over; they had given their impetus to the progress of science, they had forged another strong link to the chain of power and swiftness, which was by degrees binding the green earth with ribs of iron, and sending abroad over the seas fiery coursers, which sped like fabled monsters from shore to shore, dimming the blue billow with the smoke of their nostrils, as they triumphed over the winds and tides of the vasty deep!

Mr. Lacie was in his element now, and all exterior vexations, all beyond this, whether of pleasure or pain, were forgotten, and he walked briskly in under the grim arch of the doorway, and casting a glance of pride around the spacious, pillared warehouse, where huge piles of ponderous iron machinery were arranged in due order, he opened the door of his private counting-room with a feeling of security, for he thought that he would surely be safe from all intrusion and vexation here, and walked in. But he suddenly started back with a look of stern displeasure on his countenance; for there, occupying his own particular chair, sat the old beldame, Mother Garrity, who, leaning her chin on the knob of her tall walking-stick, watched him with the immoveable patience of a *couchant* cat, who bides its time for the appearance of the predestined mouse. Nor was she in the slightest degree moved by his aspect of displeasure; or the menace that shone in his eyes, that threatened her with a blow from his upraised cane; but still glowering at him she muttered: "Ye dare na' do it. Ould blood like the Lacie's was niver brought to shame yet for havin' struck a lone woman. Lower your stick, sir. I came here for no harm."

"What brought you here, woman!" asked Mr. Lacie, in high displeasure.

"Not for a welcome greetin', be sure of that, your honor; but I had summut to say that couldn't be said to anither," replied Mother Garrity, in her jargon, which had a high flavor of the North country dialect.

"Does Jerry—"

"Aye, your honor, it's Jerry. Hould, now, an' be after tellin' me—for I'm ould, begad, an' forget—did there ever come a time, when one of the proud ladies of your race brought disgrace on her name an' station, by matin' wid them that hadn't even a name—by rayson of bein' born out of wedlock—to give 'em in return?"

"I'll answer you; then begone. No! Rise up, and go, and if you are ever seen about this place again I will dismiss Jerry—mind you well—it will be your fault, for I will not be annoyed by you any longer," said Mr. Lacie sternly.

"I'll go prisently, your honor. Be patient, Misther Hugh Lacie. I'll niver come—on my sowl, I won't after this—if you'll only be patient an' hear me through. Don't you—mind what

I say now—don't you go an' let your dead brother's child be the first to bring shame on the ould Lacie blood. I've been watchin', begad! an' I'm not so blind that I don't see the sparkle of her bonnie eye, an' the red rose blushin' in her cheek, when *he* spakes to her"—

"What in the name of the"— shouted Mr. Lacie, but checking himself, he added in his usual tone: "There's enough of this nonsense. You poor, miserable, doting old creature, begone this moment, or I'll call in some of my workmen to put you out. Here—here's money —begone."

"Glory! your honor, I'm very poor, but I dinna thole the siller," she mumbled, tying up the half dollar all the time, in a corner of her ragged handkerchief. "But what I've got to say must be said, if I'm kilt for it; and hearken to my words, or when it's too late you's give all your riches, if you had only minded me."

"I'll hear what you have to say," said Mr. Lacie, remembering—with a sigh of pain—the scenes of the morning. He turned, and closing the door, locked it, then threw himself into a chair before the fire, and told the old crone she might speak out.

"It's about the bonnie Lady-bird, that's got hersel' snared—but hech, sirs! the aigle don't mate itself wid the rook. What would the likes of her do in a poor, starved home, like the one Jerry, poor lad—would bring her to?" said the old woman, with a leer.

"Jerry the deuce!" stormed out Mr. Lacie, "the lad has too much sense to think of such a thing, and if the sense is wanting, he has too much honor; so no more of it—no more of it! I don't believe it of him. But after all, what's the harm? God has given the lad a princely soul. He has made him noble, and true! He has genius, talent, and integrity, and his principles are as pure as the gospel. So where's the harm?" added Mr. Lacie as if arguing with himself.

"Harm!" shrieked the old woman; "Harm! If she was a poor servant girl prenticed for her vittals an' clo's—if she was a beggar—if she was outcast from womankind, wid the marks of shame upon her, Jerry Garrity's no mate for her, an' she Reginald Lacie's daughter! There's a ban on him! It would raise the dead out of their graves if she was ever brought so low as to be his wife, no matter how grand, or rich, or powerful he may rise to be. She'd better marry a man from the hulks; she'd better drown hersel' in the say, than do it!"

"What has the lad ever done?" enquired Mr. Lacie, in mute amazement, having no fears all the time for Eveleen, for he had not forgotten how that very morning he had heard her say "*Never*," as if it were wrung from the depths of her heart; but willing to probe the mysterious secret with which the beldame had suddenly enshrouded Jerry, he humored her mood.

"The lad's weel enough, but there's a black curse on him, an' it'll fall on whoever he weds, most of all on her," she replied, panting with exhaustion; "an' I warn you—you—not to let Reginald Lacie's daughter come down to that."

"There's no fear of such a thing. It will never happen. Now be quiet, and tell me if Jerry is your grandson?" answered Mr. Lacie.

"I'm content if you say that. Yes, he's my grandson. But stick to what you say, an don't let *that* happen. Aye, bedad, more's the pity! he *is* my grandson," she said, with a sullen nod, as she rose to go. "I've said my say, Misther Lacie, an' it's for you to look to it. The lad's a good lad, but the curse goes wid him like his shadow. Let him marry who he will, only not her."

"You've said your say, woman," said Mr. Lacie, also rising, "and I may or may not have reason to thank you for the warning. Be that as it may, listen to me. If you ever need assistance, send to me, and you shall have it. But never dare you set your foot within these doors again; if you do, I'll give orders to my people to expel you by force, and give you in charge of the police as a nuisance."

"Aye! aye! I'll go; I'll go. I've said my say," mumbled Mother Garrity, hobbling out—"better she'd die of a broken heart, than wed the like of him. I wish he was at the bottom of the say!—he's my torment! I love him, an' I hate him! I dare na' hurt a hair of his head, an' I could tear him like a tiger for the bitter thoughts he brings me. Och! but it's a weary, langsome day syn the blight fell on my flower! Clouds an' mist an' stormy oceans have come betune us, *caen buy deelish;* but I canna' forget the time ye wor trampled in the dust wid the world's scorn upon your bonny head! I wouldna if I could forgit or forgi' the black heart that brought the desolation to my dure. *Chorp an douil!* but it's a bad case if I don't get my full of vengeance! Hech, sirs!" she exclaimed, as in the gloom of the place, Moses Kugle came full against her from an opposite direction, and would have fallen over her, if she had not clung to an iron pillar, which broke his plunge into a prolonged stumble.

"Dunder und blitzen! What are you doing here, creeping about in the dark?" cried the old clerk, poking about for his hat, which had been precipitated from his head by the shock, and gone rolling under the grim piles of machinery. In the meanwhile, Mother Garrity had hobbled out of his way, and disappeared; and Moses Kugle, having at length got hold of his hat, put it emphatically on his head, and went in to speak to his employer.

"I'm glad you have come, Moses!" said Mr. Lacie, whose countenance wore a grave and worried expression which deepened its wrinkles, and made its harsh lines still more austere.

"I'm at your service, sir. There's nothing amiss, I hope!" asked the old clerk.

"Nothing much, Moses, my boy; nothing more than I expected when I fell heir to the charge of a woman in my old days. They're all alike, and can't help it. It's in 'em—no matter how good they be—to breed trouble. But here—I've lost time enough to-day," he continued as he took out his pocket-book and undid the clasp with his usual deliberation. After looking into its various compartments, he drew forth a soiled note, which, from the various creases in it, seemed to have passed through numerous hands; which having opened and read, he folded it carefully and gave it to Moses Kugle, who had remained silent, simply because he did not know what in the world to say.

"You know where that fine gentleman, Rolfe Estman, lives!" said Mr. Lacie—"That's right, put it into an envelope—it is safer."

"Yes, I know well enough where he lives. But what am I to do with this?"

"You are to see him, and let him know that the paper, which is a forged note on Bradshaw & Co., is in my possession; but under no circumstances are you to allow it to pass out of your hands into his. It is his work. It came to me in the way of trade, and in good faith on the part of the man from whom I got it, who received it from a merchant down in the city, who, in his turn, got it from Rolfe Estman himself.

I detected the forgery at a glance, and I have traced it to him. I wish him—for particular reasons—to know that I am the present holder of it," answered Mr. Lacie.

"Yes, yes! Dunder! but this is an ugly business! Tuyfel! a forgery! You can't afford to lose eighteen hundred dollars in this way sir!" said Moses Kugle, as he deposited the envelope in his wallet, and settled his dusty hat firmly down on his bald pate. "I may not find the man at home."

"That is likely. In that case, wait until he comes. Don't leave his room without seeing him," said Mr. Lacie, opening his desk and taking out a small compass. Alone once more, he settled himself at his table, and was soon deeply engrossed in the completion of a diagram of some improvement in machinery, which had occupied his thoughts for many days; and minutes and hours rolled unheeded by. He had just found the desideratum for which he had been so long ardently and laboriously seeking, and was in the act of illustrating the idea on his diagram, when his office door was burst open without ceremony, and Owny Travers, heated and panting, rushed in.

"I beg your honor's pardon, but I want you to come right away with me," said Owny, wiping his face.

"Come with you?" said Mr. Lacie, perplexed and fairly bewildered by this new interruption.

"Iss, sir. *Wirra!* but I'm at my wit's end entirely, an' the magistrate there waiting; an' the divil of a pagan dyin', I b'lieve; mebbe he'll be gone afore we get back to him. Don't wait to put them things away, sir! Here's your honor's cloak an' hat;" and before Mr. Lacie knew where he was, his cloak was thrown about him, and his hat crushed down, hind part before, over his eyes, by the impetuous Irishman, who ended by throwing his arm about him, and whirling him out of the door into the street in less time than it takes to write it. But having got into the open air, and recovered his breath and presence of mind together, he squared off and gave Owny a blow that made him stagger and prance backwards against the wall; but as soon as the stars got out of his eyes, he dashed —head foremost—at Mr. Lacie, and would have inflicted some damage on that gentleman's ribs with his hard skull, if he had not sprung aside, leaving Owny a free passage to the street, where he went spinning down into the mud.

"Tare an' 'ouns, sir, if it was anybody but yoursel' I wouldn't lave a whole bone in your skin!" he sputtered, as he wiped the mud from his face.

"By this and by that!—if it was anybody but you, you run-mad Irishman, I'd pummel you according to your deserts."

"You hot-headed ould Celt, I'd like to know if you was born in Holland or Jimaka?"

"Get up, you impudent rascal."

"Hard names back in your teeth, sir."

"What do you want with me? Perhaps you'll do me the favor to tell me now?"

"*Chorp an douil!* I don't care whether I do or not. It's nothin' to me, bedad, only the magistrate tould me to get some respictable gintleman that belonged to the same belief that the man does; an' faith, I didn't know anybody more of a haythen than your honor."

"What magistrate, and what man, in the name of common sense, are you talking about? If you don't tell me instantly, I'll leave you."

"Didn't I tell your honor that it was Squire Dobbin?—an' the man! sure who should it be but the one that's been sick a month past at my house? He's come to his mind, an' been roarin' for a magistrate for the last hour to take down his affydavit."

"And I should be glad to know, Owen Travers, why you couldn't have said that at first, instead of laying violent hands on me, and behaving like a madman? Come along with you! But I'm not going through the streets with you in that plight; you look like a mud-turtle," said Mr. Lacie, throwing his own cloak about Owny, "keep it on, sir, or I'll go back."

"Faix, sir, an' it's a good thing the mud caught my head instead of your honor's ribs," replied Owny, drawing the cloak around him with a sheepish air, "an' I beg your honor's pardon for my ill manners."

"I'll excuse you this time; you can't help being a torpedo, I suppose. You've got enough on your conscience, without the addition of my broken ribs," said Mr. Lacie, with a twinkling in his deep-set eyes, which was not lost on Owny Travers, who read in them a treaty of peace; and he speedily regained his good humor, and his usual careless rolicking mien, as they walked along together towards the street where he lived. He had not heard one word about Mr. Lacie's being there that morning, for the very good reason that the boy whom he had left in charge of the house, and to attend to the wants of his unwelcome guest, became so terrified by the outcries of the madman, that, without having taken time even to fasten the front door, he went away to his own home in a distant part of the city before he returned; and now, strangely enough, Mr. Lacie forgot to say one word to him about the letter from Cincinnati. Having come to the house, Owny opened the door for Mr. Lacie, and followed him in. The physician and a magistrate were sitting beside the sick man's bed. He was now sleeping heavily, having just exhausted himself with delirious struggles and ravings. Both gentlemen knew Mr. Lacie, and saluted him respectfully.

"How is he, sir?" he asked the doctor. "Has he been rational at all?"

"At short intervals he has, but the moment he begins to talk of what weighs on his mind, it arouses the wildest frenzy."

"Do you think, sir, under these circumstances, that any statement he may make would, in a legal point of view, stand good?" said Mr. Lacie, addressing the magistrate.

"If the intervals of reason were of longer duration, there's no doubt of it. It is very evident that he has committed some foul crime. In his present state, however, I suppose his incoherent sentences would scarcely criminate him."

"No. But hist! he is awakening."

"My life," said the miserable man, opening his blood-shot eyes, and speaking in a calm, composed voice, as if he were resuming the thread of an interrupted conversation, "has paid the penalty as much as if I had been hanged by the neck. But two victims is more than is needed for one murder; an' as I'm pretty nigh the grave, I'll spake out, for the good of them that's where I ought to be. I'm ready to be put upon my oath, your honor," he said, turning to the magistrate. "I'm in my sound mind this minute, but you must make haste." The magistrate, desiring the doctor and Mr. Lacie to witness the act, administered the solemn oath to the unfortunate wretch, and leaned forward to listen to his dread secret. "He was," he said, speaking slowly and distinctly, "a native of County Cork, and had been in this country five years. More than one year ago, he was working with many others on a western railroad. Among the laborers there was a party of *Far-downs*, and one day they got into a fight, and fought for three hours, with pick-axes, knives, stones, wedges, and anything that came handy. One minute the Orangemen got the victory, the next the *Far-downs*, and it was hard to tell how it would end. He was fighting hand to hand with the leader of the *Far-downs*, and finally succeeded in wresting his knife from him, after a hard struggle, and plunged it haphazard into him. He fell—he was dead. The rest, seeing their leader fall, ran off."

At this instant—while they were all listening in speechless horror to his recital, he suddenly broke off—a shuddering seized him—a wild cry burst from his lips—the mad fit was on him again, and if his ravings were to be credited, he saw the bloody image of his victim standing over him, and felt the fires of the lower world consuming him. Mr. Lacie and the magistrate withdrew, appalled, into the adjoining room, or rather shed, leaving the doctor alone, to study another phase of human misery.

"See here, my friend," said the magistrate, beckoning to Owny, "it is too bad for you to be burdened with such a guest. If he lives over tonight, he must be removed to the Almshouse."

"Oh vo! your honor, he's quite welcome to stay. I've got a sort of used to him now, an' I'd be lonesome after him," said Owny, remembering his promise to Eveleen.

"But he must be a tax on you. You are not rich."

"Faith an' I'm not—but he doesn't cost me much, I'm obleeged to your honor. A sup of water an' a drop of whisky betimes, is all he takes. No, no, let him die where God sent him."

"As you please, but it's a queer fancy; particularly as the man is a stranger to you."

"An' I hope I shall niver come across sich another while the breath's in my body, bedad!" said Owny, earnestly. "I hired a lad to 'tend him whilst I was abroad attending to my business—I'm a fruit-seller, your honor—but when I came home to-day, he had run off, scared out of his wits, I suppose."

The gentleman waited and watched patiently, until late in the afternoon, hoping that the frenzied man would have another interval of consciousness, but a dreary madness seemed to have settled on him, which found vent in horrible outcries and curses. The physician thought there was but little hope of his ever being able to complete the confession of guilt he had begun; and Mr. Lacie, after telling Owny Travers that he should send a hospital nurse to relieve him, went away, back to the factory, taking his dinner at an eating-house, on the way—and when he got once more securely in, he doubled locked the door, put up the ponderous iron bar, and went into his office, where he bolted himself in, and with a feeling of security, threw himself, weary, and almost bewildered by the events of the day, into his arm chair, where we shall leave him.

Eveleen's position was not an agreeable one. In fact—in consequence of what had happened—every act of her daily life connected with those around her, would hereafter be a sacrifice to her inclinations, and contrary to the instincts of her proud nature. Indignation and contempt were the feelings which the injury sought to be inflicted on her by Magdalene Estman and Mrs. Hunter naturally excited; and the more deliberately she reflected on their unjust and unprovoked emnity, and the unmanly, cowardly course of Rolfe Estman, the lower they sank in her esteem, and the more keenly did her resentment become enkindled; for, as we have elsewhere intimated, Eveleen, although possessing many rare and noble traits, was not a saint. But she knew full well, that she, as a Christian, must not indulge in such feelings; that she must be reconciled with her enemies before she could approach the Sacrament of the Altar; that her prayer "to be forgiven as she forgave others," would, in her present state of feeling, be not only a mockery, but the invoking of a curse on her own soul. It was her first conflict, and when she knelt down, after midnight, to her regular devotions, her mind was so fevered and distracted by the demon of unforgiveness which possessed it, that the words died on her lips. "Lord God!" she at length exclaimed, "I cannot of *myself* forgive them. I desire to do so, but it seems impossible. I dare not approach Thee while my soul is clouded by this implacable anger. Thou wilt turn Thy face away from me. I have lost Thy grace. I am in mortal sin. I am miserable. Unless I forgive, I know I can never be forgiven. Unless I am merciful, I can expect no mercy. I know all this. I cannot plead ignorance, and yet how can I forgive? It would be hypocrisy to say it with my lips, when a bitter resentment lurked in my heart. Oh, miserable one that I am, who shall deliver me?" Sleeping or waking, through the long winter night, rest did not visit her pillow, and when she arose in the morning, unrefreshed and feverish, the first thought that presented itself to her mind was flight from a house that had always been simply tolerated as a temporary abiding place, but never regarded as a home, and which had now become hateful to her, so hateful that the bare idea of living in it made her heart quail.

The breakfast bell rang, and she went down, armed in all the panoply of pride, to the breakfast table. Mrs. Hunter was nervous, but polite and attentive. Magdalene Estman pretended to be looking over the paper when Eveleen entered, and did not raise her eyes towards her; and during the meal she conversed with Mrs. Hunter on indifferent topics, in that low, silvery voice of hers, with as much *nonchalance* as if

Eveleen had been a myth, or a lay figure—in short, she ignored her presence, with an affectation of unconcern which was galling and exasperating to her high spirit.

Mr. Lacie called to see her after breakfast, and she directed the servant to invite him up into her sitting-room.

"I am very glad to see you, sir," she said, shaking the cushion of the *fauteuil* which she had rolled around to the fire for him.

"You look glad! Why, child, you look like a martyr. Have they been wronging you again?"

"No, sir. But I did not rest well last night."

"So—I didn't think it was in you to mope because two silly women had nothing better to do than to botch up a miserable lie about you."

"It is a sad thing, sir, to be obliged to lose respect for people whom I have esteemed, and what is worse, feel as if I could never forgive them, no matter how much I try."

"Don't, then—they are not worthy of forgiveness."

"That is the way the heathen do, sir, and I— it is true an unworthy one—am a Christian."

"I know nothing about it," said Mr. Lacie, with a puzzled look. "I came to tell you something which I thought would please you. I have, out on the edge of the town, a small, comfortable house, and if you choose, you can put the poor woman whom you have been assisting into it, and her boy you can send to me. I'm in want of a messenger lad at the factory, and he can have the place."

"Thank you, dear uncle," said Eveleen, lifting his hand to her lips, and then caressing it in both her own. "This will be a most pleasant change for poor Martha Brown. I know she will be extremely grateful on the boy's account, for it was only the last time I saw her that she said how easy it would make her if her son could get a place where he'd be able to learn some respectable business. But she's very poor, sir—I fear the rent will be above her means."

"Give yourself no trouble about that. She can pay the same rent she pays in Raynor's Court, and I'll turn it over to you to clothe the lad, and pay for his schooling in the summer."

"God bless you for this kindness, sir!—when shall I tell them?"

"You can send for her to come to you to-day, if you choose."

"I have no one to send, sir. Had I not better go?"

"No; you must not go there again. I'll send word to Owny Travers to come to you, and here is this letter—give it to him—then let him take a line from you to Martha Brown. If she sees fit to accept the offer of the house, you can let me know, and I'll send her the key, and number, and street, by Moses Kugle."

"Yes, sir."

"Niece," said Mr. Lacie, moving about uneasily in his chair, "I don't know how to put my words into fine phrases. I'm a rough, up-and-down man of business, and used to coming point blank to my aim. But I wouldn't harm or wound you, lass, for my right hand. The question I want to ask you is as much out of my element as if I were to undertake to make lace embroideries in my factory."

"Ask me what you will, dear uncle," replied Eveleen, while her heart beat faster.

"Perhaps, after what passed between us yesterday, I ought to be silent on the subject; but I have reasons, child—something has happened, which makes me anxious to know the truth. Has that lad, Jerry Garrity, ever made love to you?"

"Never, sir! nor have I any reason to suppose that he entertains any such sentiment towards me!" replied Eveleen, while a thrill of pain wrung her heart, and the crimson blood rushed impetuously up to her face.

"I'm glad to hear it, child. He's a noble, good lad—but it wouldn't do. These unequal matches end miserably. I should never consent to it. I am quite relieved to hear this. Now, good bye, and keep cheerful," said Mr. Lacie, going out.

"It is true," mused Eveleen, crushing back her tears. "There is nothing between us. It was a dream which must be forgotten—a memory that my woman's pride must blot out, a blossom that must wither, and go to dust, in the hidden corner of my heart, where it was born. But never in my life do I expect to meet with a being who, independent of name, birth, and circumstances, is so noble in every sense of the word. Like an invalid, my sick heart pines for home! It cannot grow strong here. It must have something about which it can entwine itself, and diffuse its feelings, or like a transplanted flower, plunged into strange earth, it will wither and perish. I *must* get back to Carrigmona. Oh, wild old sunlit hills," she cried, stretching out her arms, "I *must* come to ye. Oh, poor, noble, suffering friends, bearing your poverty and burdens as patiently as Jesus bore his Cross, I will come, and out of my abundance comfort ye. Deserted home! forsaken grave! ye shall no longer beckon for me through the dim distance: I will come, for it is not good for me to be here."

CHAPTER XII.

THREE LINKS.

Link First.

WHEN Owny Travers came that night Eveleen handed him a letter that Mr. Lacie had received from his agent in Cincinnati, and told him that although her uncle and herself were of the opinion its contents demanded some attention, they were far from placing implicit faith in the terrible suggestions it held forth.

"It might not be poor John after all," she said; "but there was no telling. There were a thousand snares by which a friendless stranger, in a strange land, might suffer shipwreck."

Owny put his hat on the floor, and having wiped his face with his handkerchief, opened the letter, and Eveleen saw, as he stood directly under the gaslight, that his face wore a sickly pallor, while his hands trembled so that she could distinctly hear the rustling of the paper. He had not as yet spoken. Her words had inspired him with a nameless dread; but as he read on, he marked his progress through the letter with exclamations of horror and incredulity.

"I wouldn't b'lieve it was Shaneen, Miss, if he was to write an' tell me so hissel';" he said, as he folded the letter up and gave it back to her. "There never was a Travers yet that need hould down his head with shame for what any of his folk did; an' if one of 'em could so far forget his ould honest name as to be guilty of what would hang him, he might hang for me, if it was my own born son. John indade! The quietest, best lad in all Wicklow, to come all the way across the ocean to get the devil in him! Oh, no! I wouldn't b'lieve it, if the Blessed Virgin hersel' was to appear this minit an' tell me so. An' don't you see, Miss Lacie, *asthore*, that this one's name is Hanlon?"

"It seems incredible also to me, Owny, knowing as I do the excellence of John Travers' character and principles. Perhaps Ally had better not see the letter?"

"Faith an' I don't see the good of showin' it to her, but there's no hidin' anything from her concernin' Shaneen, unless I tell her a lie straight up. *She's* got too much sense anyways to believe a word of it, an' mebbe it'ill give her an idee of what scrapes she'd be like to get into, if she starts on a wild-goose chase, lookin' afther John, betther than any argyment I could use."

"Perhaps you are right. But I have a dread, Owny—something heavy here"—said Eveleen, laying her hand on her heart, "which makes me wish that some one who knew John could go to Cincinnati. After all, the difference in the name is nothing, for it is easy to understand why he would wish to conceal his real name, if such a terrible thing had overtaken him."

"I'll hear what *she* says," replied Owny, looking down, and striving to master his emotion; but his lips quivered, and he again rubbed his handkerchief over his face, under pretence of wiping off the perspiration. "I'll take the letther to her, an' if she b'lieves one word of it I'll think she's gone crazed with her sorrows."

"Poor Ally!" said Eveleen, gently. "Give my love to her. Tell her that it is not because I have forgotten her that I have not been to see her. I have had my own cross to bear since I saw her. Now tell me, how is your patient?"

"*Bachal Essu!* I ha' need to be as patient as Job hissel'; to be dry-nurse, miss, to such an ungodly, overlooked sowl, and he an Orangeman to boot. He's just as crazy as a March hare, an' crazier, too," said Owny, running his hand distractedly over his head, until his hair stood on end. "I'm beat out intirely—but didn't you say, Miss Eveleen, *asthore*, that you had a bit of a note for Mistress Brown?"

"Yes. Here it is," replied Eveleen, taking the note from a small portfolio on the table. "Tell Ally to come with her; and listen, Owny —break the news in that letter very gently to her."

"May the heavens look down upon her in her sorrow! but she'll never b'lieve a word of it's bein' Shaneen. She knows him too well, bless you, to think he'd do anything mane or wicked. She may b'lieve he's dead or drownded, or imprisoned for debt, through sickness or misfortin'; but she'll never b'lieve *that*."

Ally had been extremely restless and anxious for the past few days, not having seen Miss Lacie or Owny Travers; and when he opened the door, she was just tying on her bonnet to go—attended by Jerry Garrity—in search of him. He kissed her pale cheek, and spoke cheerfully to her, saying that "between the sick man and his own business, he had been kept constantly busy, and that Miss Eveleen was not well, but sent her best love to her, and wanted her to come the next day with Mistress Brown to see her;" all of which was quite satisfactory to Ally Kane's gentle and guileless nature. But there was something he had not yet told her, and which she dreaded to ask him; and it was not until they were seated together in Mistress Brown's room, that she had almost in a whisper inquired "if a letter had come yet?"

"Faith an' there has, but it would ha' been as good for it to stay where it came from, for any satisfaction it gives anybody. Here it is, *caen buy deelish*, an' I know you'd as soon b'lieve black's white, as to believe one word of it," answered Owny, in as confident a tone as he could assume, handing it to her.

But Owny Travers was disappointed in his anticipations. Ally Kane opened the letter eagerly, and bowing her head over it, became absorbed in its contents; her lips did not move, but they saw that her face grew more wan, and distinctly heard the quick, sharp beating of her heart. At last she was through it, and she raised her eyes towards him with such a woe-begone, dreary look, that Owny got up and turned his back, under pretence of pouring out a drink of water at a table near him, and gulped it and his tears down together. But feeling that it was necessary to say something to break the painful silence, he sat down beside her, and taking her wasted hand in his, strove to comfort her in his homely fashion.

"Oh, *wirra!* it's no use, *alanna!* Cheer up, for I wish I may die, if I b'lieve a word about it's bein' him."

"He never did it; *that* I can readily believe. I'll say more. I'd pledge my life that Shaneen would rather die than be guilty of murder. But something tells me to go; there's somethin's a whisperin' that it's him, an' if it is, he's as innocent as I am. Shaneen was so gentle-hearted that he'd go out of his way any time to keep from putting his fut on a worm," said Ally, in a low, choking voice.

"The heavens look down upon ye, *savourneen deelish,*" said Owny, scarcely knowing how to dissuade her. "It's no use to fret and waste your strength on the credit of that letter, but wait until another one comes, an' then, if you still have the same opinion, I can do no better than to go with you."

"It might be too late," she said, in the same tone of voice, "too late. He's badly enough in want of comfort—poor John!—without a friend to cheer him in his prison. I must not delay. It's no use to seek to hould me back. I can go alone. Then—if—if I am wrong, I'll write you word."

Nor could all Owny's persuasions and arguments, or Mistress Brown's suggestions, move her purpose. In vain he urged upon her how impossible it was for him to go away for some days, and what a risk she was running in undertaking so long a journey alone, and sojourning in a large city without a friend or protector. Her faith and purpose were all unshaken. She told him that "Almighty God and the Blessed Virgin would guide and befriend her; there was nothing that could deter or frighten her from her aim, which was to find John and comfort him, if he was in distress." So Owny could do no more than promise to come to her in the morning, and buy her a ticket to Cincinnati, and see her safely in the cars. He promised also to see Mr. Lacie that night, and ask him to give her permission to take the letter with her, and also write a few lines to his agent, recommending her to his care; all of which the faithful and whole-souled fellow did.

"Write me word, *savourneen deelish*, as soon

as you find out about it," were his farewell words to her at the car-window, "an' if it's Shaneen, I'll come to you, if I hev to come through fire an' water."

She bowed her head—her heart was too full for speech—and the cars being in motion, she glided from his side like a pale phantom, even while he essayed to speak other words of cheer to her.

* * * * * * * *

Link Second.

For several days Eveleen's mind was anything but calm. Her natural defects interfered now so materially with the precepts of religion and its requirements, that she was miserable. She longed for the strengthening and revivifying sacraments, which, if they do not always console, teach the heart lessons of humble endurance; but she well knew that until she conquered the revolted and insubordinate passions of her nature, Christ could not reign in the kingdom of her soul. It required more heroism for her to forgive and be reconciled with her enemies, than she possessed, and she was on the point of yielding; but her Father in heaven, who had seen her struggles, and knew the purity and uprightness of her intentions, pitied her, and by His providence led the way to what she had in her inmost heart desired.

One night late, as she sat alone in her room, reading and thinking alternately, she fancied she heard a moan. She laid down her book and listened. Another and another followed in quick succession, as if some one was in great pain. She went to her door, and opening it softly, stepped out, and heard the sound repeated more distinctly. It proceeded from Magdalene Estman's bed room.

"My God! she is suffering, perhaps dying," exclaimed the generous girl, forgetting all her injuries. She snatched up a light, and hurried across the passage. She paused an instant at the door, and heard her muttering and moaning bitterly; she opened it gently, and stepping in, walked lightly across the floor to Magdalene's bedside, and found her moving restlessly, while her long black hair, unbound and dishevelled, lay scattered over the pillow, or coiled up like glossy serpents on her bosom. She tossed her arms to and fro, while her cheeks glowed crimson.

Eveleen laid her cool hand gently on her forehead. It was burning. Looking around, she saw a flask of *eau de cologne* on the toilet table. She drenched a fine handkerchief with the cooling, aromatic water, and quickly returning, bathed the poor fevered face and parched hands. Suddenly she opened her eyes, and fixed them in a wild stare on Eveleen's face. So large and bright did they look, so dark and glowing, so fierce and wandering, that she shrank away, fearful that in her delirium she might spring on her and tear her. But with a shrill laugh, and a violent shudder, she muttered some incoherent words and closed them, then turned on her side and seemed to sleep.

All resentment fled from Eveleen's breast, and she bitterly reproached herself for having entertained so unforgiving a spirit towards one who might never know a moment of consciousness again, or hear from her lips ere she passed away to the judgment, that all was forgiven and forgotten that had been painful and wounding in their past intercourse.

Sending up a fervent prayer to God that He would, in his infinite mercy, spare Magdalene's life, she hastened out of the room to awaken Mrs. Hunter, and send for medical aid.

* * * * * * * *

Link Third.

Traveling without rest day or night, Ally Kane arrived at Cincinnati in the first golden flush of the morning. Weak and weary, she felt as if she was the sport of some troubled dream, and that the splendid city which arose so grandly before her was but a part of the phantasmagoria of her vision.

Two gentlemen were conversing near her. One was pointing out to the other—who was a stranger in those parts—various objects of interest as they appeared to view.

"That is the city prison," he said, in a cheerful, hearty voice, as if he took great pride in the imposing edifice, which, notwithstanding it was erected for the accommodation of criminals who had offended against the laws and debased humanity to the last degree, was really an ornament and improvement to the city. "That is the city prison."

Ally heard him, and her dream was over. The words had aroused her to a full sense of the reality of her sorrow, and she looked out with strained and eager eyes towards the dark and massive structure, over which the sun was pouring as bright and golden a flood of light as that which sparkled on the restless river, and along the soft green meadows in the distance.

Oh, beneficent Sun! Like Him of whom thou art but the shadow, thou withholdest not thy genial and consoling brightness from those whom the world has scorned and forsaken. Like His infinite charity, thou shinest on all creatures, the just and the unjust alike; and while the guilty and conscience-stricken shun thee, and cower away into dark places, to hide from the brightness which contrasts with their pollution too strongly for endurance, the innocent and pure in heart—although the world's scorn may be on them, and the felon's chain about them—can still rejoice in thy splendor, and greet thy effulgence with thankfulness! Oh Eye of Day! What sights dost thou behold! what secrets dost thou share!

Let us follow in his path for a few moments,

that we may remember, as we gaze with happy hearts on his glory, those who need our prayers, our charity, and our love.

Through the rich damask curtains of a spacious room, which was crowded with all the luxuries and appliances of wealth, a proud young mother held her rosy babe up to catch the long, golden stream of sunshine that stole slanting over their pillows of down.

And the child crowed, and clapped its dimpled hands, and caught at the glittering rays, and the young mother laughed at its tiny efforts to grasp that which she knew all the time would elude it. And another was there whom the sun saw, but who was invisible to them. The babe in its dreams sometimes beheld this Being, but never with its mortal eyes. A tall and mighty ONE, of sweet and solemn aspect, he stood ever near the child, always watchful, and so ineffably bright in his aspect, that the sun's rays paled before it. There was but one thought of sorrow in its mighty heart—a little dark cloud it seemed, amidst a shoreless ocean of love. And that thought was of the time when the child's baptismal robe, now so stainless, would, notwithstanding his guardian care, become soiled by sin and wrinkled in all its fair proportions. For it was the Guardian Angel of the little earth-born, who from its birth to its death had been appointed by God to contend with the powers of evil for the possession of its soul. But the young mother and the crowing baby and the sunbeams sported together; and the countenance of the Celestial One grew sad, because that mother, in the midst of all her blessings, was thoughtless of God.

Not far off, on the bare floor of a comfortless garret, a woman who had once been innocent and fair, crouched on the floor. Her garments were threadbare, and her shoes were ragged. Long nut-brown hair fell rippling over her shoulders to the floor. On a broken chair before her lay two small pieces of gold, upon which her swollen eyes rested with a look of loathing. "Outcast," she murmured. "Without hope. Scorned for the poverty which the world refused to relieve. Scorned for the sin to which its uncharitableness has driven me. Scorned by those who like myself have fallen from the level of pure womanhood, because in spite of my fall I cannot be *all* like them! Scorned by the virtuous, who press their robes close to their sides when they pass me, as if I were a leper! Whither shall I fly! I have sinned, and whither shall I fly for succor! Oh, my dead mother! Oh, my virtuous father! Oh, my little angel sister! whither shall I fly to hide me from my sin?—will GOD cast me off as the world has done?" Suddenly the sun flashed through the uncurtained window, and strewed its golden benison on the prostrate form of the Magdalene, while at the same moment the sweet and solemn tones of the Mass bell floated out from a distant steeple. She lifted her poor head and listened—she gazed around her at the strange brightness, and her eyes were heavy and swollen, and two tears rolled over the fever-spot that burned in her sunken cheeks.

"It was for such as we that He suffered," she murmured. "It seems to me that I once heard He came to call sinners, and not the just, to repentance. I will arise and go to my Father—this gold will I cast into the street, hoping that some starving child or overworked woman may find it. I am fainting with hunger, but rather would I swallow molten lead than food purchased with the wages of sin. I cannot perish forever. All else I can endure but *that* thought. No! no! I cannot perish. I will go and humble myself; I will acknowledge my sin, and seek refuge among the penitents of yonder asylum. Anything but sin and eternal death." And the sun beheld a fair and solemn angel with a serene and uplifted face, issue from the air, and stand beside her. His raiment was white and shining, and his heart made loud music in heaven as it throbbed with joy at the return of this prodigal child whom he had been watching, and following, and contending for, from the hour of her birth. Tenderly he raised her up, and placed his strong arm about her, lest she might strike her foot against a stone, as she entered on the rugged way of repentance. And the sun rejoiced with the angel, and gave glory to God.

Through a window of the Cathedral sanctuary, upon which was delineated the martyrdom of St. Stephen, the sunbeams crept reverently in. There was incense in the air and the perfume of flowers. There was a marble altar, golden candelabras, and lighted tapers. And amidst it all was a DIVINE PRESENCE, and this presence was surrounded by an innumerable company of adoring cherubs, angels and glorified spirits, who, like those in heaven, cried incessantly, "Holy! holy! holy! is the Lord God of Sabaoth! Worthy of all honor, might and benediction is the Lamb that was slain!" To those men and women who come hither, bringing with them the grossness and imperfections of their human nature, this sight of ineffable glory was invisible—these solemn jubilates unheard. Some thought, as they adored, that the air over the tabernacle brightened and stirred as they gazed, and fancied they heard strange harmonies, indistinct and far away, as the deep silence throbbed like the soft waves of a ceaseless tide upon their ears. But although it was not given to them to behold the wondrous spectacle, because their boon was simply to believe, they received with this Faith a gift far more great and royal than the vision of angels would have been, which was no less than that DIVINE PRESENCE, as their food and their guest. Adored in heaven by seraphim and all the celestial company, adored on earth by angels and men, they received it, and it refreshed their souls as they journeyed towards judgment. The priest now enters, clothed in white vestments and glittering stole, to celebrate the holy mysteries. Creeping and slanting along, the sunbeams rested for an instant on the dark and sorrowful picture of Calvary behind the altar; kissed reverently the thorn-crowned head of Jesus, and quivered silently away.

And now, as Ally Kane began her search for Mr. Lacie's agent, the golden light is bursting into a prison cell. The casement was open high up near the ceiling, and a beneficent breath of air stole in with it. There was a small iron bedstead in the corner, which, with a table, a stove and a chair, completed the furnishing of the cell. The walls were of rough, white-washed stone. Near the window, under a wooden crucifix which hung against the wall, there was a picture, rudely executed and colored, but astonishingly bold and truthful in its outlines. It represented Jesus on His way to be crucified. He had fallen, bruised and fainting under His heavy burden, on the rugged road; and His enemies, fearing that he would die ere their vengeance was consummated, had seized on a stranger—one Simon, a Cyrenean—who was passing that way, and laid the heavy cross on his shoulders, compelling him to bear it.

Greatly honored though Simon was in bearing the burden of his Lord, he knew it not then, and his nature no doubt revolted against it; but after three hours of wondrous gloom, during which the earth seemed moved by some profound tribulation, and the sun shrouded its light, and all nature shuddered in affright, the maltreated stranger understood the whole mystery. The picture suggested these thoughts to whoever gazed upon it.

In the midst of the cell a man whose feet were manacled sat leaning his head on his arm, which rested on the table before him, and seemed to sleep. It was evident that his bed had been untouched all night. A plain black rosary had slipped from his fingers, and lay on the floor. He was dreaming, although not asleep, of wrecked happiness and vanished hopes. His eyes were sunken, and his pale cheeks wasted and wrinkled, although he was in the early prime of manhood, and must before his fall have been strong in hope, and in all the higher attributes of his kind. But he was now only the pale phantom of his own past, standing alone with his ignominy on the verge of that dark and unknown land, whither the judgments of man, enforced by the exactions of an inexorable law, had driven him. In two short weeks he was to die—to be hung by the neck until he was dead! Without ruth, the halter would tighten its deadly coil around that throat which had, only a few short years ago, been encircled by the arms of a virtuous mother and a betrothed bride. But he stirs. Suddenly he clasps his hands over his heart, which has been wrung by a cruel pain.

It passes away; and he stands upright, with the sun-rays slanting down on his head. He looks around with a dreary, anguished expression, and walks towards the window, clanking his chains. And beside him, calm, glorious and solemn, with a celestial pity brooding over his majestic countenance, walks another of those invisible sons of God, whom He has appointed to guard the souls of men. He had followed him from his birth to the present time, and now waited patiently for the end—which was near at hand—to convey the soul of that poor prisoner to the regions of eternal life. The sun saw this, and again quivered with joy because GOD was so compassionate.

Climbing on a chair, the prisoner stood gazing out into the distance; then, with a bitter sigh, turned away, for the fragrant breeze, the far-off blue heavens, and the sunshine, reminded him of his early days, of his mother, and his home.

"They will never know it," he murmured; "thank God, they will never know it." He paused before the picture we have described. The sunshine was on it, and it seemed to speak to his soul as it had never done before. "They put the cross of Jesus on the man's shoulders," he murmured; "am I—like that man—bearing His cross?" And he stood pondering the question, until a sweet and devout expression settled on his wasted features. In that moment he felt that his sufferings were united with those of

Jesus—his desolation, his unjust sentence, his ignominy and death; and he bowed his head with submission to what had, and what was yet to befall him.

Lovingly might the sun linger in that dreary cell; for rarely in its journey over the earth does it shine on one who, innocent of all crime, bears the unjust judgments of man, even unto death, in such a spirit of submission.

But the day waned, and the twilight was just beginning to purple the heavens. In that dreary cell the shadows lay heavy, and there was no sound of life, except a low, irregular breathing. Its occupant, wearied out by a night of unrest, had thrown himself on his bed and fallen into a deep sleep. There had been much to try him that day. Many persons, inspired by no higher feeling than a morbid curiosity, had intruded themselves on him, and stung his sensitive soul by questions and observations bearing on his case, with as merciless an indifference as if he were already dead, or as if his ignominious sentence had crushed out before death all the feelings of humanity from his living heart.

Reporters for various journals had been sketching down every word that fell from his lips, and taking note of every look, and movement, and expression, for the benefit of the public. Reverend teachers had been there, urging him to think of his soul—and abandon his old and precious faith, which, they assured him, was idolatrous, and would damn him. They besought him to confess his crime, and rebuked his sin with long and solemn faces, as the friends of innocent Job did: and so, wearied out, sick and feverish with excitement, he had fallen asleep to forget it in peaceful dreams.

The door opened softly, and a priest, preceded by the turnkey with a light, came in. They both stepped quietly when they saw that he was sleeping, and the turnkey put the lamp down and went out, while the man of God, full of tender compassion, knelt beside the bed to pray for him; for he knew that all earthly hope of succor must be abandoned, and that he must die. And yet, as he gazed on his wasted features, on the hectic glow that burnt on his cheeks, and listened to the violent irregular throbbing of his heart, he hoped that God would call him to Himself ere the day of ordeal came.

That very day the holy man had plead with the Governor of the State until his voice grew husky, for a commutation of the prisoner's sentence; and when that was sternly refused, he still plead for a reprieve, on the ground that he had been condemned purely on circumstantial evidence, and that by a short delay something might come to light—in the providence of God —to establish his innocence.

But the Governor was inexorable. He had, he said, "extended the executive clemency already too often, and not in one instance to a worthy object. He had only let loose on the world hardened criminals, who abused their regained liberty by making war against the laws and society, and using their experience only to elude vigilantly all legal restraints. He felt responsible as to the manner in which he discharged the functions of his office, to Almighty God, whose justice punished the wicked as well as rewarded the good."

As a Christian priest, he appealed to him to consider how infinitely more mercifully the condemned man had been dealt with in being fairly tried, and allowed time for repentance, than the poor wretch whom his knife had sent, with all his transgressions on his head, to the judgment.

"But he is innocent—on my life he is innocent!" urged the priest.

"Furnish legal proof that he is so, and he shall be free to-day," replied the Governor. "Without that, he must die at the appointed time. You will now be good enough to excuse me, for I have pressing business to attend to."

The minister of God could say no more. Legal proof of his innocence was wanting, and he went away with a heavy heart to the prison, where he was allowed entrance at all times.

As he passed in, he saw the drooping form of a woman leaning against the door. Her face was veiled. He paused a moment, desiring to say some little word of consolation to her, when she suddenly fell at his feet, and besought him to gain her admission to the cell of the man who was condemned to die.

"I have come a long way, your reverence, to look at him, for there's much rayson to fear he's one that's very near and dear to my heart. For the love of Jesus, take me in."

"Sit down, my poor child," he said, gently. "I will come to you presently. It is past the hour, but I may, perhaps, be able to gain you admittance. But could you not wait till to morrow?"

"Oh, sir, the heart is sore in my body, and I b'lieve it would break if I can't see him to night. Oh, sir, for the love of the Mother of Sorrows, let me in," she cried, bathing his hand with her tears. "I don't know that he's the one I'm seekin'; I only want to see, because my heart's breakin' with the fear that it is. If it is not him, I will come right away."

"Wait here, my child, and be of good courage," said the priest, leading her gently to a chair, "until I come."

He then went in and told the gaoler that there was a friend or relative, mayhap the wife of the condemned, without, beseeching admittance, and he hoped he would grant it.

The man was accustomed to those things— they were a part of his life, and did not move him—but he had learned to respect the good priest, and felt a kind of admiration for his prisoner, whose conduct throughout had been re spectable, patient and gentle; and he thought it would be a favorable opportunity to show his appreciation of it by granting this favor, even though it might involve him in some risk. So he told the Father to go up, and if it was possible to admit the stranger for a few moments, he would fetch her. Then, remembering there was no light in the cell, he lit the lamp that belonged to it, and went up with him.

When he returned, he went out to the woman, and invited her into his comfortable room, then left her, under pretense of consulting some one about admitting her, for he wished to impress on her mind that if the favor was granted at all, it was a very great one.

While the priest, pale and wearied with the emotion he had undergone that day, more than the physical fatigue, remained in prayer beside the condemned man, over whose face a strange smile was flitting, which made it beautiful, he paused in his devotions to watch him, for he knew, and thanked God, that he was having the comfort of happy dreams.

He was dreaming of home. He was there. Murmured words spoken low and joyously tell his vision. "Ah, my *colleen bawn*, Ally *asthore;* God be thanked, I am back again! The waters of the Lough are as bright and golden as the hair of *mavourneen*. Kiss me again, *mahair avourneen*, and lay your arm about your boy, my fatner; may the heavens bend down their glory on ye. * * * * There's my boat. For the sake of happy ould times, Ally *machree*, let us take a sail round by St.———" But the words died away in a troubled moan, and his hands closed over his heart. Tears were dripping like raindrops over the good *soggarth's* face.

The door opened at this moment, and admitted the woman.

With swift noiseless steps she glided to the foot of the bed, and looked down on the sleeper. She threw up her arms with a wild gesture when she saw him, clasping and wringing her hands together, and by a strong effort kept back the cry that was bursting up from her heart.

It was he whom she sought!

She laid off her bonnet and shawl, and the good priest saw a face of rare and sweet beauty, but so white and marble-like, that it looked as the face of the dead.

"It is he, sir," she whispered, as she knelt beside the sleeper; "it is my own love I've searched for so long." She lifted his hand gently, and folding hers over it, laid her head on his pillow, as if, now that she had found him, she was content to die.

Presently he awoke. Bewildered, and almost thinking that he still dreamed, his eyes rested on the golden hair that had fallen like a veil over that fair face, resting so near his own—he felt his hand clasped in a tender hold; he looked from her to the priest, then around at the dreary walls of his cell, and moved his feet, to see if the chain was still there; for his dream of home, and the reality of what he now beheld—so like were that form, and those golden tresses, to the dearest part of his vision—made it impossible to collect himself, and the thought presented itself that perhaps he had been ill, and that in the delirium of fever he had imagined all the terrible things that had happened. All would become clear presently, and he prayed God rather to die than have such dreams of delirium again.

Poor fellow! the fever that was sapping his life away gave greater vividness to the bewildering thought, and he smoothed gently the pale golden hair that lay in such profusion over his pillow.

"Be calm, John," whispered the priest, who rightly thought his mind was slightly wandering. "This is a friend, who says she has been seeking you a long time. Compose yourself, my son."

"Why does she not speak, my father? Is she dead?"

"No, no, of course not," said the priest, rising. "I will lift her up—perhaps she is overcome by weakness—there!"

"It is my love, my *caen buy deelish!*" he shrieked, as the priest raised her up. "I knew she would find me. I knew I should see her again. But she's dead! The sight of me in this place has killed her, and well it might; but oh!

my Ally, my wife, I am innocent—I am innocent before God." All the time he was caressing her, and holding her inanimate form to his bosom—for she had fainted.

The gaoler came in at the moment, to say that the prison doors must be closed for the night. John Travers—for it was he—grew suddenly calm. "Yes, my father, take her away, and do not let her come again—it will kill her, and make my trial more bitter. She was my promised wife. One more embrace, one more farewell, my darlin', then farewell forever." He laid his cheek on hers, and kissed her white lips; then, straining her in a long embrace, he laid her tenderly in the arms of the gaoler, who said he would place her under the care of his wife.

"Oh, my Father," said the broken-hearted young man, "do not abandon her. Stay by her until she recovers, go with her to her home, wherever that may be, in this great and cruel city. Console her and hear her sad history, and bring me news of—my—old father—and mother," here he broke down and burst into a passion of tears. The priest put his arm about him and kissed his cheek—he could not speak—and led him to his bed, where he sunk back exhausted on his pillow, whispering, "She must not come again!"

CHAPTER XIII.

THE BOW IN THE CLOUDS.

THE physician who was called in to administer relief to Magdalene Estman pronounced her extremely ill, and held out but a faint hope of her recovery.

"Her brain was seriously affected," he said, "and the crisis might or might not be favorable; it was impossible for him to say. It was absolutely necessary, however, for her to be perfectly quiet, and have her medicines regularly administered.

Mrs. Hunter's nerves and occupations together left her but little time to attend to the suffering girl; and beyond fluttering in and out a dozen times a day, to make a show of anxiety, deplored that Miss Estman had no female relative or friend on whom she could call in the emergency, and protest that she must sit up at night to nurse her—which she never did—she accomplished nothing. So day and night, inspired by charity, and urged by what now seemed an unavailing regret, Eveleen kept watch beside the unconscious Magdalene, cooled the fever of her brow by aromatic applications, and faithfully administered the nauseous medicines, on the action of which, the physician had declared, her life depended. And in the silence of that darkened room, how bitterly she reproached herself for having withheld her forgiveness until, humanly speaking, it might be too late. "Oh," thought Eveleen over and over again, "if I could only make her understand how, from the bottom of my heart, I forgive her, how thankful I should be! I am glad, at least, that I can serve her. I am glad there is no one to come in and usurp my place beside her." It was too true. There was no one on whom the sufferer had the least claim. Her friends were worldlings who, when they heard of her illness, said what is proper and usual on such occasions, and went on their way careless,—and forgetful at last of her existence, Mrs. Hunter sent a message to Rolfe Estman's chambers, to inform him of his cousin's illness, but the landlady wrote her a line in return, saying that "Mr. Estman had sailed the day before for California."

Three days and nights Eveleen had never left the sick room. She caught a few short intervals of sleep now and then, which, with her deep anxiety, prevented her feeling any prostrating degree of fatigue. It was near midnight of the third day, and no change had taken place in the condition of the sufferer. A dumb woe seemed to brood over the torpor that had fallen upon her, which imparted to her countenance an aspect of such hopeless sadness that Eveleen's heart was moved to the tenderest pity—and she longed for the power to penetrate that heavy slumber, which seemed to have locked her senses in oblivion. But it could not be, and with all the torture of her self-reproaches, and her deep concern for that neglected soul, which, for all she knew to the contrary, might be unprepared and unabsolved, on the threshold of judgment, at that moment; with hopes and fears alternating in quick succession, and a restless desire for the slightest favorable change, she was powerless, and could do nothing but pray and be patient. "How do I know," she thought, as she knelt by the side of the unconscious girl, holding her hot hand in a gentle grasp, "how do I know through what drear and terrible experiences her soul is passing? Her senses are not her soul. Alas, poor Magdalene! how can I tell but that a bitterness of woe, such as the human mind cannot conceive, is at this instant oppressing and crushing your affrighted spirit? How naked it is left now, that the near approach of Eternity has stripped it of the flattering unction of the vain appearances of a religious life! How sternly and solemnly, like accusing angels, must arise the neglected sacraments before you! Oh, terrible, poor Magdalene, must be the anguish that, like a bitter flood, rolls over you! Oh, that you could speak, and make known your needs! Oh, that God may deliver you from the desolation that encompasses you, and give you the grace of true contrition!"

If she had been her dearest friend, the charity of Eveleen could not have been more deeply moved in her behalf; if she had been a dear sister, whom by some act she had injured, she could not have plead more earnestly with heaven than she did, to grant her an opportunity of making her peace with her. Altogether, it was a sharp trial for the high-minded girl, an ordeal in which her heart was becoming purified, and learning one of the difficult lessons in the science of religion. As she knelt, keeping her eye fixed on the sorrowful face before her, which in those three days had grown so thin and wan, she thought she saw her lips moving, and leaning forward almost breathless to catch her meaning if she spoke, she heard her distinctly whisper, in deprecating accents, as if pleading for herself: —"Motherless, motherless. She died when I was a little babe." Then the whisper died away in sighs, and all became again silent. Eveleen bowed her head and wept. The whole story was told. An undisciplined nature had been left to its own guidance amongst the hidden quicksands of the world; it had drifted away, and almost suffered shipwreck; it must go down, and all on board perish, unless God in His dear mercy bade the storm subside, that threatened the frail bark with destruction. "I too, was left motherless," she mused, "but I had a tender, loving father, which she had not. I had the far-off memory of my angel mother, whose image was ever blended with that of Jesus and Mary, about whom she used to tell me; and I had, too, the prayers of the holy poor! And then, too, every nature differs! Some need more special graces than others; some need more guidance and bitter experience! My God! grant that the sharp experience I am now suffering may soften, for all time, the vindictiveness of my nature, and teach me never again to withhold forgiveness, even if it should not be accepted, or if it should be refused to me in return. Be merciful, oh Lord! to thy servant, and enter not into judgment with her." Thus musing and praying, the long, dreary night waned, and the dark hour that precedes the dawn came over the earth, with its death-like chill and silence. Eveleen, with a feeling of exhaustion, leaned her head on the side of the bed; her eyes involuntarily closed, and a heavy sleep stole over her wearied senses. How long she slept she did not know, but when she awoke she was lying on the sofa in her own room, and Mr. Lacie was sitting beside her.

"Where am I? Who brought me away? Magdalene will die unless she gets her medicine regularly," she exclaimed, starting up and looking with a bewildered glance around her.

"Keep quiet, niece, keep quiet," said Mr. Lacie, laying his hand on her arm, "there's no need for your presence in there."

"Is she dead?" asked Eveleen, growing very pale.

"Dead?—no, no! Thanks to your good nursing, the girl's better, and Martha Brown's with her. Did you think I intended to let you kill yourself? No! I came here this morning early, and when the servant went in to tell you, she found you on the floor. The other one had come to, and lay watching you, without being able to speak, or assist you in any way. Fortunately you needed no assistance, for you were only asleep. Then, after the flurry was all over, I heard all about your sitting up and nursing the young woman! Well, well, she's friendless, they say, and I suppose it is all right; only I won't submit to your doing more than your strength allows. No Lacie that I ever heard of was ever so base as to put his foot on the neck of a fallen foe. But she's better now, so keep quiet."

"Who says she's better, sir?"

"The doctor says so, and she says so herself."

"My God, I thank thee!" exclaimed Eveleen, clasping her hands. "I *must* go in, sir, I must, just for one moment."

"Eveleen Lacie, you are a fool! The woman's better, I say, and doesn't need you now or ever, any more. She's not worthy of so much anxiety on your part," said Mr. Lacie, much annoyed.

"Let me go, sir!" replied Eveleen, leaving him. "I *must* go. My peace of mind depends on going this moment. She may grow worse, and die."

"Good Lord!" said Mr. Lacie in a fretted tone, "they're like the wind. There's no understanding their crotchets. I suppose I must wait patiently until the sentimental interview is over. Wicked jade! I'd give her sentiment, if she was well, and I not a man."

When Eveleen entered the room, Martha Brown, whom Mr. Lacie had gone after himself, as soon as he heard how matters stood, was standing at a window, dropping some medicine in a wine-glass; and Magdalene, quiet and pale, lay exhausted on her pillow, with her long hands, listless and powerless, drooping on the coverlid, where her nurse had placed them. There was a dreamy look, softened and sad, in those large dark eyes, once so full of pride and fire, and when Eveleen, moving swiftly, came to her side, and leaning over, kissed her white lips, and whispered: "Thank God, my friend, you are better," the deeps of that haughty nature were broken up, and a flood of tears gushed from her eyes.

"Forgive me, Eveleen!" she whispered.

"As I hope to be forgiven, Magdalene, I do. Let the past be forgotten forever," said Eveleen, gathering her feeble hands together in her own; "oh, Magdalene! I have been wishing to say this to you ever since your illness. Thank God! it is said."

"Thank God," she whispered. "I have heard that but for you I must have died, and now I will tell you that it was the remorse for my cruel and ungrateful conduct to you that awoke me from the torpor of years. I saw myself, Eveleen, for the first time, in all the deformity of my hypocrisy and sin. But I was too proud to humble myself. The struggle was sharp, and ended in illness. Oh! Eveleen, I have no right to speak —I have no right to be credited, for I have been a great hypocrite; but I am thankful from the depths of my soul for being spared. I am most unworthy. Oh! Eveleen, is it true, that you forgive me?"

"From my inmost heart. Never doubt it, Magdalene," said Eveleen, stooping to kiss her forehead.

"Then, if a mortal whom I have injured can thus readily forgive me, surely my Creator, although I have outraged and insulted Him, will."

"Surely will He do so, Magdalene. He has promised it over and over again," replied Eveleen, while tears flowed over her cheeks.

"You know," she faltered, as she looked down with an humble expression, so unlike the proud Magdalene of other days that Eveleen could scarcely realize it was she, "you know there's but one course for me. I must see a priest without delay. I may die at any moment, for I feel strangely weak. Will you fetch one to me, Eveleen?"

"In a half hour Father Folliard shall be with you," promised Eveleen, "unless you have some other choice."

"The doctor said she must be kept very quiet, Miss Lacie," whispered Martha Brown, who had come to the bedside, and stood watching the interview with great anxiety. "You know, Miss, he said her life depended on being kept quiet, and said he should look to me to attend to his directions; so please excuse me for speaking."

"I am very much better. My mind is easier, nurse. But tell me, who sent her here, Eveleen?" whispered Magdalene.

"My uncle. But I must go, dear Magdalene, this moment. No offence, Mrs. Brown. You are right—she must be kept quiet;" replied Eveleen, full of a sweet and inexpressible joy, which made all the pains she had ever suffered, sink into insignificance. "Oh sweet reward!" she thought, "Lord, Thou leadest us by paths we know not of, and when Thy presence seems to have abandoned us, then it is nearest. I thank Thee for these trials whereby Thou hast tried me, and feel all unworthy of the blessed fruits they have borne." But Mrs. Brown was not so easily pacified, and having administered the medicine to her charge, she hastened out after Eveleen, and found her just at her own door.

"Don't go yourself, dear lady," she said, "you are worn out with loss of rest and fatigue—send some one else after Father Folliard. You need rest, and refreshment." But the good woman was not in the secret. She did not know the good work that Eveleen was about, or how she wished to perfect it to the end; and when she smiled to dispel her anxiety, and assured her that her advice was excellent, she went back to the sick room quite certain that Miss Lacie was too sensible not to follow it. Mr. Lacie was waiting impatiently for her return. He had rung for Nero, and ordered toast and coffee for her, which was brought up a minute or two after she came back, and of which she thankfully partook; then feeling refreshed and invigorated, she put on her hat and shawl, chatting all the while with her uncle, who evidently suspected her of being a little light-headed.

"Where in all the world are you going, niece?" he inquired.

"To walk a little way with you, sir. I need a mouthful of fresh air."

"The only sensible thing you've said to-day. But you need sleep more," he replied, putting on his hat.

"I'll take a good nap after I return," she answered. They walked together as far as Father Folliard's house, where Eveleen bade him "good day," and walked in.

"Humph! I thought there was some nonsense at the bottom of it," he muttered, giving the pavement a sharp rap with his stick. When he arrived at the factory he found a note on his desk from Jerry Garrity, stating that his grandmother had been knocked down in the street by a runaway horse, and was so severely injured that the medical men in attendance thought her life in extreme peril. "He wrote," he said, "to explain his absence from the factory, as he could not leave his grandmother, who became very much excited whenever she lost sight of him."

"It will be a good riddance for the lad, if she dies. He can never prosper with such a clog at his heels. But he's a noble fellow. He must not be hampered now," said Mr. Lacie, taking out his pocket-book. He wrote a few lines in pencil, and enclosing a twenty-dollar bill he sealed the envelope, directed it to Jerry Garrity, and calling one of his workmen, sent it off immediately to Raynor's Court. Then in the engrossing cares of his extensive and complicated business, Mr. Lacie forgot all the outer world, its cares, its joys and sorrows, except that now and then his thoughts wandered away to John Travers, and he determined as soon as the factory closed to walk down to Owny's house and make inquiries, not only relative to John and the visit of Ally Kane to Cincinnati, but also learn something of the mysterious stranger whom he had so long and generously entertained. It had now been one week since the poor girl set out on her sorrowful journey, and he thought surely by this time, tidings of some kind must have come from her. If he could only hear, he thought, that the condemned man in Cincinnati was *not* John Travers, he should feel quite satisfied, for somehow it had weighed on him more than he liked to own to himself. When Mr. Lacie got there he found Owny sitting on the door-sill, his elbows on his knees, and his face leaning on his hands, apparently lost in deep and perplexing thought, for according to his custom, whenever he was troubled or puzzled, he ran his hands every now and then distractedly through his grizzled hair.

"Hilloa, Travers, what ails you?" said Mr. Lacie, laying his hand on his shoulder.

"*Tare an' ouns*, but your honor gave me a start," he exclaimed, springing to his feet. "But I'm in luck to see you just now, sir, for I'm on the two horns of a dilemmy, that's almost banged my siven sinses away."

"What's the trouble? Any news from the girl?" asked Mr. Lacie, quickly.

"Not a sintence, your honor. I tould the poor thing when she went, that it was a wild-goose chase she was goin' afther; and not hearin' from her, I'm expectin' her back every day. No, it wasn't that, but *him*," said Owny, pointing with his thumb over his shoulder, behind him.

"Aye, bedad, he's alive an' kickin', and got his sinses back since yesterday. Faith! and he's *quite* enough now, and up and tould all he had to tell to Squire Dobbin to-day. And I feel sore puzzled about it, and don't know what in the world is movin' me, for your honor, as sure as

I'm a livin' man, I b'lieve that poor boy that's goin' to be hung, out yonder, is innocent of the murder he's goin' to be strung up for; and this fellow in here is the raal culprit. Faix! and I'm so intirely made up in my b'lief, that he's the murderer, I was jest thinkin' if I oughtn't to go right away, and try to save his life. Squire Dobbin has some such thought as well as meself, for he tould Doctor Grayson that he was goin' to write by to-night's mail. But that's not goin', your honor."

"You're right, Travers. But what does the man say?" asked Mr. Lacie, with deep interest.

"Faix! not much more than he tould before, only that his name is Hogan, and when he run from the police, the day they, the Corkonians and Fardowns got in a scrimmage on the railroad, he left his knife stickin' in the man's side. And he says that it was that knife that turned the case agin' the young fellow they took up; for the letter H—for Hogan, you know—was cut on the handle, and the other fellow's name is Hanlon, but nobody knowed the difference. You see, your honor, the poor boy, as innocent as may be, come along just after the rest run off, with the pollis in full chase, and seein' a man down, he goes up to see what he can do to help him, and there, bedad! the pollis finds him draggin' the dead man, that he thought was in a swound, to a spring near by; so they arrests him on the spot, and marches him, covered with dust and blood, to the nearest magistrate. It was no use for him to swear he was innocent, for he was caught on the spot, with the dead man's blood on his wristbands, an' his knife in the man's side; and so he was committed for trial. And all the time the trial was goin' on—the heavens look down upon us—the divil within, beggin' your honor's pardon, was hidin' and sulkin' in Cincinnati, where he staid it out, 'till the poor boy's condemned to death, and he as innocent as the child unborn. He says that he heard people say he was a dacint, likely lad, and had good edication, but he was so overjoyed—divil fetch him—at his own safety, that he niver thought 'til he was miles and miles away, how awful it was to have blood on his han', and let an innocent person suffer the pinalty of his crime. But he hadn't courage to give hissel' up, and he kept on and on, flying from his own conscience, until his money was gone, his clothes in rags, and his health destroyed. He was kilt up by favers and pains, and didn't know at all at all where he was goin', for his wits left him, till here he comes staggerin' to my dure, and falls headlong over my threshold. And that's the whole story, your honor."

Just then Doctor Grayson and the Sheriff came out of the house. They saluted Mr. Lacie, who asked the doctor how his patient was?

"He is sinking rapidly, sir. If he lives three days longer I shall be satisfied."

"Yes," added the Sheriff, "he is in the hands of a higher Law than that of man."

"I suppose some step has been taken to arrest the execution of that young fellow in Cincinnati?" said Mr. Lacie.

"Of course. Squire Dobbins wrote this afternoon. It is a sad comment, sir, on the admissibility of circumstantial evidence," replied the Sheriff.

"And no less than a bitter satire on that point of law which allows a man's innocence until he is proven guilty. How can circumstantial evidence afford legal proof of guilt I'd like to know? I hope Squire Dobbin's letter may not get there too late. Why not telegraph?"

"Oh, there's time enough! The execution—Hogan informs us—is not to take place for three weeks."

"In that case it *is* time enough. But it should be remembered that the evidence—at least as it regards dates—of a man who has been for weeks in a state of frenzy, may not be altogether reliable," said Mr. Lacie. "I hope, though, for the sake of justice and mercy, that his statement is correct."

Just then, a small boy, heated and tired, came up to the group, and holding out an envelope, touched his cap, and inquired if any of them could tell him where a man named Travers lived.

"My name is Owen Travers. What do you want?" said Owny.

"A telegraphic despatch for you, sir," replied the lad, handing it to him.

"For me, your honor?" said Owny, turning to Mr. Lacie, while every vestige of color forsook his face. "It's a mistake—but here's my name on it—*wirra!* but I'm afeard to open it. Take it, Misther Lacie, honey, and if—if—it's him—oh vo?"

"Twenty-five cents, sir," said the boy.

Owny tossed him the money, and he ran off. Mr. Lacie broke open the envelope, and while he glanced over it, Dr. Grayson and the Sheriff moved aside.

"What does it say, sir?" inquired Owny, who had been watching Mr. Lacie's compressed lips, and knitted brows.

"Come hither, Travers. Be a man. Don't speak or cry out, for there's no time for it. It is John Travers. He is to die this day week on the gallows, for the crime of the man whose life you have saved." But the shock was too unlooked for to be borne with fortitude, and poor Owny staggered forward, uttering a wild cry, and fell at Mr. Lacie's feet, as if some one had inflicted a mortal wound in some vital part. Dr. Grayson sprang to his assistance, and lifted him up, but he was quite insensible, the strong, brave, rough old man was stricken down like a weak woman by the blow. In a little while he recovered, but his limbs trembled, and he seemed to have lost the power of speech.

"Rouse you up, old friend. Owny, my old play-fellow! rouse up. John must be saved," said Mr. Lacie, grasping his hand. "There's time enough yet to prove his innocence and save him. You must go immediately and take the evening train west. To-morrow I will follow you."

"I will go with you, Mister Travers," said the Sheriff. "Here, drink this whiskey—you need it." Owen, still pale, and bewildered, drank what was offered him, and looked around him, as if just awakening from a dream. Then he arose to his feet, stretched out his arms, and shook himself, and finally covered his face with his hand and wept. No one interrupted him now, for although there were only men around him, men whose daily associations were calculated to indurate all natural softness, there was not a dry eye among them. They knew, too, that these tears would do him good.

"I must go," he said, at last. "There never was a Travers yet came to that. And to think your honor that I've been shelterin' an' killin' mysel' out-an' out, for the murderer of my own brother's son! Oh, vo! but it's too hard entirely that he's laid so low that I can't lay my hands on him, an' give him a blow that 'ud end his life; that I can't stan' up foreninst him, bate my two hard fists about his face 'till he's blind; hould me, sirs, for I feel somethin' risin' in me that makes me thirst for that man's blood—take me away, your honor! take me away"—cried poor Travers in wild excitement.

"Owen Travers," said Mr. Lacie, holding him off with his strong arm—"if the man was well and strong, before Heaven, I think I should do no wrong to let you loose on him. But he is fast going to his account, and will be judged by a more righteous tribunal than the one that condemned poor John on shallow circumstantial evidence. Be thankful that he came to you—be thankful that he was spared to tell the story of his guilt in time to save John's life. Let us waste no more time in angry, grievous words, or useless threats—but go—you cannot go too soon."

"Come, Mr. Travers," said the Sheriff, looking at his watch, "the cars leave in twenty minutes. I am going with you. Mr. Lacie, oblige me, sir, by calling at Squire Dobbins', and telling him what has happened, and where I have gone. There are two policemen within there, who have orders to keep strict guard over the prisoner, who is too ill to be removed."

"My carriage is here, I will drive you to the depot"—said Dr. Grayson. They thanked him and started, but Owny Travers, although he kept close to the Sheriff, such was the confusion of his mind, that he scarcely knew whither he was going, or for what purpose.

"Have you any money about you, Travers?" asked Mr. Lacie at the carriage door.

"Faix an' I haven't, your honor," said Owny with sudden recollection; "I put every pinny I had in the bank this mornin'."

"Take this, my good fellow," replied Mr. Lacie, placing a bank bill in his hand. "You can pay me when you come back. I shall follow you in the morning, and in all probability fetch my niece. That poor girl must need a friend."

"Thank your honor kindly—an' God bless you," said Owny in a more composed manner, as he grasped Mr. Lacie's hand. The carriage drove off, and in ten minutes from that time he was being whirled away as fast as steam could bear him, to the rescue of his young and innocent kinsman. We will not follow him through that dreary night, which seemed to the poor fellow as if it would never end, or depict the gusts of anguish that swept over his heart at intervals, as he pictured to himself all the bitterness and ignominy that had fallen around the life of the noble-hearted, high-minded son of his brother. Our duty calls us away just now to Raynor's Court, and we must leave him with his grief. You have not forgotten, patient reader, the note received by Mr. Lacie, informing him that the old crone, Mother Garrity, had been knocked down in the street by a runaway horse, and dangerously injured. It is to her bedside that our fidelity, as a chronicler of complicated events, constrains us to go. Her room is squalid and musty. The cobwebs hang in gray festoons from the damp, low ceiling, and cockchafers and snails make their way along the mildewed walls. The furniture is old and rickety. Her bed is of straw, and covered with quilted rags of every hue, picked up from the streets and gutters. Her window is stuffed with odds and ends of everything to exclude the air. The fire-place broken, and blackened with a half century of smoke and soot, is scarcely brightened by the handful of coals that gleam and flicker in the grate. A dim lamp sheds a fitful light over the squalid den. On the heap of straw and rags we have described, as the nightly resting-place of its occupant, lay the old crone, moaning, gasping, sleeping and screaming alternately. Beside her stood Jerry—the young artisan—watching and listening, in the hope that he might be able to relieve her. Suddenly—as he leaned over her—she muttered something which caused him to start back and grow deadly pale, then he bowed his ear closer to her lips, hoping to hear more of that which had raised a wild tumult in his heart. But she was silent, and in a few moments opened her eyes and fixed them with a fierce glare on him.

"Don't ye think, now, that I've got money hid away. That's what you're watchin' for! Begad, I don't own a shillin'. I don't know who'll bury me. I'm poor an' forsaken, an' the parish 'll have to do it."

"Don't be troubled about that, mother," said

the young man, gently. "You shall have decent burial. But, mother," he added, smoothing her yellow, claw-like hands, and his voice sounded low and solemn on the midnight, "you are old, and your hurts are very severe. I hope you may grow better, but I cannot tell. Should you not like to see a priest?"

"What have I to do wid a priest? No!—no! If God had saved my *caen buy deelish* from the wolf, an' she so innocent—heck! she was as pure as the hawthorn blossoms in May—it 'ud be different wid me. I want no priest."

"Who was your *caen buy deelish*, mother?"

"Ask your proud father!—heck, no! how should *you* have a father! My mind's wanderin'. Don't take account of what I say.— There's no money, remember *that*. No money. Only rags—only rags."

"I don't want money, mother," replied the young man, strangely moved. "All I want is to know something about myself. Who am I, and what am I? Tell me, mother, in the name of God—for the time may come in a few hours when you'll wish you had done so, and cannot. There's a mystery—I don't know what—just give me a clue—" and he knelt beside her.

"Ha! ha! You'd like to know, lad? Begad, honey, but you've got a proud stomach, and your low birth and poverty sets heavy on it. What would you give, now, to mate wid a Lacie? *You—you*," she repeated, with bitter scorn, "inate wid a race that never harmed a hair of a definceless woman—that never was known to destroy the virtue of a poor, innocent maiden. But it can niver be Jerry Garrity. Who should you be but my gran'son, Jerry?" she cried out, with a sharp leer.

"Let it all pass, mother," he said, while a hand of ice seemed to be grasping his heart. "I will not disturb you any more with questions about myself. I submit, in God's holy name, to my lot, and, with His assistance, will refer all my future to His divine will. But I must plead with you, mother, for your own soul. Let me fetch a priest!"

"If you bring a priest to me, begad! I'll spit on him!" she shrieked with a look of such implacable anger, that he drew back as if a flash of lightning had swept across his sight. Exhausted, she fell back on her filthy pillow, muttering and gasping. Presently all became still, and he knew by her breathing that she slept. Then he knelt to pray for her safe passage from time to eternity, for he well knew that on the very verge of time, God sometimes, in answer to prayer, vouchsafes a moment of grace, which the perishing soul responds to in sentiments of contrition so perfect that its salvation is secured at the eleventh hour. And until the gray dawn began to creep through the stained window-panes, he ceased not to plead for her. As the light became stronger, the young artisan saw but too plainly in the sunken visage and pinched features of the old crone, the signs of an inexorable and relentless hand. Then the sounds of life began to come in from the awakening city, and the whirl and turmoil of the busy day began in earnest in the streets and in the marts of trade. All heedless of the awful fact that a soul from their midst was being led by invisible messengers beyond that terrible mystery—Death—to be judged for eternal weal or woe, the busy sons of men pursued their aims: the lesson was nothing to them. What interest had they in common with an old beggar like Mother Garrity? Why should they pause to think for a single instant because such an one as she was about meeting the common fate of all? You have your answer, sir! *The common fate of all.* You could not have elucidated the problem better if you had tried all your life. But we have no time to moralize; we have already been led far beyond our limits.

Two or three old crones hobbled in to inquire after the sick woman, with whom they had enjoyed snuff and gossip together for so many years. They looked at her, shook their heads and mumbled to each other. She started from her fitful sleep, and in a fierce voice bade them begone. "They had come to rob her," she said; "but she had no money, nothing but rags."

"She's dyin' to all intints. She can't live over twelve o'clock," said one, without in the least noticing her words.

"Aye, if she do, she'll hould out 'till midnight," muttered the other. "Wouldn't you like a sup of nice hot *tay*, Mother Garrity?"

"Get away wid ye," replied the dying woman.

"Or a drap of whiskey, to put the life into you, honey?" persisted the old woman.

"Hev ye got it to gie' me? Didn't I tell ye I was poor? Go away! Begone! Jerry!" she screamed in a shrill voice, as if in sudden alarm.

"Can I help you, mother? Do you feel much worse?" he said, bending over her.

"Aye, boy—chokin'"

"Drink something warm. You have taken nothing since midnight. Here's the gruel: it is warm. Swallow a spoonful, mother."

"I can't swallow," she said, pushing his hand away. Hers was cold and damp.

"Mother," said the young man, with anguish in every feature. "Think of your soul; you are dying."

"I said my say," she said in slow, deliberate tones. "My lamb was destroyed; an' I don't hould to what you do. *I'm* no papist. But you're a fool, Jerry Garrity. You're a fool."

"Only see a priest, mother," he urged, "there's mercy to be had at the very last."

"No—no priest. It's growin' dark, Jerry. Push up the fire, lad."

"Oh, mother, it is death! Do not go away into eternal darkness. Let me fetch some one who will smooth the rough road for you—a priest of God—mother!"

"An' so, poor lad, you love me," she said, groping her hand towards him.

"Yes, mother. Who else had I to love?" said the young man in a broken voice.

"Bend your head down hether, lad, for my tongue grows thick. What's that droppin' warm on my face? Tears! Jerry Garrity, you are a fool; but I can't go away so. It's no use makin' the innocent suffer for the guilty. I done my worst to make ye evil minded an' bad, but it wasn't in ye. I'd like to ha' seen you hung. Never mind. It wasn't to be. Listen. When I die, whin the breath's clare gone from me—mind there's no money—look you under this bed. You'll find there a little woodin' box. *It is yours.* Take it and go away with it to Sir William Erle, of Carrigmona, on the shore of Lake Luggela, in county Wicklow, Ireland. Tell him that Hulda Bracken sent you, an' that she hated him to the last. I do what I do for the sake of you, that out of revenge to him I tried my best to ruin. But there's no money. Nothin' but the box. Remimber to show him the mark on your breast—them drops of blood stained into your flesh afore you were born, by rayson of a *frecht* your mother got. They haven't forgot it, I warrant ye. An' tell him I curse him," she screamed, tearing off her dingy cap, and with a supernatural effort raising herself up, while her white matted hair hung in wild elf locks about her ashen face, "I curse him livin' an' I curse him dyin', an' if so be I can, I'll curse him in my grave."

The young artisan, sick with horror, and the strange agitation of her words, was speechless, but he laid his arm gently about her, and eased her down on her pillow.

"Are you there?" she asked, in a low, faint voice.

"I am close beside you, mother. I will never leave you. Say one little prayer, mother—only say, 'Lord be merciful to me a sinner.'"

"Lord," she gasped, slowly, "show no mercy forevermore to William Erle—the black-hearted sinner. that destroyed the lamb of my bosom. Curse——" The curse died away in unintelligible mutterings and gibberings; and from that hour until midnight, when her soul sped from her body on its fearful errand into eternity, she uttered no word, and gave no sign. Then the young artisan folded her hands on her bosom, and covered her face with the sheet; after which he groped under the bed for the box, which having found—it being the only one there—he covered it with his cloak, and went to engage some person to perform the last human offices for the dead, after which he ran up to his own room under the eaves, to search into the secrets it contained, and solve the mystery which for years past had kept his heart in a wild flurry of hope and expectation. What he found we will tell by and by. But the bow grew brighter on the cloud, and he received it as a covenant of peace and promise.

CHAPTER XIV.

ALMOST PERISHED HOPES.

THE gaoler, holding Ally Kane in his strong arms as if she had been an infant, bore her swiftly through the dark corridors and down the winding stone stairs, out across a court to his own house, which, although it stood apart from the prison, was still within the enclosure of its high, massive walls, where his wife and children resided. The faithful priest, Father Grandfiel, followed close after, determined to redeem his promise to poor John: "To stay by her until she recovered, and attend her to her home, wherever that might be, in this great and cruel city." The gaoler's wife, with kindly instincts beaming in every feature of her coarse but not unhandsome face, received the sorrow-stricken and insensible stranger with unhesitating welcome; and, while she was making her comfortable in her own neat bed, questioned her husband in an undertone as to her history; but his duties were not yet over in the prison, and after briefly telling her all that he knew, he hurried away to attend to them.

"Poor young creetur!" she said, smoothing back the long golden curls from Ally Kane's face, which was as white and silent as marble.

"She's mighty purty. I swanny, if it aint a shame for the like of this to happen her. Here you, Mister,—I don't know your name, mine's Pottles—give me the hartshorn off that ar shelf. I'm afeard she's dead."

"She's not dead," replied Father Grandfiel, handing her the bottle of hartshorn, and laying his fingers on Ally's wrist. "There's life here, but it throbs very faintly. Poor child! Our Lord has given you a heavy cross to bear."

"That's what staggers me clean out," said Mrs. Pottles, rubbing the cold hand she held, and applying the hartshorn to the nostrils from whence not the faintest breath seemed to issue. "Swanny! but it's a strange way for a boss to be showing his love to his 'prentices, to be all the time bangin' and grindin' of 'em. There! I thought she gin a kind of grunt, but she didn't. Oh! my! my! the troubles of this world!"

"She will be better presently, my friend," said the patient Father. "You ought not to be surprised at the way God has of dealing with his creatures. The trials of this life purify the soul, even as fire purifies gold, and the grinding of the rough heavy mill-wheels purifies wheat."

"We ain't nither gold *nor* wheat, so that argyment goes for nothin'," replied Mistress Pottles, whose ignorance of such matters was evidently of that description which the Church defines as invincible. "Hold on thar, Mister: how's her pulse now?"

"Something stronger," replied Father Grandfiel, looking down on the still white face of the poor girl with a feeling of almost womanly pity.

"I wonder if she's got a mother," said Mrs. Pottles, as she gently smoothed poor Ally's shining tresses. "She's the born image, as she lays there, of my little Nan that died. I swanny! if it didn't e'en a'most kill me, when they nailed the poor little creature up in her coffin, and she lookin' for all the world like she was 'sleep, with her yellow curls about her face, and a pleasant smile on her little lips. Do you reckon the little ones grow any arter they go 'way from us, Mister? I hope they don't, anyways, for somehow I think I'd like to find her a baby. I shouldn't know her, if she growed," talked the good woman, while she rubbed away at Ally Kane's wrists, temples and heart, careless whether she was answered or not. Father Grandfiel—who at any other time would have been amused at her oddities—was well satisfied to let her go on without interruption, for his heart was fully occupied with the sorrows of the two friendless creatures whom Providence had so strangely thrown on his spiritual care; and while he lifted his soul in strong pleadings for them to the Throne of Mercy, the terrible woe that was impending over them was ever present, like a temptation, to shake his faith. "But, at least, even though all human comfort must forever stand aloof from them," he thought, "their

Father in Heaven may still send the angels of His love to minister to them, and give them strength to drink of that cup which refuses to pass away."

"She's better, the poor dear," said Mrs. Pottles, as Ally opened her eyes and looked with a dreamy expression around her. "Here honey, drink these few drops of wine." She swallowed the wine and tried in vain to remember where she was, or how she had come into that strange place.

"God help you, my poor child. I'm heartily glad that you are better," said the priest, making the sign of the cross over her head. But, like one who has been dreaming of things which seem so real, that the awakening appears like a continuation of the vision, she looked into his face with a calm, gentle gaze, almost wondering in its expression, then turned and looked at the woman who sat beside her, long and wistfully. Lifting her hands to her head, she pressed her temples, and thought awhile, until suddenly she remembered it all. A low, despairing wail burst from her lips, and she wrung her hands wildly and woefully over each other, but not a single tear flowed to soften the rigor of her anguish.

"My child," said the good priest, who was deeply moved, and who knew that something must be speedily done to break up this mental tension, "have good courage in the name of

God. Remember that poor John's sorrows—which are heavy enough—will be much aggravated if you become ill. You must bear up for his sake."

"Ah, Shaneen, *asthore*, why did ye ever lave the home where ye wor born; an' the hearts that loved ye an' wor proud of ye, to come amongst the could-hearted strangers of this cruel land? Better for ye to ha' been a beggar on the road side; or had your life ground out iv you in the parish workhouse than be brought to this. Oh, Shaneen, *machree*, I was always afeard your high notions would bring trubble on ye! Not that I b'lieve my darlin's guilty, for I know it was niver in him to do what they're goin' to take his life for; oh, no! Shaneen, an' God will bring it to light yet, my love, to put them that's sentenced you to confusion, an' it will kape the sod from layin' too heavy upon your heart. But oh, it was a black day you left your home, and turned your back on your native hills." And covering her face with her hands she wept and wailed, low, like a frightened child who has been shut up in the dark, until the wild passion of her woe, like any other tempest, died away in low whispered murmurs. And as it ebbed away the changeless constancy, and unwavering love of that poor heart was strengthened and somewhat comforted by the invisible, but none the less surely merciful compassion of God, who saw and pitied her dark tribulation.

"Can't your riverence save him?" she asked, lifting her head from her knees, where it had been resting.

"Alas, my child, all that I could do has been done. You must prepare yourself for the worst, nor is it the least of my trials in connection with this sad case, to be obliged to tell you so. Innocent as I believe your lover to be, there is no help for him except in the mercy of God, to which I hourly hereby commend him," said Father Grandfiel, thinking, rightly, that it was best to let her know at once the extremity of his case, rather than torture her heart with dubious words, which might imply hopes that could never be realized.

"Aye," said Mistress Pottles, "he wont be the first that's been wrongfully hung by a many. I swanny, if my neck oughtn't to be a half a mile long, I've suffered so for the poor creetures that's been hung since we've been here. Here, honey, drink some more of this wine, and I'll send out for a carriage and go home with you."

"Where am I? Home? Tell me, Father—I feel dazed," said Ally, looking after the woman, and then around her.

"This is the gaoler's house. He brought you down here after you fainted up there, and placed you under the care of his wife, who has been very kind, my child."

"*When is it to be?*" she asked, laying her wasted hand on his arm.

"This day two weeks," replied the priest in a low voice, while he turned involuntarily away.

"Two weeks!" repeated the stricken girl, rising up, and faltering as she stood before him. "There's no time to sit grievin'. I've found him, and it's jest as SHE tould me in my drame. He's bearin' HER SON'S cross, and I'm not to hinder him, but comfort him. Aye, Shaneen, my darlin', I'll stand by ye to the last. I'll not hinder ye, or make ye downhearted, when the heavens are openin' above ye like they did over the heads of them that used to be torn by savage beasts, and stoned to death by wicked men."

"The hack is come," whispered Mistress Pottles to Father Grandfiel. "Come, honey," she said, putting her arm about Ally, "I'm going to to take you home. You should stay here, but it's agin the rules. Where's your stopping place —try and remember, my poor gal."

"Here it is, ma'am," replied Ally, gently, as she drew a slip of paper from her pocket, on which the name of the hotel, and the street on which it was situated, was written.

"Good Lord!" exclaimed Mistress Pottles, as she took hold of the poor girl's hand to help her into the carriage, "you're burning hot—you've got a ragin' fever on you. Misther—" to the priest, who kept close beside his charge, "please go back there, and leave word that maybe I won't be back to-night. We'll wait for you, for I s'pose it'll be better—seeing you're the only friend this poor soul's got—for you to go with us."

Father Grandfiel, thankful to the good woman for her truly charitable intentions, hastened away to do her bidding, then returned and got into the hack to accompany them, for the two-fold purpose of complying with his word to the condemned man, and to be at hand in case his services should be required by poor Ally, who by this time was almost delirious with fever, and quite unable to hold up, which Mrs. Pottles perceived, and slipping her strong arm about her, drew her head to her bosom, and held her there until the hack drew up before the door of the hotel, as tenderly as if she had been her own sister or daughter, instead of an unfortunate and friendless stranger. Nor did she leave her that night, but after administering a composing draught, which Father Grandfiel procured for her, sat watching her, and doing all she could to alleviate her burning thirst until the sun rose; then finding the fever somewhat abated, and the suffering creature disposed to sleep, she darkened the room and slipped away. But she did not leave the house until she had commended the unfortunate girl to the care of the landlord's wife, to whom she imparted her sad story. For three days and nights Ally was too ill and weak to leave her bed, during which time she was carefully waited on, and tenderly nursed, by the women about the house, many of whom were her countrywomen, whose sympathies were warmly enlisted in her behalf. Father Granfiel came to see her every day, to bring her news of John, and direct her thoughts beyond the dreary storms of life to the only true and abiding source of consolation. On the fourth morning he came, bringing with him the Bread of Life, which replenished the feeble, fainting energies of her soul, and imparted to it more of endurance and submission than she had felt for many weary weeks. The wild waves of her stormy sorrow had almost dismantled her soul of its hope and confidence; and, like a hidden reef, or sunken rock, the sudden woe of finding her lover where he was, and realizing more than her worst anticipations had ever suggested in his regard, had nearly made shipwreck of all together, when amidst the confusion and rack of the tempest, Christ Himself came to her, bidding her not to fear, and commanding the wind and the waves to be still. And then she could look—knowing John to be innocent—her great woe more calmly in the face; she could look at it, and aye, *beyond it*, when sunshine and peace for ever more abode on the "distant hills." But we have no time to tell all she felt and thought—we have been led beyond our limits already, and must confine ourselves simply to the leading incidents of the concluding events of this strange, but true narrative.

Every day since her illness, Ally, to try her

strength, would attempt to rise whenever she was left alone, only to fall back fainting on her pillows; but on the fourth day we have just spoken of she was able to sit up and walk the length of her room. The next morning, after a quiet and refreshing night, she arose and dressed herself, and having partaken of some breakfast, she sat down by the open window to think what she should do. The soft spring air, bringing with it the smell of hyacinths and violets from the garden below, fanned her pale cheek, and revived her drooping strength—song-birds flitted through the bright air warbling as they flew, and there arose a soft murmur from the tender foliage of the beautiful trees, that shaded her window, as the wind breathed on them, that inspired her—despite of all her sorrow—with a strange and mysterious glimpse of the joyous feelings of "long ago," but it was only for a moment—an instant—and, like a song-bird, it was gone. But she got up and put on her shawl and bonnet, and stood at her door to ask the first servant who came by to get her a carriage. A man, with a trunk on his shoulder, was coming along the passage. Some traveller was going away. She saw him when he went by, and when the porter drew near, she laid her hand on his arm, and asked him, in a low, hurried voice, "would he please to get her a carriage." The man started, but he knew her—he had in the days she had been there, heard her sad story—

and he told her to "sit down and rest until he came back for her," which she did, for her knees were beginning to tremble under her. It was not long before he returned, and making her lean on him—he had a fair young sister like her across the ocean at home—he led her slowly down to the hack and helped her in.

"If I was you," he whispered, "I'd go to the Gov'nor an' beg him off."

"The Gov'nor? Who's that? Can he save his life?" she asked eagerly.

"Faith an' he's the only one that can. He don't live in Cincinnatty, but he's just stayin' here to attend to some business about a canal up yonder at Columbus. He's going away next week."

"Where is he? Where can I find him?" she asked, in a wild flurry of hope.

"I'll speak to the driver—he's a friend of me own, an' he'll take you direct to him. All you'll have to do is to ax for his room, and march straight up to it," replied her sympathizing countryman, "an' if I was you I wouldn't lave him 'till he'd give me a pardon for him." Then he held a whispered consultation with the driver, after which she was whirled away through the splendid streets and busy crowds of the Queen City of the West, heedless of the magnificence and din, intent only on the forlorn hope which was leading her to the feet of the man who held her lover's life at his disposal.

Arrived at the hotel, her sad errand was passed from one to another of her countrymen, who were employed as porters and waiters in the establishment, by the hack-driver, who placed her under the care of one of them, and told her he would wait for her, and "wished her good luck, God bless her."

"The Gov'nor is at home, up in his private parlor. Come up. This way, *acushla*," said the man, and conducted her along with as reverent a respect as if she had been the Governor's wife or daughter. At the head of a broad flight of steps he passed her on to another, with "God bless you, an' soften his Honor's heart," who hurried her down a broad hall, and gave her in charge of another, with a kindly and earnest wish that "she might get what she was seekin';" who was an old man, with grown up daughters under his own roof, and he, seeing how pale and weak she was, put his arm about her, and carried her to the very door she was to enter on her dubious and trying errand. "Christ an' His holy Mother help you, *acushla!*" he whispered, as he tapped lightly on the door.

"Come in," was the response. And she glided in—the door closed on her; and she found herself alone with this man of awful power. He was reading the morning paper, and thinking that the intruder was one of the servants of the establishment come to remove his breakfast things, he did not look up or stir until Ally Kane fell at his feet, where she knelt, pale and speechless, with her hands clasped, her great blue eyes fixed on his with an expression of imploring anguish, and her hair—her bonnet having fallen back—clustered in golden masses over her cheeks and bosom. There was something of such earnestness of purpose, and so full of the eloquence of woe in her face, that his attention was riveted in a moment, and his heart became full of a strange pity, even while his brow was knit with its habitual sternness.

"Rise, my poor child," he said, gently, "and tell me your errand."

"Oh, your Honor, this is the best place for one that's come to beg for the life of another. Save his life—they say you can, your Honor—save his life, for Christ's sake! He's innocent—don't let him die," she gasped.

"My poor child," replied the Governor, whose lip quivered, "I pity you from my soul; but I can do nothing. It is entirely out of my power to grant your prayer. I suppose you are a sister of the man Hanlon, who is condemned to die; but I tell you if he was *my own son*, he must suffer the penalty of his crime. Your friends did wrong to send you on this errand, knowing how fruitless it would be."

"He is innocent, your Honor," she answered, in a low, choking voice, "as innocent as a little child of that man's death. Oh, sir, for the love of Christ an' His Virgin Mother, pardon Shaneen! He'll go far away, where you'll never see or hear of him agin, an' I'll work for you all my days, an' sarve you an' yours like a bound slave, an' not a day'll go over my head that I won't pray for God's blessin' to fall on you an' your house. It's his life I want—his precious life; it's to save him from the shame of dyin' on the gallows, that I'd be willin' to lay my life down this minit, if it would do any good."

"This is a case in which duty makes me powerless. I *cannot* grant your prayer, however much I pity you. It is impossible," said the Governor, austerely.

"May God be more merciful to your Honor, then, than you've been to *him*," she said slowly, as she arose from her feet, feeling that her last earthly hope had been dashed out. "But when he's dead, by your word, that might ha' saved him, an' it comes to you, as it surely will, that you've hung an innocent man, you'll wish you had died in your cradle—for it is a woesome thing to have innocent blood on one's head, an' the broken hearts of an ould mother and father, that's totterin' into the grave afore their time, because their staff's broke from under 'em, lavin' alone one that 'ud give her heart's life to save his."

"Have you any friends here, my child?" asked the Governor gently, while the lines of his stern forehead grew full and corrugated; and he would have wept like a woman if he had dared.

"Friends enow," she said, "I have God an' him." So she folded her shawl closer about her, and bowing her poor head, she went away, feeling that there was nothing left for her now but to abide by John, and go with him step by step faithfully and courageously to the last dreary scene. As soon as she was gone, the Governor—deeply moved—went to his table and wrote an order to the gaoler to "give her admission to the prisoner whenever she applied for it, and grant *him* any indulgence that was not incompatible with the rules and regulations on such occasions;" which he dispatched without loss of time to the prison.

John Travers was alone when she was admitted. His head drooped forward on his breast, and one hand was thrust under his jacket, and pressed heavily on his heart, as if to keep down its tumultuous beating. His cell had been crowded all day by fresh throngs of officious and curious persons, who questioned, gazed, and talked at and to him, until he was almost maddened. But they had all gone—their morbid cravings satisfied—and he was left to wrestle alone with his bitter misery. He did not hear the light, swiftly-gliding step that came towards him, or feel the soft touch of the hand that rested on his shoulder; but when she said in those gentle tones that blended their music always with his dreams, "Shaneen, *asthore!*" he raised his head quickly, and with a cry of joy opened his arms, and folded her to his breast. He did not expect to see her again—he had begged that she might be kept away; but now that she was there breathing and trembling — no longer a dream phantom—on his breast, he thanked God that she had come.

"It is very sweet, Ally, darlin', to have you here. I shall go away easier for it," said the poor fellow.

"I am glad to hear that, Shaneen, *machree*. That's what I come for. An' now I'll tell you what we'll do 'till the time comes for us to part. We won't think of it, darlin', but we will talk about the happy days agone, and the happy day that'll soon dawn for you; but not of what comes betune. Not a word of that, *asthore*. An' there's great comfort for us in the Body an' Blood of the Lord," she said, crossing herself devoutly, "that his riverence, Father Grandfiel, who's been a good frind to me, will bring to us; for I don't intind to lave you, Shaneen, unless they tear me away from you." And as she talked, she smoothed back the clustering hair from his sunken temples, and kissed his broad, fair forehead. And then holding his hand in hers, she told him all that had happened since he came away; of her voyage, of finding Miss Lacie, and how kind they had all been; about old Owny, his uncle, and why he did not come with her—she told him everything except the history of her own wild anguish, and the result of her effort that very day to save his life.

"Ally, my darlin'," he said, when she finished her simple narrative, "there's one wish I mustn't be crossed in, an' that is, *never* to let them know, not even uncle Owny and Mr. Lacie, that John Travers an' the John Hanlon that's sentenced to be hung is the one person. Mind that now, if you love me, Ally." She promised him, and then he told her all that had happened to him since he left Baltimore. He had determined to settle himself in Cincinnati, and thought he would defer writing until he had done so to his satisfaction. Cheerful and hopeful he proceeded on his journey, looking beyond all his half-formed plans to the one aim of his life, which was to prosper and rise, and when he saw everything clear before him to return home to Ireland to fetch her, and if possible persuade his father and mother to accompany him back to the land of his adoption. Full of these buoyant hopes and an untamed energy, he was on his way to Cincinnati. He was within ten miles of the city, but having got off the cars at the last station, he was left. Anxious to get there that evening, and not heeding the distance, he started to walk, carpet-bag in hand, and such good way did he make, that ere the sun set he saw the spires and cupolas of the city gleaming not far below the hill on which he stood. The sight spurred him on—he would soon be there, and after a good night's rest, he would rise fresh in the morning for a new and steady start in life. Hastening along, he suddenly—on turning a road which led around the angle of a rocky bluff—came upon two parties of men, who were engaged pell-mell in a furious fight. He soon discovered that they were Fardowns and Corkonians by their rallying cries. He attempted to pass through them, but it was at a fearful cost, as we shall see. As if drawn into a sudden vortex, he was tossed and torn, until in self-defence he was compelled to fight his way along, or be killed on the spot. All at once, to his amazement, they fled, and as the dust cleared away he saw that they had left not only their pickaxes, wedges, fragments of clothes, and many a stout club behind them, but there in the middle of the road lay a man, either mortally wounded or dead. Humanity had ever been one of John Travers' leading characteristics, and he would have lost all respect for himself, if he had gone away without attempting to assist the fallen stranger. A little brook gurgled across the road a few yards off, and thither he determined to drag him for the purpose of bathing his face and wounds, if he had any; but while in the act of doing so, a party of armed police surrounded him, and refusing to hear a word of explanation, arrested him on the spot. He understood now the sudden flight of the rioters. In vain he protested his innocence, and declared his having met with these men was a simple accident—his torn clothes, and a bruise on his cheek and hand, refuted his assertions. Giving him in custody to two of their number, the others proceeded to examine the prostrate and insensible man beside them. Not wishing under such discreditable circumstances to give his real name, fearing that the affair might get into the papers, and unnecessarily alarm his friends, John Travers had given that of Hanlon, when he was questioned. As yet no wounds were discovered on the unfortunate victim of the riot, but upon turning him on his side they uttered a cry of horror—for there under his left shoulder, plunged up to the very hilt, they saw a knife, upon the handle of which was rudely carved the letter H. The man was dead—murdered—and John Travers was accused of the crime, and after lingering month after month in prison, broken in spirit and health, he was tried on this evidence, and convicted on these circumstantial proofs. He was condemned by an American jury, and sentenced by an American judge, to die an ignominious death, although, as we know, he was as innocent as his Honor or any of the twelve men whose verdict had sealed his doom, of the terrible crime.

Interrupted by outbursts of anguish he told the sad story from beginning to end, but she, choking back her tears and veiling her wild and impatient emotion under the mysterious power of reticence, as if to all human pangs she had suddenly grown dead and cold, soothed and cheered him; she even sang one of the sweet old home songs of their native hills, while her heart was breaking; and when the time came for her to go away—not far, she was determined on that —she told him, because she was afraid of starting up the wild woe of his heart, that she would return presently, then kissed his forehead, and went out into the gloomy corridor, where she leaned against the wall for support, and almost shrieked when the ponderous lock turning on him, seemed to grate through her poor heart, as it finally shot home into its rusty wards.

"Come down to see my Missis," said the gaoler, taking her by the arm: "she's got something to tell you." The something was to show her the order of the Governor, and invite her to stay with her *the few days that remained.* Thankful for this boon, Ally felt somewhat comforted, and having partaken of some refreshment provided for her by Mistress Pottles, she asked permission to return to John.

"There's nothin' agin' it now," said Mr. Pottles, the gaoler, who was a diplomat in his way; "since the Guvenur himself has spoke; but afore you go, young woman, it'll be necessary for my wife here to search you for the purpose— you understand it's a mere form—of seeing if you've got anything about you that's wrong— anything, in short, that could *help him off.* 'Cos you know I'm 'sponsible for his safety."

"Yes. She can search me. I have nothin'

like that. I don't think—thank God—that he'll need it. I b'lieve afore—next Friday—God hissel' will take Shaneen to glory. Somethin' tells me that. Somethin' seems to whisper that that Blessed Virgin will come to his help an' refuge."

"The poor creetur," said Mrs. Pottles, nudging her husband, "I told you it 'ud 'ventually set her distracted. But don't say nothing, Shadrack; let her think so, if it'll comfort her, poor soul."

And the weary days passed on, neither slower nor faster for the great grief and tribulation they were bringing nearer those suffering hearts. John Travers had suffered two or three strange and terrible spasms of the heart, which left him almost lifeless when they passed off; and it was plain to see that he was sinking, his vital powers succumbing, as the time drew more near. But they never spoke of it to him; Ally never left him, except at short intervals when Father Grandficl was there, administering spiritual consolation to him. Daily they received together the life-giving bread of the Divine Mystery of the Altar, and daily—while her heart was fainting and breaking under its load of anguish—she read, talked and sang their *auld lang syne* lays to him, until a deeper calm seemed to gather over his soul. It wanted only four days of the time. The gibbet was being constructed. Whenever she went down to the gaoler's house she heard the heavy blows of the hammers, and the discordant, swift grating of the saws, on and through the wood. Almost wild, she felt for the first time her desolation. Her thoughts fled to Owny and Mr. Lacie. She had promised him not to let them know; but she could not let him die without one more effort to save him, come what would of it, for there was a something urging her to write—write—write. We, who believe in the ministry of Guardian Angels, know what this "*something*," that impels us at times, means. Father Grandfiel stopped at the gaoler's house, to tell he was going away home, and that John had asked for her. She told him what she wished, and he—hoping nothing for the condemned man, however, from it—promised to stop at the telegraph office, and send a telegram that evening. "But what shall I say, my child?"

"Only this, my Father. 'It is John Travers. In three days he will be hung. Come without losing a moment; an' spake to Misther Lacie.'"

"They will hear to-morrow morning. Now the address—where does Owny Travers live?" She told him, and hurried away with a strange and lightsome feeling in her heart. But the next day passed, and no word came. The dreadful preparations were still going on. Wednesday dragged slowly along, and no tidings. Her cheeks grew thinner and her eyes heavy. She could scarcely drag herself along, nor could she sleep or eat. Outside that cell, where, for the sake of him she loved, she still exerted her energies, and wore a calm aspect, she was like one dead, only that she moved. Her wild hope was dying out—fading like a cloud in the distance, leaving her all alone on the midnight sea. Thursday came as days will, no matter what marks their track—the morning, bright and glorious, spread into noontide, which presently began to wane, and yet not a sign, and she resigned herself with a bitter pang to her trial. It seemed to be God's will that she should have this peculiar suffering, and there was nothing left for her but to abandon herself to His Divine compassion, and die when the worst was over. But that night the sheriff saw Father Grandfiel, and informed him that news had been received which would possibly delay the execution, and hurried away.

But Father Grandfiel was too faithful a shepherd of souls to impart this unsatisfactory intelligence to the condemned man, to disturb, by false or unfounded hopes of reprieve or acquittal, the solemnity of his preparation for eternity—to call him back to visions of life and hope only perhaps to plunge him back again into darker despair. Nor would he hint the circumstance to Ally, whom he had learned to regard, not only as a heroic and constant woman, but as a pious martyr—until he learned something more decided.

CHAPTER XV.

TOO LATE.

"GOD only knows how my heart yearns to impart comfort to my poor suffering children," thought Father Grandfiel, as he stood in the corridor where he had met the Sheriff, pondering on what he had heard. "But at so solemn a moment I dare not disturb their minds with hopes which may be only illusory. No, poor martyr! thou art prepared for thy transit into eternity, if ever mortal was; thou hast been purified by a fiercer ordeal than fire, and it will be well with thee through Christ. And thou, poor Ally! who sufferest so bravely and meekly the will of God, and bearest thy heavy cross with such rare patience!—it would be cruel to add other thorns to thy crown by suggesting a prospect which will, I fear, end only in deep and bitter despondency! Tender Father and Sovereign Lord, into Thy hands I commend them!" Sighing deeply over the woes he could not remedy, the good priest went over to the gaoler's house to tell Ally—who was there—that he was going, and that he would come between five and six o'clock in the morning to administer the holy communion to John Travers and herself—to him as his Viaticum; then blessing her, and bidding her be of good courage, he lingered a moment after she went out, to impress on the minds of the gaoler and his wife the necessity of remaining perfectly silent on the subject of the startling news brought by the Sheriff that evening, lest in all its mystery and uncertainty it should come to Ally's ears.

"Another day," he thought, as he walked away from the prison, "and the bitter trial will be over for them. It is glorious, in such bitter straits, to know that the dear and abiding mercy of God is strong and abundant enough for all our needs."

But Father Grandfiel—although he was a most prudent and saintly man, to whose heart the salvation of souls was the first aim—believed also in human means, and was not one to remain passive when there existed the slightest prospect of serving the distressed; so, when he left the prison, he determined, with characteristic mercy, to go direct to the Sheriff's house in quest of further intelligence. When he rang at the door, the girl who opened it informed him that "the Sheriff was with the Governor."

"When do you think he will be in, my child?"

"He's just sent word home not to expect him to-night, sir. It's something about the young fellow that is to be hanged to-morrow."

"Thank you." replied Father Grandfiel, turning away. "So," he thought, "the Spirit of

God is moving upon the troubled deep. I can do nothing but pray, and I will betake myself to an audience with Him in the Sanctuary, where I will plead with Him to vindicate justice and show mercy by proving the innocence of that man even at the eleventh hour." And excited by strange and undefined hopes, which, if he had analyzed, would have seemed childish, he betook himself to the foot of the Altar—having first partaken of some necessary refreshment—where he spent the greater part of the night.

In another part of the city, in the operator's room at the telegraph office, sat the Governor of the State, the Sheriff, and two distinguished lawyers, one of whom had prosecuted John Travers for the commonwealth, and one of whom defended him. Two dispatches had reached them that evening; the first signed by Mr. Lacie and the magistrate Dobbin, of Baltimore, to the effect that the condemned man who awaited the execution of the sentence of the law in Cincinnati, was innocent; that the real, guilty criminal was in Baltimore, and had confessed his crime. The second was from Wheeling, signed by the Sheriff of Baltimore, who informed them that all proceedings in the case of John Travers must be instantly stopped; there was ample and legal proof of his innocence, "which would be forthcoming in twenty-four hours." They were waiting in almost breathless silence for a reply to a message they had dispatched a few moments before to Mr. Lacie. Presently a sharp click from the battery announced its arrival. The Governor grasped the slip of paper, and read:

"The man Hogan is yet alive. His deposition is formal, being made under oath before a magistrate. The Sheriff will be there in the morning. Mr. Lacie is also on his way."

This was from the worthy magistrate to whom Mr. Lacie had deputed the authority of opening and replying to any dispatch sent to himself from Cincinnati.

"I fear we were on the verge of a fatal mistake, gentlemen," said the Governor, gravely, "a most fatal mistake. Tell them to forward the man's deposition without loss of time," he continued to the operator, while Ally Kane's anguished face came gliding like a phantom into his memory, silently reproaching him for having, in his judicial career, almost deified human justice.

"It is on the way, in safe hands," was the reply brought by the lightning. And there those men—high in the ranks of intellect and morals, without reproach in their vocation, honorable and high-toned in their views, who would have shrunk from giving an undeserved blow to a dog, yet who in the short-sightedness of human justice had condemned an innocent man to a cruel and ignominious death on what they considered *conclusive circumstantial evidence*, and that only—sat eager to repair the wrong, and earnest in their endeavors to secure a perfect acquittal, until the gray dawn stole through the windows; then when there was no more that they could do, they took a carriage and drove to the *depot*, to meet whoever might arrive from Baltimore.

John Travers had passed a sleepless night. The agony of his vigils was known only to Almighty God. The bitterness of his undeserved fate, the sudden and dark eclipse of his aspiring manhood, the ignominy and shame of his last hour, rolled like tempestuous floods over him. How often during that night, like a mirage in the desert, arose the fair scenes of his mountain home! How plainly he saw the old father and mother whom he—God help him—in the honest pride of an honest heart had forsaken! And there was no refuge but an ignominious grave for him! How could he bear it? He fixed his bloodshot eyes on the picture of Simon the Cyrenean, and thoughts arose which stayed his wild woe. "Whose cross is that they place on His shoulders?" "The cross of Jesus Christ?" "Who has placed this heavy rugged cross on me?" "Men." "By whose permission?" Aye, John Travers, by whose permission? "The permission of God, who gave up His only Son to the death of the cross, to ignominy, insult, abandonment, and all manner of torture, for thee! Is the disciple greater than his Lord?" "Could I see clearly that it is for Thee I suffer, my Lord, I could suffer bravely and without murmuring."

'It is for Me. They have laid My cross on your shoulders. It is for My glory." "Remember me, then, oh, Lord, when all human aid forsakes me." "This day shalt thou be with me in Paradise." It was thus the angels of God ministered unto that poor prisoner in his bitter agony. The wildness of his woe subsided, and a soft slumber, so like exhaustion that it could scarcely be called sleep, stole over him. His head rested on his breast, and whenever he started in his sleep, which he did frequently, the manacles on his feet clanked with a dreary sound. And during the short interval that he slept, a strange dream came to him. He thought that he stood on the verge of a fathomless abyss, from whose depths arose the hollow, surging sound of rushing waters. He was obliged to cross this gulf, but how? If he attempted to gain the other side unaided, he must certainly perish;—and still he lingered, trembling and breathless, but still urged on by some unseen and irresistible power. At last he stood dizzy and afraid on the very limits of the ledge; when lo! he saw Ally on the other side, attended by a fair and solemn Angel of great stature and resplendent beauty, stretching out her arms to help him over—but alas! they were too short to reach him. Then he saw the Angel lift her in his strong arms, and hold her out towards him over the abyss. Reeling, and almost ready to drop into the dark gulf, he grasped her hands, and in another moment he was in safety on the other side; but Ally was gone—he was alone with the Angel who gathered him to his side, and led him away into a strange country. With a start, he awoke, and she was there waiting beside him. Silently she kissed his forehead, and smoothed back the thick curls, which had grown long and clustering in the prison, from his face, and would have spoken had she dared trust herself. She pointed to his clean linen, and other things she had brought in—the clothing in which he was to array himself for the last time, and which she had laid on a chair near by.

"It'll be a sore day for you, Ally, *asthore*." he whispered. "Forgive me for bringin' this dark sorrow on you.'

"Don't talk so, Shaneen, an' niver fear for me; an' as to forgivin,' what have I to forgive *a suilish machree?* Our partin' will not be for long, an' though you're *mo seact n-anam astig tú*,* I'd niver hould you back, now that the gates of heaven are swung back for ye, *asthore!* Only think, Shaneen, that afore the sun goes down on ten thousand aching hearts this day, you'll be there," said the girl in low, sweet accents, while her own heart was enduring such pangs as no pen can describe.

"It's not so hard to die, *a suilish machree*," he said, while a red spot flamed on each wasted cheek, "as to know all the same of my dyin'.

---
* Seven times as dear as the heart that's within me.

But God look down upon me, and forgive me. His will be done!"

"That is right, *alanna!* Have courage. You die a martyr, my own true love—then die like a man! I'm goin' now for some flowers to brighten up this sorrowful place for our Lord an' Comforter, who is comin' presently. Let us thank God now an' forever, Shaneen, that HE sticks to us when all the world forsakes us! Have courage, *asthore.*" And she turned away, to hide from him the deadly pallor that she felt stealing over her face, and hastened out into the corridor, where she staggered and faltered along, almost blind with the mist that arose to her eyes, and must have fallen prostrate on the stone floor, if the gaoler, seeing her condition, had not met her, and thrown his strong arm around her.

"Come, now, cheer up. It mayn't be so bad after all—that is," said he, correcting himself, "not so hard to bear as you expect."

"I am better now," she said, commanding her energies, and standing upright. "It was only a wakeness. I'm expectin' Father Grandfiel. Will you give me a few roses?"

"There! there! Sit down, child. Of course I'll give you some roses. Wait here. I won't be gone a minit," said the gaoler, who hurried away to do her the small favor she asked; "though," thought he, "what she can want with roses sich a time as this beats me. But

Papists are strange critters, and I remember now of seeing flowers on the altars in their churches. Well, it's none o' my busiuess—'every man to his taste,' as the old woman said when she kissed the cow." Ally waited for him until he returned, not only with roses, but with clusters of the common but purely beautiful white lily. When she returned to the cell, John Travers was already dressed in what used to be his holiday attire, and was kneeling, with his eyes fixed on a small crucifix, which for the last few days had never left his hands. His handsome, manly face was very wan, but never in his happiest days had he looked more noble—never had the likeness and image of God shown out more nobly in his visage than on that morning in the felon's cell, which he expected to leave in a few short hours for the gibbet.

"Mother of Sorrows," was the cry of Ally's wrung heart, "but how can I ever bear it? But you tould me on the say that he was carryin' your SON's cross, an' I wasn't to hinder him; an' I won't to the last." And no sigh escaped her lips, but with noiseless steps, and light fingers, she arranged the flowers on each side the crucifix on the table she had prepared for the most holy sacrament—her own crucifix, that she had brought from Ireland with her. Over the table hung the picture of Simon the Cyrenean, bearing the cross of Jesus. Just as her simple and touching arrangements were completed, in gushed the golden sunlight, shedding a fair effulgence over the spot. Somehow, at the same instant, a feeling of peace crept into the soul of the sorrowing girl; she could not define it, she knew not whence it came, and she thought she was either dying or going mad. Father Grandfiel now entered, bearing in his bosom the Lord of Life, under the pure and spotless veil of the sacred host. He was very much agitated, but they did not observe it, for all their thoughts and feelings were concentrated on Him whom they were about to receive, their consolation in in sorrow, and the rod and staff that was to comfort them in the shadow of death. He blessed them both fervently, then deposited the Blessed Sacrament on the place prepared for it, and having arrayed himself in surplice and stole, proceeded with the solemn and soul-touching rite. He had got as far as the "*Ecce Agnus Dei,*" when there came the sound of many feet along the stone floor of the corridor. They both heard it. Ally bowed her head lower on her breast, and a sudden shiver—almost imperceptible—passed over John Travers' form. They thought, although it was too soon for *that* yet, that those who were to have charge of the terrible preparations of the day were coming to begin their work. But Father Grandfiel approached them, and in another moment they had received the Bread of Life. "It is I, be not afraid," He whispered, as He entered within their hearts; and they, recognizing His voice and presence, grew calm, and humbly reposed on His Divine strength.

The approaching footsteps had paused at the door, and a low and distinct sound of sobbing was heard from the corridor, and there seemed to be a struggle, and earnest whispers; then Father Grandfiel was beckoned away, and all was still for at least a quarter of an hour. The good priest then returned to them, looking pale and excited. A gentleman of stern and dignified aspect accompanied him in, to whom he whispered, "For God's sake, let us be cautious, sir. If it is told to him too suddenly, he might die or lose his reason."

"You are right, sir. Break the matter to him as gently as possible. I can wait—I can wait," was the answer.

"Ye are not strong, my dear children," said Father Grandfiel, "do not kneel any longer now." They arose, and John Travers sunk exhausted on his bedside. Ally stood beside him, determined to cling there to the last.

"How is it with you, John, my dear child?" said Father Grandfiel, laying his hand on his head.

"I don't be afraid, Father, thanks be to God. I b'lieve He'll give me courage to die like a Christian man," replied the noble young fellow, "only I'm in dread that my weakness 'll make me look like a guilty coward."

"Yes, my child, that is a portion of your bitter cup. But do you know I think sudden joy is harder to bear than the worst grief that can befall us."

"Mebbe so, your reverince. It's a great consolation to me to *know* my innocence. I would rather die a victim than a criminal. Glory to God, my hand is clane of blood—aye, even of the blood of a brute beast. But I confess it's hard to go 'way and lave her, an' know that my life, after all my fond hopes, has been a failure. An' I think, Father, it's a duty I owe to them I lave behind me, to lift up my voice to the last agin' the cruel law that's condemned me to death," he replied in a firm voice.

"Injustice is hard to bear, my child; but Almighty God's Providence never slumbers nor sleeps, and He is able even now to deliver you out of this cruel strait," said the good priest, trembling at the effect that even these faint suggestions of hope might have on him. But the poor fellow had too long bidden adieu to all earthly hope, or human aid, to heed them. His faith in the mercy and justice of man had been wrecked; he could believe all things of God, of whom they could not bereave him, but for himself man could do nothing, and he simply replied in a low voice:

"He will deliver me. Don't forget Ally, *a suilish machree*, all the kind lovin' words I give you to take home." But Ally did not heed him then. She had comprehended, with her quick woman's wit, the accents of hope; she had recognized that grave stern face as that of the Governor before whom she had knelt a few days before. What was *he* doing there at that hour? She leaned forward, and laying her hand on Father Grandfiel's arm, fixed her large bright eyes on his face with a look of wild hope, and eager, intense anxiety in every lineament.

"Plase God—spake out for Christ's sake, your reverince—is it a reprieve?" she gasped.

"In one moment, my child. John," said Father Grandfiel, laying his arm tenderly about him, "your courage was good to meet death under the most terrible form, but how would it be if I were to tell you good news?"

The young man started—a deep flush crimsoned his face, and instantly receded, leaving it as white as marble. He pressed his hands over his heart, which had given one wild, bursting throb; but he did not speak; he only fixed his eyes on the agitated face of the priest with a look of speechless inquiry.

"Be calm, my dear child. Lift up your heart and be glad. Almighty God has been pleased to bless your patience and submission. You are not to die to-day. There are friends of yours without, powerful friends who are waiting to see you, to tell you how Divine Providence has, in a wonderful manner, made everything clear."

"Providence! friends!" he said, in a wondering, bewildered sort of way. "Not die to-day! The Lord be good to me, but that's the cruelest of all; to put it off, for me to go through all the dark bitter way agin. Ally, *a suilish machree*, what does it mane?"

"Here's one can tell you, *asthore*," whispered Ally in faint, low accents, as the Governor approached them. "Rise up, John, *alanna*, here's the Governor of the State itsel' come to you;" and she put her frail arm about him, as if she could help him. Others now entered the cell, and in their midst was a struggling, half-frantic old man, who broke away from them, and with a loud cry sprang forward and clasped John Travers to his breast. But John, pale and bewildered, only looked from one to another, and said, "It's a long way for you to come, Uncle Owny, to sup such sorrow. Take care of Ally. You know we were to be married at Easter, an' she'll be like a widow when I'm gone."

"Oh, vo! listen to that, will you? His heart's broke intirely. I don't b'lieve he knows me, as much! Shaneen, lift up your head, you've got a right to, *a bouchal dhas!* You're not to die. Ax the Governor there. The raal murderer's found, an' confessed his villainy, the *overlooked boucaun.*"

"It is true, John Travers," said the Governor, stepping up and taking his hand. "You are free. There's nothing against you; and I have come with these gentlemen to express our sorrow

that you were brought into such peril, and say
that all we can do, publicly or privately, to make
amends to you, that we intend doing with the
help of God."

He comprehended it now.

"My God, I thank Thee!" he cried in trembling accents. "Too late! too late!" he murmured, as he fell slowly and heavily back in
Ally's faithful arms; his head was pillowed on
her bosom, and she would have fallen under his
weight if the gentlemen present had not taken
him from her and laid him on the bed. Too late,
indeed! When they lifted him a dark stream of
blood was oozing from his lips. The shock
had, notwithstanding all the tender care they
had used, been too great for his debilitated and
diseased system; a blood-vessel was ruptured,
and the days of the unfortunate John Travers
were numbered. We will not portray the deep
anguish of Ally, or the frantic grief of Owny
Travers—it would carry us beyond our limits;
nor describe the deep and terrible excitement
that prevailed throughout the city, when the
history of the case was made known in all its
painful and afflicting details. If the hoary murderer whose evil passions had brought this ruin
on the innocent had been within reach, no law
could have saved him from the fury of the pop-
ulace; for their high sense of justice was outraged, and not few or whispered were the
threats they made against the jurors who con-

demned John Travers, and the judge who sentenced him to die. But the legitimate object of their fury was not there—fortunately for themselves, as well as him—and the storm subsided as all storms eventually do.

Tenderly, and while he was still unconscious, John Travers was removed to a pleasant room in the gaoler's house, where, it is useless to say, nothing was left undone for his relief and comfort, that deep sympathy, and devoted affection, friendship and science, could accomplish. The next morning Mr. Lacie and Eveleen arrived, and lost no time in seeking their humble, but dear friends; and then Ally, wan and wasted to a mere shadow, relinquished her place for a few hours at a time, to rest, while Eveleen, with a sister's true tenderness, and a Christian lady's gentle courage, watched beside the pillow of the dying man. We say dying—we mean that he was sinking without hope of recovery; he might live weeks and months, but human justice had been too tardy; when it was ready to repair the great wrong, it was, as he had said, "too late."

CHAPTER XVI.

HOW IT ENDED.

For two days they expected John Travers to die, but he lingered through the third night neither better nor worse, in a cold, speechless torpor, which shut out all expression of life from his eyes, and held his limbs motionless. The hemorrhage had been easily managed, and he did not seem to suffer, but the medical man gave no opinion; in fact, his symptoms were so strange, that he with all his science had not been able as yet to form a diagnosis of the case. He knew that his nervous system had received a terrific shock, but whether the result was catalepsy or simple inanition, he could not say, for the sick man gave no sign in reply to the inquiries that were addressed to him. There was one thing that comforted the faithful friends who never left him, and softened their anguish with an unutterable tenderness. It was the expression of his white face, which was one of utter peace, such as we sometimes see on the face of a dead child. But John Travers was not unconscious. He heard the faintest whisper in the room; he recognized every hand that touched him, and his faculties were alive to every emotion, although he had no power to burst the marble bonds that held him in thrall. With all the keen, sentient powers of his dumb life, his soul never ceased its grateful jubilate to Almighty God, who had delivered him from all imputation of crime, and an ignominious death. Those he loved would not now go to their graves with their heads bowed down with shame. God had in His Divine Providence dealt wonderfully and mercifully with him, and with a cheerful spirit he submitted himself to the Divine will, even unto death. "Out of the depths" of his silence—like the dumb stars —he offered such praise to God as no human tongue could have expressed. It was an ecstacy of sudden peace, sanctified by devout and patient love. He would have spoken, if he could, to have alleviated the fears and anxieties of his own true love, Ally Kane, and his other friends, especially Owny, who would sit for hours beside him, weeping like a child, and ceasing only to run his hands through and through his hair, until not a single hair retained the position assigned to it by nature. But John Travers, as we have said, heard and distinguished each voice. He could not see them, but he knew that they were there, waiting patiently with him the will of God. He heard them telling each other, over and over again, the strange story of his deliverance; he knew that his old uncle, Owny Travers, who had not been near the Sacraments for forty years, had been so humbled and softened by the blow, that of his own accord he sought the confessional and poured out his sins of years, where they were obliterated, and where, after a searching ordeal, the soul which had grown polluted and disfigured became pure and healed. He heard Mr. Lacie, who had been deeply moved by these events, and who knew but little of God, except as one of the facts of a commonly received belief, talking and listening with wonderful docility to Father Grandfiel, as they sat, late in the night, watching beside him. And he knew that he had not suffered in vain. He could not but note the kind and almost tender concern that the gaoler and his wife exhibited in his regard, and not few or brief were the prayers he offered for their conversion. He well knew that he was their guest, and his plea was, "Lord, I was sick and in prison, and they visited me! I was a stranger, and they took me in."

On the third morning after this deep and strange insensibility had fallen on him, Eveleen came early, to take Ally's place, while she went to Mass at the Cathedral to receive Holy Communion. Mr. Lacie accompanied, or rather followed her in a few moments, being obliged to stop at the Post Office to inquire for letters from home. Owny Travers was persuaded by them to go and seek some necessary repose, for he had been watching all night. Mr. Lacie and Eveleen went to the bedside together, to look at the patient.

"Poor John!" said Mr. Lacie, laying his hand lightly on his head, "I shall never cease to regret that it was I who urged him to leave his humble and respectable home in Ireland. Hilloa, Eveleen, what's this?"

Eveleen saw it—the crimson blood—as it slowly suffused his marble-like countenance, and it seemed to her that he must speak. She knelt beside him and grasped his hand; but alas! the tide of life fled back—fading away to a deathly white, leaving them hopeless as before.

"But," said Eveleen, "it *is* a change—a new symptom! Anything seems better than this death-like torpor. It is the very saddest thing I ever knew," she added, as she smoothed back the dark clustering curls from his temples, sprinkled some *eau de cologne* on his pillow, then sat down near Mr. Lacie, beside the open door that let in the rich fragrance of a gay little *parterre* of sweet-scented, old-fashioned flowers. Eveleen was knitting some little present to leave as a "forget-me-not" with Mrs. Pottles, whose whole-hearted kindness, and the efficient aid she had rendered her humble friends in their distress, had won on her regard. Mr. Lacie began to fidget. Eveleen looked up, but he settled himself immediately, and began one of those *unheard* whistling solos, which, most of all outward signs in the world, is the least calculated to deceive an acute observer, touching one's tranquillity of mind. But Eveleen went on with her knitting; at last he drew a letter from his pocket, the rustling of which, as he opened it, made her lift her eyes. He put on his glasses deliberately, and spread the letter on his knee. She felt called on to say something.

"A letter from home, sir?"

"Yes. It seems to me that the whole world's gone mad. I never heard of such a freak."

"Nothing wrong, sir, I trust, in your business?"

"Business! Do you think, child, that all my human emotions are turned to iron? If you do, you're mistaken."

"Oh, no, sir. The history of your love for me proves the contrary. But who is the letter from?"

"It's from Moses Kugle. Here he writes me word that the murderer, Hogan, still lives, and is in the hands of the authorities of the State of Ohio, the Governor of the State having sent on a requisition for his body; but he is too far gone to be moved, and the gallows will be cheated of its lawful prey."

"Poor wretch!" murmured Eveleen softly, "may he repent!"

"Ahem!" said Mr. Lacie, after a pause of a minute or two; "I have no objection to his repentance, but I trust he'll recover strength enough to be hanged. The man he murdered was not his only victim. That noble creature laying there like the wreck of a strong, swift, beautiful ship, is another; and that poor, silent, pale child—Ally Kane—who looks more like a lily beaten down by the storm, is another! And look at old Owny! Dang it! the man'll go blind with crying, and rub all the hair off his head in the bargain. If ever a wretch deserved hanging he—that man, Hogan—does. That's all about that. But here's what brings me all standing. Moses Kugle goes on to inform me that the old weird-woman, Garrity, is dead; and it was discovered, by a bank-book hid away in her bosom under the rags, after she died, that she had on deposit in the Savings Bank over four thousand dollars; which, as there was no will, her grandson fell heir to. But," continued Mr. Lacie, laying down the letter on his knee, and bringing his fist emphatically down on it, "this is not the strangest part of the business. After the old hag is buried, here comes Jerry into the factory, one morning, and tells Moses Kugle he's going away, and to please say to me it was a matter of more vital importance to him than his very life that led him to take such a step, and begged that I would trust him, and think as well as I could of him until he returned, when he would explain all. Now," asked Mr. Lacie, folding up the letter, "what in the name of all mischief has got into the lad? Does he think that four thousand dollars will last forever? What say you, Eveleen?"

"I can form no conjecture," said Eveleen, without looking up. "Does Mr. Kugle say anything about Mrs. Brown and her little boy?"

"No," growled Mr. Lacie, his brows lowering black and heavy over his eyes. "It is a thousand pities for a youth of such noble promise to become a vagabond on the face of the earth. His ambition and genius will wilt, he'll become a mere commonplace man, satisfied if, by some ignoble drudgery, he earns the bare necessaries of life. Don't you think so?"

"No, sir," replied Eveleen, in a low but firm tone, and glad she felt that the entrance of some one, who was approaching the house across the court, would put an end to a conversation which she, being quite unprepared for, found herself unequal to. It was Father Grandfiel's light, quick step she heard, and now he entered, followed in a few moments by Ally Kane, who spoke in her gentle, humble way to Mr. Lacie and Eveleen, then took her place by the bedside of her lover. As she folded his hand in hers, and leaned over to kiss his pale, silent lips, a sudden low cry escaped her. All gathered eagerly around to know the cause. Again that glow of life suffused his face, and there was a perceptible quivering in his eyelid. Father Grandfiel asked for brandy and water, and attempted, as he had done several times before, to pass a few drops of it through his clenched teeth. They yielded slightly to the pressure of the spoon, and he swallowed the stimulant.

Pale and almost breathless, beautiful Ally watched every movement with all the intensity of her deep and well-tried love. She felt that a crisis was at hand, but she knew not whether it would eventuate in life or death. She hoped for life, and in the sudden tumult of her joy plead with the Help of Christians for her lover's recovery. Then human hope spread out, like a mirage, its last bright and cheating illusion before her mind's eye. Fair was the vision, as fair as the last gorgeous splendors of the setting sun, which are so soon followed by dim shadows and dark night. She believed that John would live. She would conduct him back to the fond embraces of his aged and desolate parents: the air of his native hills would restore him to strength —then they would be married at Easter, and in their humble and quiet happiness forget the bitter sorrows of their sojourn in the land of the stranger. She laid her white cheek on his broad forehead and caressed his head with her hand. Presently she heard him whisper, so low that none but herself distinguished the sound:

"Ally, darlin', where be you?"

"Thanks be to God, Shaneen *asthore*, that He sent His holy angels to waken you from the dumb sleep you were in. Cheer up, *avourneen*, an' have good courage. The heavens above ha' given ye back to me, an' to your ould father and mother. I niver left ye, Shaneen *asthore;* where I am now, close beside ye, I have mostly been from the first. Oh, darlin', there's happy days in store for us yet under the thatch of our ould home over the ocean," exclaimed Ally in her wild joy, which diffused over her wan and wasted countenance a beauty so unearthly that every one observed it. He drew her face down to his and kissed it; then, pushing her gently from him, he looked around on the earnest, anxious, familiar faces of those who had been faithful in their friendship to the end.

"Friends! the blessin' of God rest with ye forever more," he whispered in a feeble tone, as his languid glance rested for an instant on each countenance, "an' may HE reward ye out of the abundance of His love. Glory to His name for such friends. Pardon me for the trouble my headstrong ambition has given ye all. My breath seems low—Father, I am in haste—there's sum'at I have to say."

"Leave us together, my friends," said Father Grandfiel, gently—for he saw plainly how it was. "Have courage, Ally, my child—your bitter trials are almost over," he added, laying his hand on her head; while she—poor child—thinking his words boded only good, went away with Eveleen's arm about her, with a light, elastic step. But, alas! for her hopeful, trustful heart! Well for her that it was stayed on heaven! It was indeed near its last bitter pang.

When they were summoned back to his bedside—after a brief interval—there was something in his face that they could not understand. It was Death. John Travers was dying; sweetly, softly, and pleasantly passing away to that land where "the wicked cease from troubling, and where the weary are at rest." It was a great shock to them all when Father Grandfiel told them what was coming; nor could they believe it fully until the physician, who came in at the moment, examined his case, and, turning away, told old Owny, who happened to be nearest to him, that "he was sinking fast, and was past all hope of recovery."

Father Grandfiel went away to fetch the oil of extreme unction, and the holy Viaticum, to comfort and strengthen the dying man on his solemn journey through the narrow pass of death. Old Owny could bear no more; he felt that his grief would pass all bounds if he stayed; so, with what energy he could command, he restrained all outward emotion, and, going up to John's bedside, he knelt down, and grasping his hand, said:—

"Good bye te'ye, *a bouchal dhas*—don't forgit me, *asthore*, when ye come to the end of your journey. I'm goin' back to the ould people at home, Shaneen—let that comfort ye—an' I'll be a father to *her*—niver fear that. Niver be cast down, but take your own brave heart wid ye, lad—an' the angils 'ill make your place aisy in heaven—" He could say no more, so he leaned over and kissed John Travers' wan cheek, then hastily left the house. John's dying eyes, filled with such tenderness and wistfulness as only dying eyes can express, followed him until he was out of sight. He then, in low whispers, thanked one and all for their kindness to him in his strange sorrows, and desired to be left alone a few moments with Ally, who, without letting fall a tear, had crouched herself close to his pillow, when her last earthly hope was dashed out by the physician's fiat, her tortured heart finding its only relief in those dry, quick sobs, which indicate a grief too deep for tears or words.

"Ally, *a suilish machree*—God help thee!—come closer to me. Put thy arm about me, an' lift my head once more to thy faithful breast—but never grieve so, *asthore*, nor let the salt tears rain down on my face, for it is the holy will of God that separates us; an' oh! Ally, my true love, suppose it had been *that other partin'!*" he whispered, while a shudder at the horrible fate he had escaped passed over him. "Spake to me, Ally, and tell me ye don't begridge me the blessed life an' unclouded pace I'm lookin' for'ard to, through the mercy of God, beyond the grave?"

"Don't lave me, Shaneen—don't go away from me afther all," she cried, in heart-broken accents.

"It's only for a little while we'll be parted, *caen buy deelish*," he said, fondly. "Remimber the ould heart-broken father an' mother at home! Oh, Ally, the thought of them is very bitter to me now—but ye can sweeten the draught if ye will, so that I can go away in pace."

"How, Shaneen, oh! how can I comfort ye in this darksome pass? If it's my life itsel', I'm willin' to lay it down for ye, *asthore*," she cried.

"It's not to lay down your life, *asthore*, but to take it up, an' endure it bravely for the sake of them that'll soon be left desolate an' childless in their helpless age. Promise me this, Ally, my love."

"With the help of the Holy Virgin, I will, Shaneen. Yes, yes! to live wid my heart goin' on breakin', for the sake of them you love, is the last an' best I can do for ye," she murmured.

"But for the dear love of Christ, Ally, *asthore*, niver let a word of what befell me here reach them. Kape it off from their poor ould hearts, an' tell them—after givin' my heart's dutiful love to them both—that I died askin' the blessin' of God upon them, and in pace with all men. Now, *caen buy declish*, give me the partin' kiss, and if so it be, as some think, I'll be often with you, when you sit pale and sorrowful, in the lonesome nights that are comin', thinkin' there's none to comfort ye. Good-bye—pray for my repose, and offer up some of your communions for me!"

"Oh, Shaneen, I cannot go—do not send me away!" she cried, clinging to him.

"*I am no longer mine*, Ally. The last few hours—oh, Ally, remimber it is into Eternity I am passing, to be judged. These few hours that are left must be given to preparation—to the sundering of all earthly attachments—to the quieting of all distractions! Even now I hear the footsteps of Father Grandfiel. The parting is bitter, but let your strong love help me by silence an' prayers"— * * * * * * *

That evening a sweet, soft slumber stole over John Travers, who throughout the day—fortified by the Divine Sacraments, and a deathless hope—had been awaiting, with calm courage and in patient silence, the last struggle that would release his soul from his body. Ally sat close beside him, holding his hand in hers, but never disturbing him by word or look. Like a holy image of patience, she guarded his ebbing life from all that could come between his soul and Heaven. As the day waned, her o'er-wearied eyelids closed, and laying her cheek softly on the hand she held, she thought she would rest her head a moment; but her overtaxed energies demanded more, and ere she was conscious of it, a deep sleep had fallen on her senses. Some one coming into the room with a light awakened her—the hand she clasped was cold; she started up, and leaned over to look at his face, and fell, with a low sorrowful wail, on his silent breast. He was dead. His spirit had passed away in sleep—from dreams he awoke to eternal day. *

* * In a day or so, the turf, with its violets and daisies, was broken in a quiet, shaded nook in the Catholic cemetery, to deposit the body of John Travers, whose strange sorrows had won such general sympathy that men of all ranks, who had never seen him, followed him to his last resting-place with steps as reverent, and faces as sorrowful, as if each one had sustained an individual loss. Father Grandfiel's discourse in the Cathedral was eloquent and touching concerning the virtues and touching history of the deceased; nor did he fail to impress lessons of forbearance, justice, and human kindness on the hearts of his hearers, by pointed allusions to those events of which John Travers had, in the strength of his innocence, in his noble young manhood, unsullied by a single vice, become the victim. The sacrifice of propitiation for his repose was offered amidst sighs and many earnest prayers; the organ pealed forth the solemn dirge, accompanied by voices that lifted up the uttered words with great power and sweetness to the Throne of God. Then all was over, and in a few weeks forgotten, except by a little company—amongst whom was a pale, sorrowful girl, and an old man who never left her—who were on their way back to their native land — Ireland. We recognize them. There is Eveleen Lacie, fair, beautiful, and full of high courage, which certain lines of sadness cannot erase. Near by, on the deck of the noble

steamer, sits Mr. Lacie, smoking a cigar quite comfortably while he reads a newspaper two weeks old. The pale, silent maiden, who sits all day looking out towards the luminous horizon, is Ally Kane. She answers gently when she is spoken to, and when old Owny wraps her cloak about her, and sits down to tell her some cheering tale, or relate his travels to foreign lands, with many a queer expression and odd remark, she seems to listen; but as yet she has not smiled. She will never smile again. Not because she is unresigned, or at war with the will of God, but because the great and bitter grief she had known had crushed out the life of gladness from her heart. Let us leave her in her holy patience which endured unto the end. It would lead us far beyond our limits to tell the sequel of her history. Suffice it to say that she fulfilled her mission faithfully. She saw the parents of her buried love depart in peace, having comforted and served them until they no longer needed her; then she quietly transferred her care and devotion to old Owny, who was growing infirm and ailing, and to the suffering poor around them. So she went on, like a bruised flower which breathes fragrance from the wounded part, and making shine, through her night of sorrow, many beacons of hope to the stricken which day would have hidden from them:

> "For darkness shows us worlds of light,
> We never see by day."—MOORE.

Mr. Lacie and Eveleen had been a few days at Carrigmona. He was already beginning to yawn and talk of home. She was recovering her healthy cheerfulness, and had really quarrelled with him once or twice, which invariably had the happiest effect on him. One morning, as they sat over their lunch, engaged in one of these racy arguments, Graff, who was quite in his dotage, ushered in two gentlemen, one being a little in advance of the other. Mr. Lacie arose. The other advanced, holding out his hand with a courteous air. Mr. Lacie recognized him.

"I am happy, indeed, to find that you have returned amongst us, Mr. Lacie."

"Thank you, Sir William Erle," replied Mr. Lacie stiffly. "I am here only for—God bless my soul! Jerry Garrity! is it—is it your ghost?—what?—how?" In another moment the young man was folded to Mr. Lacie's heart.

"No longer Jerry Garrity, Mr. Lacie," replied Sir William Erle, with dignity, "but Gerald Earle—my long-lost son."

"Your son! Gerald Erle! How? Is *this* the secret that perished on my brother Reginald's lips?" exclaimed Mr. Lacie, as a host of recollections thronged his mind.

"Even so, Mr. Lacie," replied the repentant man, drawing him aside. "It was a tale of wrong. I was guilty. The victim of my guilt perished, as did her child shortly after. Old

Hulda Bracken, her grandmother, whose age I had so cruelly desolated, watched like a tigress for her revenge, and stole away my only child. I suffered, and after the bitterness of suffering came repentance, and in my anguish and humility I asked a sign from Heaven. It was this. If my repentance was accepted, let my child be restored to me, if only to gaze for a moment on him. One day a stranger came into our silent, darkened abode. He asked to see me. I sent for him to my library. So fair and noble did he appear to me, so gentle and self-possessed in his bearing, that a sigh of regret escaped me, that he was not my child. It was for such a son I had yearned and dreamed of. He brought a small box under his cloak, which he placed on the table between us. He led the way to his business. At first I listened coldly, then as he made things plainer he did not speak fast enough for me. I grasped his arm, and shook him, in the wild anguish I felt to know more. He wept. He could say no more, so tenderly did he pity me; but he opened that box, and emptied its contents before me! My God! there were all the proofs—the woman's written confession, written in the form of a curse, to let me know that it was *she* who had avenged the wrong her child had suffered. There was the little suit in which he was clad when he was stolen away, and his mother's miniature, which to please him she had that evening hung about his neck by a tiny chain of gold.

"There was but one proof wanting. There was a mark on his left breast of drops of blood. I besought him to bare his breast. There it was! I had found my son—found him all that I could have hoped, all that I desired. Oh, sir, there was great joy in that desolate house. The shock of happiness almost killed Lady Erle;—but I cannot tell you all now. I only desire to acknowledge the deep sense of gratitude I feel towards you, for your fostering care of my boy, when you supposed him to be grandson of the old woman, Garrity."

"He deserved it all, Sir," interrupted Mr. Lacie gruffly, while he wiped his eyes.

"And he told me also, sir, the story of his love for your beautiful niece"—

"Aye, he deserves her, too; he's welcome to her—that is—dang it! I don't know what I'm saying! Jerry—Jerry! Hilloa! Where's Eveleen? Where's your young lady, sirrah!" said Mr. Lacie turning to Graff, who had perched himself in the window seat.

"Dar dey go, walkin' togedder like two turtle-doves down to de Lake—ki yi!" answered Graff, with a short laugh, "an' here's two teaspoons I found in Miss Eveleen's cup, and dat signifies a weddin'." * * * * *

And so in time there was a wedding. Eveleen Lacie became the bride of Gerald Erle, whose noble qualities, true piety and brilliant genius, lost nothing by his change of name and position.

Their bridal tour was to the United States, whither Mr. Lacie was compelled to return on business, where he soon became as much immersed as ever in his gigantic schemes in the manufacture of machinery. Moses Kugle never fully recovered from the paroxysm of astonishment into which the *denouement* of Jerry's history threw him, and his marriage with Eveleen seemed a myth which he could not understand. He found some relief for his excited feelings in purchasing a magnificent set of pearls for the bride, which he presented to her in his own peculiar way—the handsome case being wrapped round with a piece of coarse brown paper that he picked up in the counting-room. We are happy to relate that Magdalene Estman's conversion was no evanescent thing, but an affair of steady progress, which slowly and gradually changed her character into one which was unostentatious and edifying. Mrs. Hunter still flutters and chatters, and mixes the world and her religion together in such a jumble that it is a marvel where one begins and the other ends.

Mrs. Brown and her son, rescued from want and death by Eveleen's noble charity, are living and prosperous.

When years afterwards Mr. Lacie came to die, he remembered the holy death of John Travers, and sent for a priest—a saintly man—who prepared him for his transit from this life to eternity. His dispositions were good, his faith firm, and his hope humble; and he passed away, trusting in the infinite compassion of HIM who had died for him; then Eveleen and her husband inherited all his wealth that was not left to charity, and Carrigmona became hers in her own right. Moses Kugle still carries on the manufactory. It was Mr. Lacie's last wish in regard to his earthly affairs. * * * A plain marble shaft, crowned by a cross, marks the spot where John Travers sleeps. His strange sorrows are yet bearing abundant fruits. The stranger who is in trouble and the forsaken prisoner are often visited for his sake, and on the hill-sides of Carrigmona the cry of the oppressed and suffering is heard no more. The martyr-like sorrows of John Travers, the fervent faith and active charity of Eveleen, the holy patience of Ally, and the virtues of Gerald Erle, will live in many righteous fruits, when they shall have passed away.

THE END.

www.ingramcontent.com/pod-product-compliance
Lightning Source LLC
Chambersburg PA
CBHW030403230426
43664CB00007BB/728